One Size Does Not Fit All

In the day-to-day work of higher education administration, student affairs professionals know that different institutional types—whether a small liberal arts college, a doctoral intensive institution, or a large private university—require different practical approaches. Despite this, most student affairs literature emphasizes a "one size fits all" approach to practice, giving little attention to the differing models of student affairs practice and their diversity across institutions. In the second edition of this influential book, leading scholars Kathleen Manning, Jillian Kinzie, and John H. Schuh advocate an original approach by presenting 11 models of student affairs practice, including both traditional and innovative programs. Based on a qualitative, multi-institutional research project, *One Size Does Not Fit All* explores a variety of policies, practices, and programs that contribute to increased student engagement, success, and learning.

New to this Revised Edition:

- Refinement of models in light of recent NSSE data and current developments in higher education, including budget cuts and the economic crisis,
- Updated information throughout about model assessment and techniques to renew divisions of student affairs,
- A deeper analysis of how models of student affairs practice relate to institutional mission and purposes,
- End-of-chapter discussion questions to guide thinking about ways to incorporate models in one's own context,
- An entirely new Part IV, including chapters on "Catalysts and Tools for Change" and "Redesigning Your Student Affairs Division."

Kathleen Manning is Professor and Program Coordinator of Higher Education & Student Affairs at University of Vermont, USA.

Jillian Kinzie is Associate Director, Center for Postsecondary Research & NSSE Institute at Indiana University, USA.

John H. Schuh is Director of the School of Education and Distinguished Professor at Iowa State University, USA.

One Size Does Not Fit All

Traditional and Innovative Models of Student Affairs Practice

Second Edition

Kathleen Manning, Jillian Kinzie, and John H. Schuh

Routledge
Taylor & Francis Group

NEW YORK AND LONDON

This edition published 2014
by Routledge
711 Third Avenue, New York, NY 10017

and by Routledge
2 Park Square, Milton Park, Abingdon, Oxon OX14 4RN

Routledge is an imprint of the Taylor & Francis Group, an informa business

First edition published 2006 by Routledge

Library of Congress Cataloging-in-Publication Data
Manning, Kathleen.
One size does not fit all : traditional and innovative models of student affairs
    practice / Kathleen Manning, Jillian Kinzie, John Schuh. — Second edition.
    pages cm.
    Includes bibliographical references and index.
  1. Student affairs services—United States. I. Kinzie, Jillian
(Jillian L.) II. Schuh, John H. III. Title.
   LB2342.92.M36   2014
   378.1'940973—dc23   2013027915

ISBN: 978-0-415-84318-8 (hbk)
ISBN: 978-0-415-84319-5 (pbk)
ISBN: 978-1-315-88535-3 (ebk)

Typeset in Adobe Caslon Pro
by Apex CoVantage, LLC

Printed and bound in the United States of America by Publishers Graphics,
LLC on sustainably sourced paper.

Contents

PART I

THEORETICAL AND HISTORICAL FOUNDATIONS FOR MODELS OF STUDENT AFFAIRS PRACTICE

1

INTRODUCTION
Models of Student Affairs Practice

Effective student affairs practice requires, in our view, an intentionally selected organizational, foundational, and pedagogical structure. Without this deliberate selection, student affairs professionals cannot meet the goals of their division or institution. We believe that student affairs divisions that operate without an explicit, intentional structure, or those that are serendipitously structured are not positioned to achieve full educational effectiveness and advance student success. By aligning goals with form and function, student affairs divisions can more purposely identify their objectives and the optimal ways to achieve them. In other words, how the student affairs division and practice are structured will make an enormous difference to the overall purpose of student affairs. The choice of model and the deliberations on that choice can influence how decisions are made, programs are instituted, and policy is set within a student affairs division and its institutional context.

One can no longer assume that one style of student affairs practice will be congruent with the mission and ways of operating for a particular institution. Highly selective liberal arts colleges require a different approach to programming, environmental management, and policy development than a large, research institution. A women's college will undoubtedly require a different developmental approach to practice than the one used in a coeducational, comprehensive public institution. In addition to differences by institutional type and size, institutional goals and desired educational outcomes also influence choices in student affairs practice. For example, institutional goals for a learning-centered campus or regarding student empowerment suggest different purposes and approaches to student affairs practice.

The purpose of this second edition of *One Size Does Not Fit All: Traditional and Innovative Models of Student Affairs Practice* is to delineate 11 different models upon which student affairs professionals can tangibly, pedagogically, and philosophically organize practice. The models presented in this book are divided into two categories, traditional and innovative (see Table 1.1). The traditional models contain three sub-categories (out-of-classroom-centered, administrative-centered, and learning-centered) and the innovative models are divided into two sub-categories (student-centered and academic-centered).

The traditional models (extra-curricular, co-curricular, functional silos, student services, competitive and adversarial, and seamless learning) reflect the early priorities of the student affairs field. The programs, services, and activities of these models focus on out-of-class initiatives and efforts that are often independently organized by student affairs professionals and the students with whom they work. The traditional models are often administratively focused and attend less, if at all, to learning and engagement goals. The innovative models (ethic of care, student-driven, student agency, academic-student affairs collaboration, and academic-driven) focus on student-centeredness, student learning and engagement, and/or collaboration and coordination with academic priorities. The models were derived from four sources: research from the Documenting Effective Educational Practice (DEEP) project, site visits to institutions and consultations with

Table 1.1 Models of Student Affairs Practice

TRADITIONAL	INNOVATIVE
Out-of-Classroom-Centered	Student-Centered
Extra-curricular	Ethic of Care
Co-curricular	Student-Driven
	Student Agency
Administrative-Centered	
Functional Silos	Academic-Centered
Student Services	Academic-Student Affairs Collaboration
	Academic-Driven
Learning-Centered	
Competitive and Adversarial	
Seamless Learning	

student affairs units, the student affairs literature, and the experiences and observations of the book's authors. The origin of the models and inspiration for this book emerged directly from the authors' intensive site visit work at 20 educationally effective institutions in Project DEEP. We were struck by how these institutions had profoundly different models of student affairs practice than what we understood. These reflections and analyses suggested that the literature on student affairs practice had not fully documented models in use nor in particular those associated with high levels of student learning and success.

The models can be "read" or understood by identifying the center of action for each category and sub-category. In other words, who or what is at the center of the effort within the model—students, administrators, learning, academics? Who or what is the focus of the programs, services, policies, and management considerations of the model? What is the relationship between student affairs and other campus units, in particular faculty, academic affairs, or other units including learning support services and the library? Is the emphasis on a collaboration between student and academic affairs or is there a different function or group at the center of the model's efforts? Because we assume that there is no one right way to organize student affairs functions, the identification of the focus of activity and energy for each model is an important consideration.

"Pure" and "Hybrid" Forms of the Models

For the purposes of this book, we present the models as clearly delineated, separate models of student affairs practice. It is important to point out, however, that student affairs professionals would be hard pressed to find an institution that has any of the models in a "pure" form. For the sake of defining and understanding the different approaches to student affairs practice, we describe the models more definitively than observed in the field. The presentation of the models in this way allows us to delineate their properties, discuss their strengths and weaknesses, and examine their potential. Student affairs practice is often, if not always, a hybrid or combination of two or three different models. Mixing and matching models by incorporating ideas from several approaches allows student affairs professionals to pursue creative and flexible practice. Regardless of whether the model is a "pure" or "hybrid" form, one size of student affairs practice does not fit all circumstances. We believe that the nature of the offices lend themselves to different approaches within a student affairs division. For example, a registrar's office may reflect a student services approach while the office of international programs uses an academic-student affairs collaboration approach and both offices could be in the same division that, in general, is guided by learning-centered models of practice. Institutional type and mission and a variety of circumstances (including the campus leadership, historical structure, budget models, and personality and administrative style of the senior student affairs officer) strongly influence the model employed within a student affairs division.

In our work with the models of student affairs practice, people often ask about the number, type, and size of institutions that use the different models. These models are offered here as descriptions rather than prescriptions of what models are found at specific institutions. The sources of information upon which the models are based (i.e., the DEEP Study, site visits and consultations, student affairs literature, and authors' experiences and observations) provide insight about how and where these models are most effective. For each model, we make suggestions about where that model might be found but the choice of fit to institutional mission is best made at the local level. The appendix of this volume contains the Models of Student Affairs Practice Inventory that institutions can use to assess their current model or models of student affairs practice. This tool can guide the actions necessary to change from one model to another (see Appendix B).

How Higher Education and Student Affairs Professionals
Have Used the Models of Student Affairs Practice

Experience and feedback from the first edition of this book provided insights into the ways that the traditional and innovative models are used within higher education. They have been employed as ways to

- *Understand the organizational structure of student affairs divisions including as a framework upon which to strategically plan, train staff, and shape professional development across the division*

(Kuk, 2009; Kuk & Banning, 2009; Tull & Freeman, 2008). Organizational theorists have posited that it is impossible for higher education administrators, including student affairs professionals, to achieve their goals if they do not understand "how colleges work" (Birnbaum, 1991). These models help student affairs professionals understand the division and larger institution by providing a framework upon which to fashion theory and practice.

- *Situate student affairs divisions in the context of institutional mission.* A consistent theme throughout this book and one expressed in the student affairs literature is the importance of synergy between student affairs and institutional missions. In order to be effective, student affairs divisions must fit the mission of the institution in which they are located (Kuh, Schuh, Whitt, & Associates, 1991; Kuh, Kinzie, Schuh, Whitt, & Associates, 2005/2010; Schuh, 1999; Whitt et al., 2008).

- *Craft a foundation for deepening the educational impact of campus programs including the first year experience, leadership programs, and student employment* (Guthrie & Osteen, 2013; Osteen & Coburn, 2012; Perozzi, 2009). Student affairs, as an inter-disciplinary field with a wide variety of functions and services, requires principles upon which to organize its practice. These principles may include student-centeredness, involve-ment, learning, engagement, student development, academic priority, and service provision, among others. Regardless of the choice, it should be deliberate and one that is reflected in the theory and practice that guides program choice, policy decisions, environmental management, and service delivery options within the division.

- *Improve academic and student affairs collaboration, a current pri-ority in higher education* (Cook & Lewis, 2007; Jessup-Anger, Wawrzynski, & Yao, 2011; Kezar, 2003a, 2003b; Whitt, 2011). Current models of student success, learning, retention, and engagement outline the importance of collaboration between academic and student affairs. In this book, we discuss the ways that a collaborative effort increases the opportunities for student success, learning, and engagement. Accordingly, we discuss the detrimental effects that prevail when a competitive approach to student and academic affairs is adopted.

- *Understand the way that change occurs in higher education institutions, including the role of leadership* (Kuh, Kinzie, Schuh, Whitt, & Associates, 2005/2010; Kuk, Banning, & Amey, 2010). When student affairs professionals fail to understand the dynamics of change within organizations, the potential for affecting student success and learning is limited. Higher education institutions are dynamic organizations that exist in rapidly changing, often volatile environments (Manning, 2013). When student affairs professionals understand the greater organizations and environments in which they exist, these educators can craft creative ways to affect change.

- *Reorganize and transform student affairs divisions to better achieve the goals of student learning and engagement* (Kuh, 2009; Reason & Kimball, 2012; Seifert, Arnold, Burrow, & Brown, 2011; Smith & Director, 2006; Sullivan, 2010; Wawrzynski, Heck, & Remley, 2012). As with anything, over time student affairs divisions can become "stale." Programs that were successful in the past may not be successful given today's college students and institutional priorities. Higher education professionals have used the models presented in this book to reorganize and transform their divisions to ones that are more effective. These reorganization efforts include student affairs divisions in international contexts. Throughout the book, we urge student affairs professionals to (a) examine the desired goals of the division, (b) coordinate those goals with or have those goals guided by the institution's mission, and (c) make a choice of model based on the goals of the division and institution.

- *Determine the location of student affairs programs, functions, and services within the college or university institutional structure* (Franklin, 2009; Marine, 2011; McCoy, 2011). Whether one is discussing multicultural student services, recreational programs, transgender student services, or any of the many programs and services within divisions of student affairs, there are a number of choices regarding reporting lines and organizational structure. The traditional and innovative models of student affairs practice can provide a rationale for ways to organize departments and units in ways that provide effective learning opportunities and services for students.

- *Suggest a framework for student learning assessment* (Schuh, 2007; Schuh & Gansemer-Topf, 2010). In this time of assessment and accountability, student affairs divisions, similar to other areas within higher education, must demonstrate that their services, programs, and initiatives bring value to the learning experience of students. Successful student affairs divisions engage in the reflective and improvement-oriented processes of assessment. Without data about the effectiveness of programs, services, policies, and initiatives, student affairs professionals cannot determine whether their efforts are having the desired effect. Assessment efforts are further aided by the existence of a structure or model of student affairs practice upon which to base theory and practice.

- *Teach graduate students and new professionals about feasible models of student affairs organization and administration within different institutional types* (Torres, 2007). People new to the field may not have the experience and knowledge necessary to imagine the different ways that student affairs can be practiced. The models provide a conceptual approach to consider the ways that student affairs practice can be achieved. For those new to the field, knowledge about the different models of student affairs practice can open possibilities about existing and new ways to achieve student affairs and institutional goals. The models can also provide a tool for graduate students and new professionals to assess their dispositions and to consider the models in which they can most effectively apply their talents and interests.

Why This Book Is Essential to Student Affairs Practice

The student affairs field has grown significantly over the past 20 years. The literature covering the different areas of student affairs theory and practice is more complete, roles are more clearly defined, and ways of operating more finely honed than at any previous time. This book, which delineates a wide range of student affairs approaches, represents the growth evident in the field and attests to the developing sophistication of student affairs practice.

Despite the increased literature upon which to base practice, student affairs remains a grassroots field in some circles. There are some who believe there is little need for theory or conceptual models. The belief that simply the "right frame of mind" or common sense is adequate for effective student affairs practice, unfortunately, continues. Similar to other areas of education, people within and outside the field believe that attitude, rather than theoretical expertise, can guide high-quality student affairs practice. In our view, research and professional development in the student affairs field continue to render this "common sense approach" obsolete. Although an appropriate fit for some institutional contexts, the traditional models for student affairs practice, by and large, reflect the common sense legacy within the field and in many respects are "yesterday's story." The innovative models, in contrast, provide an approach that uses current theory and research to guide effective student affairs practice.

Audiences

We recommend this book to several audiences: senior student affairs officers seeking to transform and/or renew their divisions; master's and doctoral graduate students pursuing degrees in higher education and student affairs administration; institutional leaders (e.g., presidents, provosts) seeking to better integrate academic and student affairs; staff involved in planning, professional development, and accreditation; and those seeking frameworks for assessing student affairs practice. Although the goals of each audience are different, each can gain something from the discussion offered here. Senior student affairs officers can discover ideas and creative solutions to long-standing issues. Graduate students can better understand how organizational structure relates to the achievement of educational objectives, including learning goals. Senior officers, particularly those with limited or no prior experience in student affairs, can better understand the priorities of the student affairs field, challenges faced by this group of professionals, and ways that educational objectives are achieved.

Organization of the Book

The book is divided into four parts: an introduction, discussion of traditional models, delineation of innovative models, and discussion of ways to bring about organizational change and transformation. In the first part, "Theoretical and Historical Foundations for Models of Student Affairs Practice," Chapter 1 orients the reader to the organization of the book and describes the ways that the models of student affairs practice, as outlined in the first edition of this book, have been used by student affairs professionals. Chapter 2 introduces the concepts of student engagement and success, specifically in the context of the National Survey of Student Engagement (NSSE). The importance of student engagement is linked to efforts to raise the quality of student learning in college and the role of student affairs in this effort. Chapter 3 outlines the history of student affairs and places that history in the organizational context of higher education. The second part, "Traditional Models of Student Affairs Practice," includes Chapters 4 through 6. These chapters discuss traditional models with which student affairs professionals are most likely familiar. These approaches are discussed in the historical student affairs literature, although they are rarely discussed as models of practice from which to choose. Instead, they are discussed as the one "way" to manage student affairs. Chapter 4 outlines the traditional models of extra- and co-curricular. The administratively centered models of functional silos and student services are discussed in Chapter 5. The models in Chapter 5 have administrative priorities at the center of their effort, and Chapter 6 discusses learning as the center of attention of the traditional models. The third section of the book, "Innovative Models of Student Affairs Practice," presents the models of student affairs developed after Project DEEP. Several of these models may look familiar to student affairs educators who have sought ways to increase student engagement and success on college campuses. Some innovative models have been in existence at institutions but, prior to the first edition of this book, have rarely been clearly delineated in the field. Instead, if they have been discussed at all, they were treated as "exceptions." Chapter 7 covers the student-centered models: ethic of care, student-driven, and student agency. Chapter 8, the second chapter summarizing the innovative models, presents the academic-centered innovative models. The two models in this category are the academic-student affairs collaboration and academic-driven. The fourth and final part of the book, "Changing and Transforming Your Student Affairs Division," contains Chapters 9 and 10. These chapters, new to this edition, discuss organizational change and ways to reorganize and transform student affairs divisions. These chapters are not meant to be prescriptive but, rather, as a means to share ideas about the opportunities and challenges that accompany efforts to renew student affairs divisions. Throughout the chapters, an emphasis on ways to increase student engagement and success remains a continuing theme. Finally, readers may be guided in their thinking about ways to incorporate the models through discussion questions offered at the end of each chapter.

New to the Second Edition

The second edition has several additions to the context shared in the first edition.

1. All chapters have been updated with the latest research on student engagement, success, and organizational theory pertaining to student affairs.

2. With an emphasis on change toward innovative models, Chapter 9: Catalysts and Tools for Change covers techniques that student affairs divisions can use to change their model of practice from one style to another. Models of organizational change are presented in the context of higher education administration and student affairs practice. Examples and practical advice provide easily understood ways for student affairs professionals to transform their division model.

3. Chapter 10: Redesigning Your Student Affairs Division presents the various ways that student affairs divisions are organized. Advice on the issues to consider when reorganizing the

division to achieve increased student engagement and success is offered.

4. The content of the second edition is enhanced with data collected from the National Survey of Student Engagement subsequent to the publication of the first edition. Connections are drawn in the various chapters among the concepts of student engagement, assessment, and strategically planned educationally rich experiences.

5. Insights from institutional consultations, conference presentations, and other opportunities to discuss the models of student affairs practice have been incorporated into the second edition.

Summary

As professionals who have been involved in higher education administration for the majority of our professional lives, we are convinced of the importance of student affairs to students' success. In this context, we do not simply mean success to graduation. We know that student affairs professionals are intimately involved in the personal and professional success of college students. College is a time of potentially enormous growth and development. We offer these models as a way to, in the context of institutional type, mission, and objectives, organize student affairs to effectively encourage that growth.

2

STUDENT ENGAGEMENT AND SUCCESS

Relationship to Student Affairs Models and Practice

Concern about student success in college remains high. Legislative bodies, accreditation commissions, and the broader public are scrutinizing institutional graduation rates, questioning disparities in completion by race and income, unequivocally calling for improvements in the undergraduate experience, and insisting on greater accountability for student learning outcomes. The demand for evidence of student learning and institutional effectiveness has steadily increased since the mid-1980s, when several influential reports appeared, beginning with *A Nation at Risk* (National Commission on Excellence in Education, 1983) and its postsecondary counterpart, *Involvement in Learning* (Study Group on the Conditions of Excellence in American Higher Education, 1984).

More recent attention has intensified on college graduation rates as the definitive assessment of institutional effectiveness and student success. Improved graduation rates were high on the agenda of Education Secretary Spellings's national commission on higher education in 2006 (U.S. Department of Education), then the 2008 Higher Education Opportunity Act called for wider disclosure of institutional graduation rates for consumer information, and the Obama administration set a goal that by 2020, America will again have the highest proportion of college graduates in the world. Pressure to increase graduation rates has also been stepped up as state legislatures explore budget incentives for colleges and universities to improve rates and many have invested in initiatives to monitor and increase college completion rates. According to Cook and Pullaro (2010), graduation rates have increasingly been viewed as the accountability measure of both student and institutional success.

The fact that nearly half of all college students in the United States will not complete their degree within six years, suggests that much remains to be done toward improving student success (Tinto, 2012). The focus on improving graduation rates has prompted institutions to attend broadly to matters of educational quality, and in particular, to experiences associated with student retention and success. Coincident with the pressures to improve postsecondary completion rates, higher education has also been criticized for failing to prepare students adequately for a 21st-century economy, not providing civic learning and democratic engagement as a part of every student's college education, and lacking evidence about college contributions to student learning (Arum & Roksa, 2011; Association of American Colleges and Universities [AAC&U], 2007, 2012). All these pressures have made it increasingly important for colleges and universities to focus on what matters to student learning and success as well as organize the undergraduate program to provide a greater range of students enriched experiences and the opportunity to succeed.

The Link among Student Engagement, Learning, and Success

The current focus on student success in college is informed by a deep research base. Several widely disseminated publications lay out the key concepts associated with student success and effective institutional performance, including "The Seven Principles for Good Practices in Undergraduate Education" (Chickering & Gamson, 1987) and Education Commission of the States's *Making Quality Count in Undergraduate Education* (Romer, 1995), which fleshes out related factors and conditions in more detail. These publications plainly indicate that colleges and universities have a responsibility to do more to foster student learning. Kuh, Kinzie, Schuh, Whitt, and Associates (2005/2010) asserted that "educationally effective colleges and universities—and those that add value—channel students' energies toward appropriate activities and engage them at a high level in these activities" (p. 9). The consistent message across these volumes is that enhancing student success should be the main priority at all institutions of higher education.

Broadly defined, student success in college encompasses academic achievement; engagement in educationally purposeful activities; satisfaction; acquisition of desired knowledge, skills, and competencies; persistence; educational attainment; and post-college performance.

Student affairs organizations have issued similar calls for increased focus on student learning as primary undergraduate goals. The push for reform outlined in the ACPA's (1996) *Student Learning Imperative* focused on total student learning as an institution's principal academic mission. Additional reports, such as "The Residential Nexus" (Association of College and University Housing Officers International Residential College Task Force, 1996), recommended that student learning outcome goals influence administrative functions and programmatic models in campus housing. *Powerful Partnerships: A Shared Responsibility for Learning* (AAHE, ACPA, & NASPA, 1998) outlined principles for possible collaborations for student learning. More recently, *Learning Reconsidered* (ACPA & NASPA, 2004) promoted the integration of all higher education resources to educate and prepare the whole student. Publications reflecting on the origin of the field (Roberts, 2012), recommitted to the role of students affairs as educators and the importance of building partnerships with other educators for the benefit of students.

These publications sound a common call for specific actions and collaborations to raise the quality of student learning in college. Together, they point to the following institutional conditions important to student success: (a) a clear, focused institutional mission, (b) high standards for student performance, (c) support for students to explore human differences and emerging dimensions of self, (d) emphasis on the first college year, (e) respect for diverse talents, (f) integration of prior learning and experience, (g) ongoing application of learned skills, (h) learning-centered pedagogy, (i) active learning, (j) integrative culminating experiences, (k) assessment and feedback, (l) collaboration between student and academic affairs and among students, (m) quality time on task, and (n) out-of-class contact with faculty. Many of these practices have taken root to varying degrees in colleges and universities across the country. For example, most institutions concentrate resources on first-year students. Other institutions established learning communities, particularly at urban and commuter campuses, as an effective way to connect students to their peers and faculty. Service learning and related forms of community involvement have gained prominence in the undergraduate experience. These types of university programs and practices increase student engagement (defined as the time and energy students devote to educationally purposeful activities) as well as lead to greater institutional effectiveness and, ultimately, student success.

Student engagement in educationally purposeful activities is a key component to student success in college. What students do during college, the extent to which they are engaged in activities that, as research indicates, contribute to learning and personal development, matters to student persistence and success (Kuh, 2001a, 2003; McCormick, Kinzie, & Gonyea, 2013; National Survey of Student Engagement [NSSE], 2002). Therefore, educationally effective institutions, those that align practice and policy around student engagement, are more likely to realize higher levels of student success (Kuh, Kinzie, Schuh, Whitt, & Associates, 2005/2010). In addition, the effect is greater when these practices are linked and integrated.

Although we have some sense of what is emblematic of educationally engaging and effective practice, it is helpful to extend this view to images of what student affairs looks like from a student engagement and success perspective. What are the features of a student success-oriented model for student affairs? Is there one best model? In this chapter an exploration of research-based models for student affairs practice is introduced in three parts. First, the student success framework that anchors the work and defines the important components of student engagement is outlined. Second, the links between student engagement and success and student affairs models are made explicit. Third, the research that provided data and ample inspiration to think deeply about models for student affairs practice is described. The chapter concludes with insights into student affairs practice at educationally effective institutions.

The Concept of Student Engagement

At the nexus of concern about student success and institutional effectiveness is student engagement. Research on the impact of college on students shows that the time and energy students devote to educationally purposeful activities is an important predictor of their learning and personal development (Astin, 1993; Pace, 1980; Pascarella & Terenzini, 1991, 2005). Simply put, what students do during college has a greater influence on what they learn and whether they graduate than who they are or even where they go to college (Kuh, 2001b, 2003; NSSE, 2002, 2003a). Pascarella and Terenzini (2005) reaffirmed that the impact of college is primarily determined by individual student effort and involvement in the curricular and co-curricular offerings on a campus. Although students bear a major responsibility for gains derived from their postsecondary experience, in that they must be active, reflective participants in their learning, the institution shares the obligation to educate and guide students to be involved in activities that matter for their development and learning. In fact, individual campus ethos, policies, and programs are critically important. According to Pascarella and Terenzini (2005) the implications for institutions are considerable: "since individual effort or engagement is the critical determinant of the impact of college, then it is important to focus on the ways in which an institution can shape its academic, interpersonal, and extra-curricular offerings to encourage student engagement" (p. 602).

According to Kuh (2001b), the concept of student engagement originates from Pace's (1982) measures of quality of effort and Astin's (1985) theory of involvement. Student engagement represents two key components. The first is the amount of time and effort students put into their studies and activities that lead to the experiences and outcomes that constitute student success. Second is how institutions of higher education allocate their human and other resources as well as how they organize learning opportunities and services to encourage students to participate in and benefit from such activities. Since colleges and universities have a direct influence over the institutional conditions and practices that foster student success, this second dimension of engagement represents a point of influence for institutions.

Student engagement is associated with many of the desired processes and outcomes of higher education. For example, high levels of student engagement are associated with a wide range of educational practices and conditions including purposeful student-faculty contact and active and collaborative learning. Student engagement occurs when institutional environments are perceived by students as supportive and affirming and where expectations for performance are clearly communicated and set at reasonably high levels (Astin, 1991; Chickering & Gamson, 1987; Chickering & Reisser, 1993; Kuh, 2003; Kuh, Schuh, Whitt, & Associates, 1991; McCormick, Kinzie, & Gonyea, 2013; Pascarella, 2001; Pascarella & Terenzini, 1991, 2005). These and other factors and conditions are related to student satisfaction, learning and development, persistence, and educational attainment (Astin, 1984, 1985, 1993; Bruffee, 1993; Goodsell, Maher, & Tinto, 1992; Johnson, Johnson, & Smith, 1991; McKeachie, Pintrich, Lin, & Smith, 1986; Pascarella & Terenzini, 1991, 2005; Pike, 1993; Sorcinelli, 1991). More recently, Harper and Quaye (2009) summarized research and practice on the needs of diverse students, exposed worrisome engagement trends among these populations, and offered practical guidance for institutions willing to accept responsibility for the engagement of all students. The authors' most salient points are the importance of placing the onus for student engagement on faculty, staff, and administrators and for attending to diverse students' needs.

The National Survey of Student Engagement (NSSE)

With the development of the National Survey of Student Engagement (NSSE) in 2000, student engagement emerged as a research-informed intervention to improve the quality of undergraduate education (McCormick, Kinzie, & Gonyea, 2013). NSSE provides an assessment of (a) the extent to which students are engaged in empirically derived high-quality educational practices, and (b) what they gain from their college experience (Kuh, 2001b). The survey broadly documents dimensions of quality in undergraduate education. Student engagement measures have been positively correlated with educational gains, grades, retention, satisfaction, and graduation rates (see Hu & Kuh, 2002; Kuh, 2003, 2008; Pascarella & Terenzini, 2005). These findings demonstrate the promise of efforts to increase student engagement. Moreover, student engagement results can assist administrators and faculty at participating institutions to understand and enhance student success on their campus and can assist others to learn from the national research project. Survey results can point to areas of the undergraduate experience where institutions can effect change and impact the extent to which students are involved in educationally effective practice (NSSE, 2003a, 2004a, 2012). This emphasis assists faculty, staff, administrators, students, and others to identify the tasks and activities associated with higher yields in areas of desired student outcomes. Beyond the practical value of the survey data, the NSSE project has helped introduce the language of effective practice, student engagement, and quality in undergraduate education into higher education institutions (Kuh, 2003; McCormick, Kinzie, & Gonyea, 2013).

Although most colleges claim to offer high-quality learning environments for students, few can directly demonstrate their impact on student learning (Kuh, 2001a; Miller & Ewell, 2005). Instead, many institutions point to educationally enriching opportunities they make available (e.g., honors programs, co-curricular leadership development programs, and collaboration on faculty research) as evidence for high-quality learning. However, many of the experiences are limited to small numbers of students. In effect, these experiences leave larger populations disconnected from peers and educators and excluded from enhanced learning experiences (Kuh, Kinzie, Schuh, Whitt, & Associates, 2005/2010; Kuh, 2008). Consequently, students are less likely to get meaningfully engaged in learning and more likely to leave college prematurely. Institutions can be more intentional about encouraging more students to participate in educationally purposeful activities.

Student Success and Student Affairs

Student engagement is an important precursor to student success. Student success is broadly defined as retention, graduation, and educational attainment (Kuh, Kinzie, Schuh, Whitt, & Associates, 2005/2010; Kuh, Kinzie, Buckley, Bridges, & Hayek, 2007). Thus, successful students persist, benefit in desired ways from the college experiences, are satisfied with college, and graduate. Although policy makers and legislators may define student success more precisely as the percentage of students who earn a college degree in four years, other educators and researchers define student success as the extent to which students make gains in critical thinking, effective reasoning, problem solving, application of knowledge, inclination to inquire, integration of learning, and leadership. Despite the differences in definitions of student success, all are dependent on students being engaged in educationally purposeful activities.

The inclusion of educational gains and learning outcomes as determinants of student success is characteristic of a student-centered learning paradigm. According to Tagg (2003), the learning paradigm college is one in which the institutional mission is to create conditions that produce learning, not simply deliver instruction. In the learning paradigm, the focus is on the quality of exiting students and their learning skills and not the quality of entering students. In this framework, student success results in colleges and universities that focus on developing students' talents.

Student growth and development have long been goals of student affairs. As will be discussed in Chapter 3, a central commitment of student affairs practice expressed in the statement of Principles of Good Practice for Student Affairs (ACPA & NASPA, 1997/1999) is the development of the whole person. This value incorporates a belief in the appreciation of individual differences, lifelong learning, and education for citizenship, assessment, and pluralism. Moreover, *The Student Learning Imperative* (ACPA, 1996) pointed out the importance of student affairs professionals working cooperatively with academic affairs both in and out of the classroom to foster student learning. These student affairs principles are not only congruent with contemporary trends in education, such as the learning paradigm, but align with a comprehensive view of student success as the promotion of student learning and development. A student success perspective creates a context in which student affairs enacts its educational role and influence.

The Role of Student Affairs in Persistence

Student affairs often has been assigned responsibility for persistence— an early and essential factor in student success. In fact, for decades, many colleges and universities have delegated student retention programs and other student success initiatives to student affairs professionals (Tinto, 1996, 2012). Many of these programs, including extended orientations, developmental courses, and enhanced programming in residence halls, are created and staffed by student affairs practitioners and are not integrated with the academic experience. This practice is problematic if it absolves other institutional units of the responsibility for student persistence and concern for student success. However, student affairs professionals at most colleges and universities are well positioned to establish the campus conditions that affirm students as well as provide the programs and services to meet their academic and social needs outside the classroom. For example, new student orientation and fall welcome week activities equip students with the skills they need to acclimate. Peer mentoring, study groups, and tutoring programs foster interdependent learning. Notably, persistence efforts are even more effective when accomplished in full partnership with academic affairs and other institutional support structures.

Although a number of the programs and other initiatives listed previously such as residence hall programs, student activities, and orientation, have been part of the student affairs portfolio for years, other programs have emerged in more recent times that also contribute to student persistence and have been assigned to student affairs wholly or in part. Many of these student experiences were found at DEEP project institutions, which will be described later in this chapter. Among them were learning communities, service learning and volunteer experiences, study abroad, leadership development, undergraduate research opportunities, diversity initiatives, tutorial programs, and capstone experiences. Assuming that these student experiences will be implemented at increasing numbers of colleges and universities and enriched on campuses where they already exist, one of the challenges for institutional leaders is to position them organizationally where they can have the greatest impact on the largest number of students. Lessons can be learned from DEEP institutions about how to make these organizational decisions.

The involvement of student affairs in student success and persistence is congruent with the traditional mission of student affairs. The field's underpinnings emphasize concern about students, including the promotion of student development and learning, acquisition of leadership skills, appreciation of diversity, and attention to retention. Despite a direct role in student persistence, there have been many calls for reform in student affairs related to collaborating with academic affairs, enhancing student learning outcomes, and affirming student affairs contributions to the educational mission. These reform efforts indicate that student affairs practice can do more to promote student success, persistence, and graduation.

Student Engagement and Success: A Framework for Exploring Student Affairs Models

In the preceding sections, the relationship between student affairs, student engagement, and success was drawn. These concepts form the basis for the student affairs models for practice discussed in this book. Our interest in and examination of student affairs models originated in the context of the DEEP project (see Chapter 1). DEEP was an 18-month study to understand successful educational practices at 20 different colleges and universities—all of which had higher than predicted student engagement scores, as measured by the NSSE, and higher than predicted graduation rates (see Appendix A for an explanation of the methodology). Findings from the project and details about the methodology employed can be found in *Student Success in College: Creating Conditions That Matter* (Kuh, Kinzie, Schuh, Whitt, & Associates, 2005/2010). A much abbreviated follow-up study was conducted with the DEEP institutions five years later in 2010 (see, Kuh, Kinzie, Schuh, & Whitt, 2011).

Specifically, the examination of student affairs practice from a student success framework began with the expectation that educationally effective institutions have distinct approaches. In fact, one simple question launched our examination: Is there an ideal model for student affairs practice at educationally engaging institutions? The following questions furthered our examination of student affairs practice:

1. What does student affairs look like at colleges and universities with high levels of student engagement?
2. What role does student affairs play in promoting student success and, in particular, higher than predicted graduation rates?
3. What similarities in student affairs practice exist across institutions that promote student success well?
4. Is it possible that widely divergent approaches to student affairs can work equally well to foster student success?
5. How do these approaches differ from established student affairs models?

Although the DEEP research project was not designed as a study of student affairs, as we visited institutions, conducted fieldwork, and interviewed respondents, we began to take note of and scrutinize approaches to student affairs at these institutions. In fact, several members of the research team theorized independently about the distinctiveness of student affairs units at DEEP institutions. During data collection and analysis, we found ourselves reflecting on the characteristics and trends in student affairs that warranted additional investigation. Toward this end, we reconsidered the DEEP data and project findings with an eye toward developing an enriched understanding of student affairs practice in educationally effective institutions with higher than predicted student engagement and graduation rates.

The DEEP Study

Since the DEEP research served as a touchstone for the models presented in this book, a brief introduction to the project is in order. The DEEP research originated from a concern that, despite an ample body of research demonstrating the importance of student engagement and effective educational practice, many colleges and universities have little experience in intentionally creating the conditions that promote student success. In addition, few schools have effective mechanisms for linking information about student experiences to efforts to improve academic programs and student support services. However, some colleges and universities are clearly doing better than others in the creation of powerful student success-oriented learning cultures. The research approach for the DEEP project was influenced by a time-honored practice in the for-profit sector: study high-performing organizations and adapt the most effective practices. Valuable lessons can be learned from organizations that stand out for their effectiveness. This principle is useful for higher education since information about what works in undergraduate education can help all institutions improve the conditions for student success. In sum, DEEP discovered and described the policies and practices of institutions with strong records of student success and documented and shared the practices that enhance the quality of undergraduate experiences. (See Appendix A for sampling procedures.) The DEEP project launched in 2002 through the support of Lumina Foundation for Education, the Center of Inquiry in the Liberal Arts at Wabash College, and the higher education member organization formerly known as the American Association of Higher Education (AAHE). The project findings generated considerable interest in the field of higher education, and in 2010, the researchers were interested in gauging the extent to which the conditions for student success still held and if new findings emerged. A follow-up study conducted with the institutions five years later revealed that the conditions for success still held and that certain practices such as an unshakeable focus on student learning and an ethos of continuous improvement were critical to sustaining effective practice (Kuh, Kinzie, Schuh, & Whitt, 2011). All the institutions had maintained their high levels of engagement, and half had increased their retention and graduation rates since the first study. Even more, one of the key new findings was the importance of developing enhanced partnerships between student and academic affairs to advance student success. The value of partnerships for addressing student persistence concerns, collaborating with academic affairs to more effectively address student learning needs, and increasing opportunities for student and academic affairs to be at the table for institutional decisions about learning and accountability for educational effectiveness was being enacted at higher levels than during the first visit.

To have achieved higher than predicted levels of engagement and graduation represents something meaningful beyond students' entering characteristics. Specifically, students at these institutions take greater advantage of the educational opportunities than students at other institutions (Kuh, Kinzie, Schuh, Whitt, & Associates, 2005/2010). Although these institutions are certainly doing well by their students, it is important to note the caution issued in *Student Success in College* (Kuh, Kinzie, Schuh, Whitt, & Associates, 2005/2010). DEEP institutions are not the "best" or the "most educationally effective" of the more than 700 four-year colleges and universities that had participated in NSSE by 2003 (the potential sample of institutions for inclusion in DEEP). Yet, their performance is noteworthy, and they offer many examples of promising practices that could be adapted at other institutions.

Student Success in College (Kuh, Kinzie, Schuh, Whitt, & Associates, 2005/2010) provides extensive illustrations of the specific practices and cultural features at the DEEP institutions that contribute to student success. Many of the practices employed at these institutions were innovative, homegrown ideas that clearly distinguished the institution. The University of Maine at Farmington's Student Work Initiative was created to fund more on-campus jobs so that their mostly first-generation students who had to work while attending college could do so while establishing meaningful connections to faculty, peers, and staff on campus. Resident assistants at Longwood University were trained to introduce new students to the educational mission of the institution as well as provide peer advising and academic support in the residence halls. The learning communities established at the University of Texas at El Paso facilitated peer interaction among the institution's predominately commuter students. These practices were thoughtfully designed with the institutional context and students' needs in mind.

Although many of the DEEP schools developed unique programs to facilitate student success, what is perhaps good news for all colleges and universities is that many of the successful programs found at DEEP schools exist in some form at most colleges and universities. For instance, several DEEP schools had great success with first-year seminar programs, mentoring programs, student and academic affairs collaborations, undergraduate research programs, and learning communities. However, what sets the DEEP schools apart is the range and quality of their initiatives, the extent to which all students are touched by enriched educational experiences, and the degree to which practices are integrated and linked to one another.

In addition to documenting specific educational programs and practices like those described previously, the DEEP research team also identified six overarching conditions and properties that were shared by these institutions. The six conditions for educational effectiveness (see Table 2.1) are interdependent elements that work in complementary ways to promote student success. The value of these elements was reconfirmed in the 2010 follow-up study (Kuh, Kinzie, Schuh, & Whitt, 2011).

The importance of several of these conditions is immediately obvious. For example, it is not surprising that DEEP schools enact an "unshakeable focus on student learning." Student learning is at the core of daily activities of everyone on campus. Student affairs professionals

Table 2.1 Six Conditions That Matter to Student Success

1. "Living" Mission and "Lived" Educational Philosophy
2. Unshakeable Focus on Student Learning
3. Environments Adapted for Educational Enrichment
4. Clear Pathways to Student Success
5. Improvement-Oriented Ethos
6. Shared Responsibility for Educational Quality and Student Success

Source: Kuh, Kinzie, Schuh, Whitt, & Associates (2005/2010).

at Miami University work collaboratively with academic affairs administrators to ensure an array of educationally enriched opportunities in their living learning communities. These six properties and conditions accompanied by the effective educational practices demonstrate the breadth of practices associated with student success. If adapted appropriately, these conditions enable colleges and universities to create and sustain cultures that support student success.

The elaboration of effective educational practice assists educational policy makers and college and university administrators, faculty, and staff to enhance the conditions for student success. However, as we reflected on the DEEP findings we concluded that they serve as important principles for contemporary student affairs practice. This prospect actually captured our attention early in the course of the research project as it seemed that the 20 DEEP schools had unique, nontraditional approaches to student affairs. Our work in this volume uses the richness of the DEEP data and findings as a means to consider and outline innovative models for student affairs practice from a student engagement and success point of view.

Educationally Effective Practice and Models for Student Affairs

In the chapters that follow, we elaborate on ways to organize student affairs for student engagement and success. We begin our consideration of educationally effective models for student affairs practice with a discussion of six traditional models generated through analysis of the student affairs literature: extra-curricular, co-curricular, functional silos, student services, competitive and adversarial, and seamless learning models. Following the discussion of the traditional models, we then introduce five innovative models that grew out of the DEEP research: student-centered ethic of care, student-driven, student agency, academic-student affairs collaboration, and academic-centered. In addition to the DEEP findings and student affairs literature, these models are based on our combined experience as instructors in student affairs preparation programs, researchers in higher education, and student affairs professionals.

We learned through the DEEP research and demonstrate in this text that there is more than one way to practice student affairs. In fact, we hope that this book opens up a long-term conversation about the many potential models of student affairs practice. Most importantly, from the DEEP research came the insight that the nature and mission of student affairs on these campuses were tailored to meet the student's needs, fit with the culture and mission of the campus, and focused on student learning. There is no magic organizational model for student affairs practice. Rather, careful consideration of the campus culture, hard work, thoughtful reflection, and a clear understanding of how student affairs can facilitate student success are essential ingredients in developing student affairs organizations that truly are effective.

3

ORGANIZING STUDENT AFFAIRS

A Second Glance in the Rearview Mirror and a Look Further Ahead

How student affairs should be organized and where student affairs units are best positioned on an institution's organizational chart are topics that have been discussed over many decades without yielding a definitive answer. Several reasons may contribute to this situation. First, student affairs, as a professional endeavor, is younger than the academic and business aspects of higher education in the United States, which began with the advent of higher education in the 13 colonies. To the extent that classes were taught, ledgers were balanced, and the physical plant kept up to at least tolerable standards made these areas of endeavor (academic and business affairs) necessary. It could be argued that student affairs work actually began the first time a faculty member talked with a homesick student about the transition to college, or maybe that student affairs began because presidents needed help regulating student behavior (Rhatigan, 2000). Second, regardless of when or why student affairs work began, Fenske (1989) provides an insightful analysis of why student affairs has struggled with its professional identity, and why its future has been in doubt from time to time. He pointed out that the primary clientele of student services, college students, are the "most transient" (p. 29) of all of an institution's constituencies. He observed that it only took five years from the height of student unrest in the late 1960s for students to be characterized as an uninvolved generation that "adhered to political conservatism" (p. 29). The shift in view about students was one that largely influenced student affairs work, requiring it to be the unit most responsive to students' needs.

Third, there is some debate as to what constitutes student affairs. Whereas few would dispute that faculty members should deliver courses, evaluate student projects, and be engaged in research and other scholarly activities, or that the physical plant staff maintains institutional facilities, what constitutes student affairs work is somewhat more debatable. Functions that are part of the student affairs division on some campuses may be positioned organizationally elsewhere on others. For example, does the office of international programs belong in student or academic affairs? Is the operation of the student union a function of business affairs or student affairs? The answers to these questions depend on institutional culture, history, and personalities. There are no right or wrong answers to these questions and others that relate to what belongs in a division of student affairs. Fourth, there even is debate about the appropriate title for the senior student affairs office. Tull and Freeman observed the following about Chief Student Affairs Officers (CSAOs):

> CSAOs, in the past and present, carry a variety of titles including: vice chancellor, vice president, dean, and director. CSAO titles carry a variety of labels including: student services, student affairs, student life, student development, and campus life. (2008, p. 266)

This chapter provides a foundation for later discussions in this book about the organization of student affairs work and how the various approaches to student affairs we found in our study of 20 high-performing colleges and universities were developed (Kuh, Kinzie, Schuh, Whitt, & Associates, 2005/2010). The chapter is divided into two parts. The first part provides a brief, historical look at the development of student affairs with an emphasis on its organization and structure. The second part examines selected issues that influence the organization and functions of contemporary student affairs divisions of institutions of higher education.

Selected Historical Highlights

The historical highlights provided in this section offer an overview of how student affairs has developed as an integral element in institutions of higher education, along with academic, business, and external affairs.

From a tentative beginning, when student affairs officers were not even certain as to what their position's responsibilities would be (Rhatigan, 2000), student affairs practice has evolved into complex, sophisticated work, often involving large staffs, substantial budgets, and thousands of square feet of facilities to manage. A challenge student affairs has faced over the years is to determine its niche, given that practitioners in this field include counselors, advisers, budget analysts, managers, public relations specialists, and more. The historical highlights reflect this changing role of student affairs on many campuses to where it is today—a partner in the education of students.

The Foundation of Student Affairs

Two foundational documents were central in laying the groundwork for the functions of student affairs practice, including The Student Personnel Point of View, 1937 (American Council on Education [ACE], 1937, as cited in National Association of Student Personnel Administrators [NASPA], 1989) and The Student Personnel Point of View, 1949 (ACE, 1949, also cited in NASPA, 1989). Although this historical foundation was established decades ago (see Rhatigan, 2009, and Schwartz, 2002, for details about the work of early deans) for the kinds of services, programs, activities, and experiences commonly provided for students on college campuses, consensus has not emerged on how these functions should be organized, to whom staff should report, and how oversight for these functions could best be provided (Sandeen & Barr, 2006). For example, student housing is a function that can be located in student affairs, business affairs, both, or neither. Other units, including enrollment management, campus recreation, intercollegiate athletics, and international programs, to name just a few, commonly found in student affairs divisions are often located in other administrative divisions (Kuk & Banning, 2009) (see Council for the Advancement of Standards in Higher Education, 2013). Kuk and Banning's observation on student affairs provides an excellent summary: "The ongoing issue of what constitutes student affairs as an organizational unit on a given campus is not directly related to any obvious organizational factor other than organizational history and the desires of institutional leadership" (p. 315). These authors added, based on their empirical research, that there is little evidence of a common organizational form or structure.

Rhatigan (2009) concluded that The Student Personnel Point of View, 1937 (NASPA, 1989) is, in fact, the foundational document for student affairs work. Along with The Student Personnel Point of View, 1949 (NASPA, 1989), these documents provided a framework for the profession, identified appropriate functions that were part of student affairs work, and established a philosophy upon which student affairs practice was developed. Prior to their adoption, individuals had served in such roles as deans of men and deans of women, and many of the functions of these individuals were quite similar to those of student affairs practitioners today (Rhatigan, 2009; Rhatigan & Schuh, 1993), but apparently without regard to a preferred organizational structure.

The Student Personnel Point of View, 1937. The Student Personnel Point of View, 1937 (ACE, 1937; NASPA, 1989), the document that shaped the core values of the profession (Nuss, 2003), identified a number of activities and functions that were part of student affairs work, but did not prescribe a specific organizational structure. The document observed,

> The effective organization and functioning of student personnel work requires that educational administrators at all times (1) regard student personnel work as a major concern, involving the cooperative effort of all members of the teaching and administrative staff and the student body; and (2) interpret student personnel work as dealing with the individual student's total characteristics and experiences rather than with separate and distinct aspects of his personality or performance. (NASPA, 1989, pp. 53–54)

The document recommended that the functions be coordinated; in other words, staff work to collaborate and avoid redundancy in efforts. But no organizational structures or organizational approaches (e.g., a freestanding unit, part of academic affairs or some other organizational structure) were recommended.

In the 1937 Student Personnel Points of View (NASPA, 1989), the authors urged coordination between instruction and personnel work and synchronization between business administration (e.g., student loans, dormitories (the term of the day), dining halls, and other functions related to fees and services) and personnel services such as admissions, orientation, and student activities. The perspective reflected in the 1937 document, particularly as "student personnel" (the document's term) related to instruction, is interesting in that the authors urged a philosophy that educational institutions "consider the student as a whole" (NASPA, 1989, p. 49).

The philosophy asserts, "an effective educational program includes in one form or another the following services adapted to the specific aims and objectives of each college and university" (p. 51). A long list of services followed this introduction, including orientation, housing, food service, extra-curricular activities, supervision of social life, and so on. The authors also pointed out that new ways of organizing student personnel services were being developed, but none were identified specifically.

Although the 1937 statement authors were concerned about the education of the student as a whole, they also pointed out that student learning be ceded to those responsible for instruction. This new, at the time, approach required that some responsibilities previously assumed by faculty now be undertaken by staff. While they were concerned with the education of the "whole student," they emphasized the out-of-class experiences of students as their domain, and left student affairs practice as it related to instruction as merely a coordination, not integrated, function.

The Student Personnel Point of View, 1949. A dozen years after the publication of The Student Personnel Point of View, 1937, an updated version was published with only two members of 1937 drafting committee participating in the document revision (Rhatigan, 2009). In this statement the authors identified several "generalizations" (their term) about student personnel work:

1. Campus resources should be interrelated.
2. Specialized functions should be organized.
3. Equal attention should be given to process as well as administrative functions.
4. Student affairs staff should participate in institutional administration, as should students.

5. Men and women should be available in all personnel departments.
6. Programs should be evaluated.
7. Effectiveness should be determined, in part, by institutional setting. (pp. 39–46)

As student affairs practice (still termed "student personnel work") evolved, recommendations concerning the organization and administration of the functions under the student affairs umbrella changed to the extent that the authors recommended that "a single administrative head" (NASPA, 1989, p. 40) be appointed to lead the overall student personnel program. The statement added "a personnel administrator should be free from responsibility for any one function or service in order that he [*sic*] may be able to deal effectively with overall program development and coordination on a college-wide basis" (p. 40). Sandeen and Barr (2006) concluded that this statement was intentionally broad, and was not intended to dictate how student affairs professionals should approach their work.

Expansion and Growth

The 1950s was a decade of growth and development in student affairs. Mueller (1961) provided guidance about the administrative organization of the "personnel division," as she termed it. She indicated that a basic core of functions should be part of this division: social functions and activities, student government and disciplinary action, and student personnel records. She added, "personnel workers will always participate in—but not have full responsibility for" (p. 139) a number of other functions, including orientation, counseling, housing, student health, placement, and admissions, to name just a few. Her advice on how these functions should be organized was very basic:

> Let us say, therefore, that on any campus a stable and well-publicized structure for personnel functions is imperative. Some centralization is necessary, and some decentralization is equally important in order to distribute the responsibilities and to reach the largest number of students directly. (1961, p. 143)

She also pointed out that faculty and students should be involved in the delivery of services and make important contributions to student affairs. Mueller emphasized that a "personnel division" was necessary on campus. She asserted:

> The main reason is that an individual, especially a professional, needs the support that a work structure gives to his [sic] ego-integration processes. The organization, whatever it is, identifies him to himself as well as to his colleagues, his family, and his friends. It lends status, and by means of it, his superiors know where and what he is and how to give orders to him. (1961, p. 134)

The 1960s: A Tumultuous Decade

As student affairs work grew in complexity, the issue of whether or not a student affairs division should exist was resolved. Divisions of student affairs were created, perhaps in part because the issues of the day were complex and exhausting. Among them were students feeling disaffected by the increasing size and complexity of their institutions, civil rights, inhibitions on free speech, the Vietnam War, and court cases that challenged the position that institutions stood *in loco parentis* in their relationships with students (Caple, 1998; Rhatigan, 2000; Thelin, 2003, 2004). Sandeen (2001) pointed out that many faculty "welcomed release from what they considered bothersome advising duties or some vague responsibility for student behavior" (p. 184). Regardless, Chandler (1973/1986), while identifying some of the challenges of student affairs administration, asserted that the units comprising a student affairs division should be headed by a vice president and that student affairs should be a major component of the university organization.

Campuses continued to grow in enrollment in the 1960s and civil unrest and controversy marked the last part of the decade. "Campus dissent became violent in a number of instances and occasionally was met by repressive responses that worsened matters" (Rhatigan, 2000, p. 19). Student affairs staff members, in the middle of this difficult period of time, were charged with keeping order on campus while at the same time preserving free speech. As contentious and violent as the decade was, student unrest had waned by about 1973 (Thelin, 2004).

One organizational issue that was addressed and resolved during this period was whether student affairs should be organized using a dean of men/dean of women model. Crane (1963/1983) asserted a practical rationale for the division of male and female offices, urging that services for men and women ought to be kept separate. His advice did not prevail, and the offices were merged into a dean of students model, an administrative restructuring that had been urged by W.H. Cowley in 1934 (Schwartz, 2002). Deans of men, according to Schwartz, fell victim to the desire for increased efficiency as institutions of higher education grew in size and complexity, and to the increasing emphasis on the professional education of student affairs practitioners. The dean of women position was eliminated for other reasons. Schwartz (1997) asserted that "the position of dean of women was an inevitable victim of the pervasive hostility that greeted women in general on campus, while the position of dean of men assumed new administrative importance" (p. 432). Although the position of dean of women disappeared, those who served in this role should not be forgotten, for, as Rhatigan concluded,

> We have forgotten their essential courage in the face of formidable circumstances, their dedication in attempting to open new fields of study to women; their persistence even in failure; the stereotype they rose above; the ethical standards evidenced in their work and writing; and the example they set for all who followed. (2000, pp. 10–11)

Rhatigan (2009) added that deans of men tended to rely on their experience and intuition while deans of women took a more scholarly approach to their practice. In the end, deans of students tended to be selected from former deans of men.

1970 to 1990: Adjustment and Accountability

Thelin (2003, p. 16) characterized the two decades from 1970 to 1990 as an era of "adjustment and accountability." A number of functions were added to the student affairs portfolio either wholly or in part. Federal legislation such as Section 504 of the Rehabilitation Act of 1973 was intended to make the campus accessible for students with disabilities who, in many cases, had not been welcome on college campuses. Title IX of the Educational Amendments of 1972 was passed to ensure that opportunities for women were equal to those of men. Who was to lead the campus response to these mandates? In some cases it was student affairs, and, consequently, the portfolio of student affairs administrators grew. But with this growth came questions of accountability and the need for assessment. Ewell (2009, p. 5) offered a cogent summary of the assessment movement in higher education:

> In 1987, the so-called "assessment movement" in U.S. higher education was less than five years old. It had in part been stimulated by a combination of curriculum reform reports that called for greater curricular coherence, the use of powerful pedagogies known to be associated with high learning gains, and knowledge about student outcomes and experiences (Ewell, 2002). But it had also been given impetus by the growing interests of state governments in using newly available tests and surveys to demonstrate return on investment.

More states were mandating through legislation that public institutions develop approaches for assessing student learning (Burke, 2004). The federal government also weighed in on the assessment movement by requiring that institutions demonstrate evidence of educational effectiveness through the process of accreditation (Miller, 2012).

As institutions' budgets were severely tested, first by runaway inflation in the late 1970s and then by recession in the early 1980s, the question of accountability grew. How could institutions demonstrate that they were using their resources wisely? Questions related to accountability also were asked of student affairs units, which often tried to ignore the questions or change the subject. This reaction on the part of student affairs may have triggered concern about where student affairs units belong in the institution's organizational structure and, perhaps more importantly, what philosophy guides student affairs practice.

The Twenty-First Century: Increasingly Diverse Students and Institutions

The current century is marked by a number of initiatives that had the effect of diversifying the student body of many colleges and universities. This resulted in broadening the portfolio of student affairs as efforts have been undertaken to provide support and assistance for increasing numbers of students who historically did not participate in postsecondary education. Thelin and Gasman (2011, p. 17) concluded, "The traditional image of the student as 'Joe College' was supplanted by women, Native Americans, African Americans, Asian Americans, Hispanics and Americans older than twenty-five as integral members of the higher education student profile." For example, 57% of all students enrolled in degree-granting institutions in 2012 were women, compared with 29% in 1947 (U.S. Department of Education, 2012, Table 198). Similarly, the number and percentage of students from various racial groups (African Americans, Hispanic [the term used by the U.S. Department of Education], Asian Pacific Islanders, American Indians, Alaska Natives, and students of two or more races) grew from 15.4% of all students in 1976 to 36.1% in 2010 according to the U.S. Department of Education (2012, Table 237). Slightly over 10% of all undergraduate students were identified as having a disability in 2007–2008 according to the Digest of Educational Statistics (U.S. Department of Education, 2013, Table 242). And, one other area of growth in the diversification of U.S. higher education is the number of foreign students enrolled in the United States. In 1980–1981 nearly 312,000 international students were enrolled in U.S. colleges and universities. This number grew to just under 700,000 students in 2009–2010 (U.S. Department of Education, 2012, Table 236).

Concomitant with increasingly diverse students pursuing higher education is a more diverse set of institutions that offer postsecondary education (Griffin & Hurtado, 2011). Particularly dramatic has been the enrollment of students in for-profit institutions, which has grown from 21,679 students who enrolled in such institutions in 1967 to more than 2 million students enrolled in for-profit institutions in 2010 (U.S. Department of Education, 2011, Table 198). Significant growth also has occurred in student enrollment in online courses (Radford, 2011). These data are particularly meaningful in that they suggest that as higher education experiences a diversification in the students it serves, and diversifies its delivery modes, new and innovative ways will need to be identified for the delivery of student affairs programs, services, and experiences. Indeed, the current approaches that are being adopted are still in a state of flux and as Crawley (2012) points out, it is unclear who is responsible for supporting online learners.

Contemporary Focus on Student Learning

As the 1990s unfolded, a number of volumes were released that helped refocus student affairs. These included the works of Boyer (1987, 1990); Kuh, Schuh, Whitt, and Associates (1991); and Pascarella and Terenzini (1991). These publications advocated a renewed emphasis on the undergraduate student experience and provided empirical evidence that the out-of-class experience of students contributed substantially to their learning and growth. One could argue that these volumes set the stage for additional reports that challenged colleges and universities to reemphasize student learning. Included in this set were *The Student Learning Imperative* (American College Personnel Association [ACPA], 1996) and *Powerful Partnerships* (American Association for Higher Education [AAHE], American College Personnel Association [ACPA], & National Association of Student Personnel Administrators [NASPA], 1998). The former advocated a renewed emphasis on student learning as a focus of student affairs practice. The latter suggested ways that various units of higher education could work together to enrich the student experience.

Although this call for collaboration was well received by many institutions (see Schuh & Whitt, 1999), the fact is that a collaborative approach had been advocated by Shaffer in 1961 (1961/1986), long before the 1990s. Of course, if these documents were to have their most potent effect on the undergraduate experience, the question naturally would arise, where does student affairs belong in the organizational structure of a college or university? If learning is the emphasis, would it make sense to place student affairs within the portfolio of academic affairs, since student learning had always been the territory of faculty and academic administrators? Or would it make more sense to continue the development of separate units of student affairs (e.g., a vice president reporting to the president), which had been the case since the 1950s and 1960s when the complexity of student affairs had emerged and developed? Although the organizational locus of student affairs continued to depend on local (meaning campus-based) factors and issues, further advice related to organizational practice, particularly as it could advance student learning, was provided in the document *Principles of Good Practice for Student Affairs* (ACPA & NASPA,

1997/1999). The authors asserted that the principles contained in this document were designed to "guide the daily practice of student affairs work" (ACPA & NASPA, 2004, p. 1). Building on the work of ACPA and NASPA was the volume *Good Practice in Student Affairs* (Blimling, Whitt, & Associates, 1999) that emphasized the diversity of approaches to student affairs practice. As Reisser and Roper pointed out,

> To accomplish the necessary congruence with the conditions of their campus, student affairs professionals need to develop approaches specific to their own fiscal condition, human resource level, political context, historical legacy, unique mission, and particular social conditions. (1999, p. 114)

Factors Affecting the Organization of Student Affairs

A number of current issues have had an effect on the organization of the current student affairs division. Sandeen (2001) identified a set of factors that influence how a student affairs division is organized, but found no single organizational model. Included in his factors are institutional mission and culture, professional background of the student affairs staff, student characteristics, presidents and senior academic officers, academic organization, financial resources, technology, and legislation and court decisions. The organizational model should be designed to carry out the unit's educational, leadership, management, and service goals. Accordingly, Sandeen called for periodic reviews of organizational relationships and functions, so that student affairs would remain contemporary in its organization and functions.

Given that a wide variety of factors influence what student affairs units do and how they are organized, are there common models for student affairs organization and practice? Dungy (2003) observed that the traditional model for student affairs has been as a stand-alone division with the senior student affairs administrator reporting to the president, whether the organizational structure was centralized or decentralized. But she also pointed out that some institutions have combined academic and student affairs into one unit, headed by the provost or vice president for academic affairs. She acknowledged some institutions originally had this organizational arrangement in place but reverted to a freestanding student affairs division with the senior student affairs officer reporting directly to the president.

To whom should the vice president for student affairs report (titled senior student affairs officer [SSAO] for the purpose of this discussion)? Should the SSAO report directly to the senior institutional officer (president) or the senior academic officer (provost)? Ambler (2000) provides various perspectives on this subject, but in the end concluded that the structure is not as important as the relationships, coalitions, and collaborations that can be developed through the work. In their study of 240 institutions, public and private, Kuk and Banning (2009) found that most commonly the SSAO reported to the president (65.5% of those responding), with the balance having other reporting relationships. Thus, over one-third of those responding had a different reporting relationship.

Conceptualization of Student Affairs

At least three different approaches to student affairs that work and affect the organization of student affairs have emerged over the years. These include student services, student development, and student learning. In some respects, these approaches to conceptualizing student affairs are quite similar to an analysis of student affairs philosophical documents conducted by Evans and Reason (2001). They concluded that student learning, development of students, and service to students are clear themes of the 13 foundational student affairs documents they analyzed.

Student services. Although not taking the format of a fast food operation feared by Crane (1963/1983), this concept of student affairs practice, in effect, holds that student affairs provides an array of services to students that are part of their collegiate experience. But these experiences largely stand independently of one another, without much thought given to the total student experience. Some might think of student affairs using a student services approach as a series of discrete, independent units, in that if students are interested in improving their health, they can use the facilities of the recreation building for exercise.

If they catch a cold, they go to the health service for treatment. If they want to establish an organization related to promoting student wellness, they can go to the student activities office for a list of procedures they need to follow in establishing a student organization. Under this conceptualization of student affairs, the units in student affairs are loosely coordinated, and one could make the case that they can be scattered around the administrative landscape without much effect on their performance.

Student Development. In this way of conceptualizing student affairs, the units of student affairs work together to provide a coherent, cohesive out-of-class learning experience for students. Students who are interested in improving their health might consult with the student health service wellness coordinator but also could work with an exercise consultant in the recreation program and touch base with the food service nutritionist on diet issues. The staff of these units would work together to provide a coordinated set of experiences to help students achieve their goals. This approach might be guided by a psychosocial theory of student growth, with the recognition that the learning that occurs in the classroom is the domain of faculty. This conceptualization of student affairs is likely to be organized as a freestanding division of the institution.

Student Learning. This approach to student affairs conceptualizes the student experience as an integrated, coordinated set of experiences that begins when a prospective student contacts the institution for information about applying for admission. Campus visits for prospective students are coordinated with faculty. Residential programs involve faculty. Courses for students new to the institution (first-year students or transfers) are co-taught by student affairs staff and faculty. This concept of student affairs work lends itself to partnerships being formed regularly to advance the student experience. It also calls into question if the units that are typically found in a student affairs division ought to be part of the senior academic officer's portfolio or freestanding. A case can be made for either, but the guiding question used to frame the work of these units is, how will what we do contribute to what students learn? For students interested in improving their health, in addition to the coordinated approach taken by student health, campus food services, and campus recreation, the students also might take courses for credit and a summer internship program with an off-campus local parks and recreation office.

Institutional Mission

Lyons (1993) offered a particularly insightful commentary on what influences student affairs work by his assertion that the mission of the institution is the most important factor that determines the shape and substance of student affairs. Lyons added that how the work of student affairs is structured, how its responsibilities are defined, how it is valued, and how it relates to the work and culture of an institution can vary greatly from one college or university to another and even within an institution. Hirt, Amelink, and Schneiter (2004) illustrated this perspective in their study of student affairs work in liberal arts colleges (LACs). They found that student affairs practice differed at LACs compared with that at other types of institutions, concluding that "student affairs work at LACs is collaborative, team-oriented, positively challenging and often requires professionals to take on additional responsibilities" (p. 102). The role of mission provides a foundation for thinking about how student affairs ought to be organized and how the work of student affairs staff can contribute to advancing the institution with which they are affiliated. Hirt (2009) went on to assert the influence of institutional mission in how student affairs is shaped and organized.

Building on the work of Lyons, Barr (2000) identified factors that influence an institution's mission, and, hence, that of student affairs. These included such factors as an institution's affiliation; its characteristics, history, focus, and governance; whether it is part of a system; the geographic location; and whether it is linked to other institutions through such activities as shared library facilities or dual enrollment policies. Furthermore, in an examination of principles of good practice in student affairs, involving a survey of chief student affairs officers at four-year colleges and universities, Doyle (2004) concluded that student affairs must demonstrate to the institution that it holds itself accountable to achieving the institution's mission as well as the division's mission. Doyle asserted that student affairs must do a better job of using resources to effectively achieve institutional missions and goals.

Developing an Organization to Support Student Learning

One of the contemporary strategies for organizing student affairs considers the extent to which the student affairs division supports and enhances student learning. Blimling, Whitt, and Associates (1999) reaffirmed the commitment to being student-centered and pressed for institutions to redefine their mission in terms of students and what students learn. Also building on the principles of good practice, Doyle found that

> student affairs divisions were most successful at incorporating principles of learning based on direct interaction with students, including (1) engaging students in active learning, (2) helping students develop coherent values and (3) building supportive and inclusive communities. (2004, p. 375)

But, he cautioned that while student affairs divisions are skilled at building relationships with students that help improve learning, units are less adept at creating organizational structures that contribute to the overall enhancement of student learning.

Forming Partnerships. One important feature in thinking about the student affairs organization of the future is the extent to which the organizational structure and culture will provide the nimbleness and flexibility to create partnerships as appropriate to advance student learning. What might illustrate the nature of these partnerships? Obvious examples are partnerships that provide learning components to such traditional student affairs functions as residential life, student activities, orientation, and student health services. Who exactly comes together to form these partnerships will depend on the exigencies of the individual institution, but the partnerships certainly have the potential to add richness to the student learning experience more so than if the various units went about their work independently of one another.

One of the ways Schroeder (2003) suggested to achieve an effective, institution-wide approach to student learning is the development of partnerships between academic and student affairs. Whitt (2011) added, "Academic and student affairs partnerships have the potential to create such environments by calling on those who work most closely with students—in class and out of class, and in curricular, co-curricular, and extra-curricular activities—to collaborate in designing, implementing, and improving student learning" (p. 484).

In spite of the challenges to forming partnerships (Schroeder, 1999a, 1999b), success stories serve as models in forming partnerships that serve students well and ultimately enhance learning. Ballard and Long (2004) provide advice on how to focus an entire institution on student learning, of which collaboration between academic and student affairs is an essential ingredient. In developing goals for their university, the first goal centered on students and required collaboration between academic and student affairs. A telling observation came from the provost: "When I evaluated our academic programs related to student success, it became clear to me that Academic Affairs must do more and we could not be successful without a strong partnership with Student Affairs" (p. 17).

A programmatic example of the development of a partnership is the formation of a joint initiative between an academic department (psychology) and a women's center to provide sexual assault education, prevention, and victim services (Yeater, Miltenberger, Laden, Ellis, & O'Donohue, 2001). Engstrom and Tinto (2000) identified learning communities and service learning as initiatives that are dependent on partnerships and can transform our institutions into learning-centered organizations. They also identified activities ripe for partnership and collaboration, including first-year experience programs, persistence efforts, career development initiatives, leadership development, and multicultural education efforts. Factors such as mutual respect, equality, trust, and shared learning are important ingredients in the development of partnerships between student affairs and faculty.

Perhaps as potent as any set of outcomes that resulted from partnerships are those reported by Whitt (2011). She indicated that partnership programs in the curriculum and co-curriculum yielded a wide range of learning outcomes. But she also cautioned that partnerships are not a panacea and the literature in this area is not grounded in empirical evidence.

Merging with Academic Affairs. An alternative to forming partnerships with academic affairs is for student affairs to be organizationally merged or combined with academic affairs. In a merged model, the senior student affairs officer reports to the provost, increasing the likelihood that the various needs, problems, and priorities of student affairs will gain greater appreciation and support from academic deans and faculty (Sandeen & Barr, 2006). Kuk (2009) indicated that at many research institutions, the SSAO's reporting relationship has shifted away from the president to the provost or senior vice president of the institution.

Price (1999) provided observations about what a merger with academic affairs meant for the student affairs division with which he was associated, and raised a number of questions for consideration of a possible merger. Among them are the following:

1. Is the merger initiated by the possibility of budget savings or an enhanced, integrated learning environment?
2. Is the provost committed to interaction among student affairs staff and deans and academic staff?
3. Will the provost be an advocate for out-of-class learning to the president and other institutional leaders?
4. Are student affairs staff and academic administrators willing to abandon their traditional roles and take risks that might cause discomfort?
5. Are key quality-of-life functions (housing, food service, student union) under the supervision of business affairs?
6. Does the senior business officer value student affairs and out-of-class learning?
7. Does the president have experience with or value student affairs and out-of-class learning? (p. 81)

Conclusion

This chapter provides a brief perspective on the history and organizational development of student affairs over the years. As the functions of student affairs were developed and refined, no universally accepted organizational model has emerged. Rather, student affairs evolved from a dean of men/dean of women model to a dean of students model. Beyond that, how the division of student affairs is organized and to whom it reports have been influenced largely by the history, culture, and needs of specific institutions. Contrasted with academic affairs and business affairs, student affairs has struggled to find its place within the organizational structure of colleges and universities.

Various perspectives on how student affairs should be organized, to whom student affairs should report, and precisely what functions should be included in the student affairs portfolio, are likely to be the focus of spirited debate in the future. What is clear is that there is no one best way to do "student affairs," but rather, the effectiveness of the activities of student affairs units will be determined by a variety of factors, including some of those described in this chapter.

PART II

TRADITIONAL
MODELS OF
STUDENT
AFFAIRS
PRACTICE

4

OUT-OF-CLASSROOM-CENTERED TRADITIONAL MODELS

Entering the student center, one is struck by the vibrant colors of the student organization banners hanging from the ceiling. The banners advertising club and organization events and the din from students milling around imply that extra-curricular activities abound at this institution. Student leaders frequently claim that they learn more out of the classroom than they do in it. This point of view is proudly backed up with the conviction that "no one checks your GPA after you graduate. But everyone looks at your resume for leadership, involvement, and out-of-classroom experience."

The student activities office has an elaborate system of student leadership. The most coveted positions include orientation leaders, admission ambassadors, and resident assistants. Students vehemently state that they would undertake these positions whether or not they were paid. The life-skills experience, sense of achievement, and fun gained, they state, is its own reward. As expressed by one student, "this is what college is all about."

A stroll through the student center gives one the impression that this space is dedicated to students. While an occasional faculty member grabs a cup of coffee or light meal, few faculty sit with students at the tables in the atrium. Faculty state that the student center "is a place for the students. We do most of our interaction with students in the classroom or in our offices. It works fine. They have a space where they can pursue their activities, and we have our space where we pursue the academic mission of the institution."

In 1931, Robert C. Clothier made a measured plea for educators to develop a student personnel function within higher education institutions. The recommended definition of this proposed area was:

> Personnel work in a college or university is the systematic bringing to
> bear on the individual student all those influences, of whatever nature,
> which will stimulate him [*sic*] and assist him, through his own efforts, to
> develop in body, mind and character to the limit of his individual capac-
> ity for growth, and helping him to apply his powers so developed most
> effectively to the work of the world. (1931/1986, p. 10)

This early statement of student personnel work made no reference to
this work occurring solely in or out of the classroom environment. In
fact, all members of the college community (e.g., "professor, instructor,
dean, registrar, adviser, coach, proctor, yes even janitor" [p. 10]) were
called upon to perform the roles of student personnel. "*Student affairs*
refers to the administrative unit on a college campus responsible for
those out-of-classroom staff members, programs, functions, and services that contribute to the education and development of students"
(Javinar, 2000, p. 85, emphasis in original).

Despite the early calls for student personnel work (later called
student affairs) to occur throughout the institution, the models that
emerged were extra-curricular or out-of-classroom approaches. "The
particular province of the student personnel concern was the extra-
curricular. Extra in this instance meaning not only *outside of* or *beyond*,
but to many *peripheral* and *unnecessary*" (Brown, 1972, p. 42, emphasis
in original). Rather than a true emphasis on the whole student, the
emphasis was on the psychosocial experiences of students (Nuss, 2003).
As early as 1937, *The Student Personnel Point of View* (ACE) delineated functions of student affairs. Looking at this list, many or most
of the suggested activities (e.g., supervision of extra-curricular activities, development of religious life activities, coordination of financial
aid, provision of food service, administration of student discipline, and
assistance to students trying to clarify purposes) take place in an out-
of-classroom environment. Whether in the residence halls, campus
activities offices, or recreational sports fields, student affairs-sponsored
programs, services, and policies supported the academic functions of
higher education (NASPA, 1989).

This chapter delineates the historical and theoretical underpinnings
of the extra-curricular and co-curricular models, traditional models
of student affairs practice (see Table 4.1). In particular, the strengths
and weaknesses of these models are discussed to situate the models in

Table 4.1 Models of Student Affairs Practice

TRADITIONAL	INNOVATIVE
Out-of-Classroom-Centered	Student-Centered
Extra-curricular	Ethic of Care
Co-curricular	Student-Driven
	Student Agency
Administrative-Centered	
Functional Silos	Academic-Centered
Student Services	Academic-Student Affairs Collaboration
	Academic-Driven
Learning-Centered	
Competitive and Adversarial	
Seamless Learning	

past, current, and future student affairs practice. Underscored by a predominantly psychosocial student development approach, the out-of-classroom models are based on the assumption that student affairs and academic affairs missions, functions, and pedagogies are independent from one another. With limited or no overlap with academic affairs, student affairs pursues educational goals that fundamentally differ from the academic mission. Throughout this chapter, illustrations of the extra-curricular and co-curricular models are offered through vignettes outlining examples of programs, policies, and organizational structures of student affairs. These vignettes are set apart from the remainder of the chapter text by italics. The accounts and names in these vignettes are, of course, fictitious.

History and Theoretical Assumptions of the Out-of-Classroom Models

"For years student personnel workers have identified themselves as educators who are concerned about the total student and whose role involves primarily the out-of-class activities" (Brown, 1972, p. 42). The prefix "extra" to the word curricular implies that these activities are supplemental or outside the academic enterprise. The guiding philosophy of these models is that faculty and others who deliver the academic program are responsible for students' intellectual development and student affairs staff address the noncognitive elements of student development. Partnering across organizational lines is not common in this approach. The academic and student affairs staff cede responsibility to each other and tend to stay out of each other's way. Well-prepared, professionally trained people who strive to stay focused on their work and not interfere with that of others on campus do the work of the various units. What would a campus that embraces the extra-curricular and co-curricular models of student affairs practice look like? What programs would be sponsored? What activities would students participate in?

> *High Involvement College (HIC) has a well-developed student affairs division. Well-versed in student affairs practice, the staff of HIC has spent years expanding and developing a wide range of out-of-classroom experiences. While some experiences such as community service, share similar learning goals (e.g., development of critical thinking) with the academic mission, the majority of student affairs-sponsored programs are not academically focused.*
>
> *The offices housed under the Division of Student Affairs include career development, student activities, orientation, community service, student center, residential life, athletics, and judicial affairs. Bridges between the student affairs staff and faculty members are nonexistent to tenuous. Each year, a concerted effort is made to involve faculty in campus life. These efforts include attempts to recruit student organization advisers, orientation participants, and residential life living-learning sponsors. But, on the whole, faculty see their role as separate and distinct from the out-of-classroom mission espoused by the student affairs division.*

In retrospect, today's student affairs educators may wonder at the choice to split in- and out-of-classroom learning. The evolution from the provision of practices and services to an emphasis on learning can be traced through the founding and seminal documents of the student affairs field.

> The *Student Personnel Point of View* [1937] was framed in terms of practices in which professionals should be engaged, whereas *A Perspective on Student Affairs* [1989] suggested that student affairs work should focus on student learning and developmental outcomes that support the academic mission of institutions. (Shutt, Garrett, Lynch, & Dean, 2012, p. 67)

With the current emphasis on student learning, such a strict separation is ill advised (AAHE, ACPA, & NASPA, 1998; ACPA, 1996; ACPA & NASPA, 2004; Blimling, Whitt, & Associates, 1999; Keeling, Wall, Underhile, & Dungy, 2008; Kuh & Ikenberry, 2009).

The out-of-classroom models of student affairs practice established a medium in which practitioners constructed a rich array of opportunities for students. Using both models, student affairs professionals historically have

> infinite settings outside the classroom which provide the student with opportunities to clarify values and purposes, confront ideas, emotions, and issues, bring new information to bear upon situations or new ways to organize information, accept the consequences of behavior, and grow in ability to lead and relate to others. (Appleton, Briggs, & Rhatigan, 1978, p. 47)

Rhatigan (2003) speculated that the impetus for a model of extra-curricular services and programs originated with the 1937 *Student Personnel Point of View* (ACE, 1937). "By outlining so many separate services, they [the 1937 authors] failed to see how this would affect relationships with other divisions and how specialization would undercut the idea of wholeness central to the espoused philosophy" (p. 17). The out-of-classroom models reflect a perspective that a student's college experience can be neatly apportioned into elements associated with the formal, credit-bearing curriculum that leads to majors, minors, concentrations, and degrees, and into out-of-class experiences leading to psychosocial development. Cognitive development occurred within the classroom through individualized study, writing, reading, and activities related to critical thinking and the development of liberally educated citizens (Bloland, Stamatakos, & Rogers, 1994). Social, emotional, and spiritual development, among others, occurred out of the classroom through club and organization involvement, leadership development, campus employment, programming, and environmental management.

Despite its pitfalls, the out-of-classroom models provided and provide, where still practiced, significant value for the student affairs field. The possibility of outside the classroom experiences creates an educational medium in which to promote a wide variety of knowledge, skills, and perspectives. In such settings, students are exposed to diverse populations of people, acquire leadership, work collaboratively with peers, and gain confidence and expertise.

The Extra-Curricular Model

The extra-curriculum, based on an experiential approach to learning (Chickering, 1977), offers opportunities to apply knowledge to real situations. Students define and pursue common goals, meet financial obligations, participate in democratic decision-making, and contribute to conflict resolution. Student affairs efforts in career development, counseling, student activities, living-learning environments, student government, and leadership training openly encourage students to gain understanding by using and applying knowledge (Knock, 1988).

> *The rich and varied campus life of HIC is a draw for prospective students. While academic goals are important, the presence of world-class performing arts, scholarly and popular lectures, annual campus wide weekend celebrations (often centered around major athletic events), and major concerts builds a rich campus community. Furthermore, the services offered through career development workshops and offerings, enrollment management gains achieved through orientation, and the student responsibility taught through the judicial program have long-lasting developmental effects. Extending beyond the campus walls, a policy of reduced fees for community members enriches the local environment as well.*

The approach offered in the vignette reflects the philosophical approach of pragmatism, a long-standing underpinning of student affairs practice (Knock, 1988). The whole student philosophy, rooted in the theory to practice approach in student affairs, dates back to John Dewey (1904, 1916, 1940). But, the earliest out-of-classroom models were not based on a philosophical view of educational practice. Nor did they originate with the founders of the student affairs field. Students invented these earliest models of student affairs practice.

> Student life and the activities of students in the colonial colleges were dominated by religious activity, a strict moralistic discipline, and a classical curriculum. . . . From the mid-eighteenth century to the mid-nineteenth century, literary clubs and debating societies were the common form of organized student activities. Students had found that the classical curriculum did not provide a means of discussing the political and social issues of the time and established these groups as a supplement to the curriculum. (Saddlemire, 1988, p. 262)

The literary societies evolved into judicial bodies, Greek organizations, debate clubs, and campus publications. Social fraternities, founded in 1825, expanded as a system to include sororities and provide housing (Nuss, 2003). As such, the personnel functions of early higher education were established outside the confines of the curriculum and academic mission of higher education institutions. With the founding of the first student union at University of Pennsylvania in 1901 (Saddlemire, 1988), out-of-classroom activities under the purview of administrators were clearly recognized. This focused interest in out-of-class learning progressed through the 1960s and 1970s as the student affairs field grew.

At HIC, student affairs practice primarily occurs in the residence halls, student unions, athletic fields, and other nonacademic-based facilities and locations. Similar to the earliest student affairs professionals, HIC student affairs staff take advantage of the rich out-of-classroom learning opportunities by developing leadership development programs, student activities, and structured student staffing patterns. Clubs and organizations are an excellent venue to teach leadership skills. Student government, Greek organizations, recreational clubs, and ethnic affinity groups provide a medium in which students work collaboratively, gain new knowledge, practice unfamiliar skills, and interact with persons different from themselves. HIC has leadership offerings including retreats, organization officer training sessions, a resource library, a speaker series, and a noncredit class taught by student affairs professionals. Student affairs staff have proposed a leadership minor to be taught by their staff but faculty have rejected the proposal as not being sufficiently academically focused.

Theoretical Foundations of the Extra-Curricular Model

The early extra-curricular model was built on a foundation of psychosocial student development (Chickering & Reisser, 1993; Erikson, 1968; Josselson, 1987; Sanford, 1962), leadership theory (Komives, Lucas, & McMahon, 2013; Kouzes & Posner, 2002; Roberts, 1981), student involvement (Astin, 1990, 1991, 1993, 1999), and organizational theory (Birnbaum, 1991; Manning, 2013; Weick, 1976). The evolution of student personnel workers as educators in the 1960s and 1970s provided an opportunity for a unique theoretical perspective,

student development, to define the work of student affairs practitioners. This theory had particular saliency for out-of-classroom learning
situations.

Psychosocial Student Development. Chickering (1969), Chickering
and Reisser (1993), Erikson (1968), Gilligan (1982), Josselson (1987),
and Sanford (1962) are developmental theorists who offered theoretical efficacy to the out-of-classroom models. Chickering's (1969) seven
vectors (i.e., developing competence, managing emotions, moving
through autonomy toward interdependence, developing mature interpersonal relationships, establishing identity, developing purpose, and
developing integrity) (Chickering & Reisser, 1993) inform programs,
services, policy, and environment management within the out-of-
classroom models. Out-of-classroom activities are not simply ways to
entertain students but a means to develop their social competence and
identity development. On campus student employment is not inexpen-
sive staff coverage but a vehicle through which students develop purpose and integrity. Discipline procedures need not be a punitive means
to control students but a way to challenge students about maturity and
interdependence. Out-of-classroom activities came to be defined as a
student development curriculum different from academics but important to a student's education all the same. Some in the student affairs
field would argue that the out-of-classroom curriculum was "equal to"
the academic curriculum. The debate about whether student affairs
is equal to, supportive of (NASPA, 1989), or complementary to the
academic mission continues today in some circles.

Residence life settings are particularly apt locations in which to
pursue out-of-classroom goals. Students who have never shared a
room live in close proximity to another person. Idiosyncrasies, personal values, and habits are up for negotiation and discussion in such
a close environment. Students who serve as residence assistants and
other paraprofessional staff learn significant lessons about themselves
and others as they counsel students about personal issues, help their
peers negotiate the campus environment, and respond to crises. Sanford's (1962) theory of "challenge and support" has particular relevance
in settings where professional and paraprofessional staff work in close
proximity to students. In the extra-curricular model, residence halls
are often considered "off limits" by faculty and nonresidence staff.

Students, on the other hand, call these facilities "home." They make connections to a community, which results in lasting relationships. The satisfaction (or lack of satisfaction) they find in these environments profoundly shapes their college experience.

Written from a female psychosocial perspective, Gilligan's (1982) theory provides conceptual strength to the out-of-classroom models. Her emphasis on the primacy of relationship building gives direction for social and emotional development for students and professional collegiality and development among student affairs professionals. The interpersonally rich field of student affairs has gained significant understanding from Gilligan's theory about the role of relationships in human development. Residence hall living, using Gilligan's theory, can be organized around perspectives about the limits of responsibility to others. Student behavior can be understood in the context of possible choices about relationship building or autonomy. Gilligan opened the door for student affairs professionals to embrace relationship-oriented development models of mattering and marginality (Schlossberg, 1989). These models provide theoretical efficacy for understanding development in the relationship rich out-of-classroom context.

Leadership Theory. The development of students' leadership skills and aptitude is a major purpose of the extra-curricular model approach to student affairs. When students serve as residence assistants, orientation leaders, or career development assistants; attend leadership retreats and workshops; and obtain advising through their leadership roles in clubs and organizations, leadership is taught. This leadership is linked developmentally to the growth of democratic values, citizenship, and commitment to community (Hamrick, Evans, & Schuh, 2002).

Breen (1970) conducted one of the first published surveys of campus leadership programs. His study found that successful programs (a) involved students in the planning, (b) involved the student activities office in a major role, (c) employed weekend retreats as a popular model, and (d) utilized group work and experience-based learning models. Subsequent surveys and research on leadership programs confirmed the substantial involvement of student activities offices in these efforts. The skills, attitudes, and approaches taught through these early leadership efforts still have some relevance, but recent models such as servant leadership, moral leadership, and collaborative leadership

(Komives, Lucas, & McMahon, 2013) place an emphasis on relationship, ethics, and civic development rather than simply task accomplishment or leadership skill attainment.

> *When a student leader at HIC is asked how she manages her time, she may admit that it is a struggle. A student leader's weekly schedule can typically involve 12 to 15 hours per week of out-of-classroom involvement. Leaders may be compelled to skip an occasional class for important meetings with the president or provost. Faculty, when encouraged to excuse a student leader from class, may have mixed feelings about students who are asked by college administrators to split their time and focus between in- and out-of-classroom activities. Faculty priorities for students may include academic excellence, graduate study, or research. Extra-curricular involvement may appear to be a frivolous add-on. Student leaders, on the other hand, believe that out-of-classroom experiences will yield the best results for their future careers.*

Student Involvement. Alexander Astin, based on empirical evidence from the Cooperative Institutional Research Program (CIRP), developed a theory of student involvement. CIRP was established in 1966 and continues to this day. This continuous data collection on student opinions provides a wealth of information on what matters to students, what influences their growth, and how student affairs professionals can influence successful learning outcomes for students. Astin defined involvement as the "amount of time and physical and psychological energy that the student invests in the learning process" (Astin, 1999, p. 588). Astin addressed both academic and social involvement but the theory has particularly been applied to the out-of-classroom environment (Wolf-Wendel, Ward, & Kinzie, 2009). Astin offered the following example as a way to illustrate the concept:

> A highly involved student is one who, for example, devotes considerable energy to studying, spends much time on campus, participates actively in student organizations, and interacts frequently with faculty members and other students. Conversely, a typical, uninvolved student neglects studies, spends little time on campus, abstains from extracurricular activities, and has infrequent contact with faculty members or other students. (1990, p. 518)

Involvement is influenced by the degree, time, and intensity of exposure to the college experience (Astin, 1993). Astin shared five basic postulates regarding student involvement. The first, as noted previously, involves the physical and psychological energy invested. The second postulate holds that "involvement occurs along a continuum." The third postulate speaks to the quantitative (i.e., how much) and qualitative (i.e., the degree) features of involvement. The fourth states that learning is "directly proportional to the quality and quantity of student involvement" in the activity or program. The fifth postulate is that "effectiveness of any educational policy or practice is directly related to the capacity of that policy or practice to increase student involvement" (Astin, 1999, p. 519).

Astin, in his theory of student involvement, treated student time as one of the most important institutional resources on a college campus. Because learning is dependent on student investment of time and energy, college administrators and faculty should consider this finite resource seriously. What activities can student affairs educators craft to achieve vital educational gains for students? How can students make optimal use of their finite resources of time and energy to achieve their learning goals? How can the campus environment be shaped in a way that enables student learning?

Student involvement is often confused with student engagement, the focus of the National Survey of Student Engagement and the DEEP study upon which the models presented in this book are based. "Student engagement represents the time and effort students devote to activities that are empirically linked to desired outcomes of college and what institutions do to induce students to participate in these activities" (Kuh, 2009, p. 683). In making a distinction between student engagement and student involvement, Wolf-Wendel, Ward, and Kinzie (2009) outlined the contributions that Astin's theory of involvement made to the student affairs literature:

- It emphasizes academic, out-of-class settings and extracurricular activities.
- It focuses on the individual and the activities that individual undertakes to become involved.
- The theory can be a foundation upon which to develop programming and other means to provide more opportunities for students to build a successful college experience.

- Research on student involvement has linked the concept to nearly every positive outcome of college. (p. 412)

In these ways, student involvement provided a strong theoretical base upon which to base the out-of-classroom learning on college campuses.

Organizational Theory. Higher education institutions have been described as dualistically organized into a hierarchy of administrators and a collegium among faculty (see Table 4.2) (Alpert, 1985; Birnbaum, 1991; Manning, 2013). This dualistic structure is amplified in the extra-curricular model because different cultures, ways of operating, and standards of practice are employed by student affairs educators versus faculty.

Table 4.2 Coexisting Bureaucratic and Collegial Aspects of Higher Education

ORGANIZATIONAL ELEMENT	COLLEGIUM	BUREAUCRACY
Structure	Fluid	Rigid and stable
Authority	Expert, decentralized, emanates from the discipline and expertise	Legitimate, centralized, emanates from the position
Goals	Ambiguous, changing, and contested	Unified
Relationships	Autonomous	Inter-related to others
Purpose	Teaching, research, and service	Achieve organizational goals and maintain standards of performance
Institutional purposes	Primary	Secondary
Context	Aligned or seek alignment with national and international communities	Aligned or seek alignment with local communities
Coupling with other departments	Independent	Loose and inter-dependent
Change	Change adverse	Use change as a way to achieve institutional goals
Long range	Tenured	Non-tenured
Measures of effectiveness	Measurable product for teaching, research, and service difficult to achieve	Demand measurable product

Source: Manning, 2013; adapted from Alpert, 1985 and Birnbaum, 1991.

The hierarchy or administrative "side" of the institution is characterized by standardization, routinization, and coordination. The collegial faculty and academic "side" of the institution uses consensus decision-making, leadership as first among equals, and expert authority. Applying these ideas to the extra-curricular model, college life can be divided into the psychosocial out-of-class hierarchy and academic collegium. The existence of these two disparate organizational forms interferes with attempts to integrate student-learning goals throughout the institution. Faculty speak a different language than administrators. Communication between the two groups follows contradictory norms of practice. The goals for both "sides" are different—sometimes conflicting. This dualistic structure creates a circumstance where distinct in- and out-of-classroom goals and practices emerge. College community members belonging to these different organizational structures in the same institution often disagree about the importance of out-of-classroom involvement, role of the extra-curriculum, and language used to describe college life. This circumstance is amplified with high tuition and its accompanying enlarged in- and out-of-classroom demands. Student time is at a premium.

With the presence of these two vastly different organizational approaches, it is no surprise that the extra-curricular model developed as a separate entity to the academic purposes and goals. A flaw in viewing the institution this way is that students experience the college more holistically than the dramatic separation of the curricular and extra-curricular assumed by faculty and staff (Kuh, Schuh, Whitt, & Associates, 1991). A second flaw in this dualistic approach is represented in the quantum organizational theories of Wheatley (2010) and Zohar (1997). Contemporary models of organizations emphasize connection, dynamism, collaboration, and attention to the whole. Allen and Cherrey (2000) linked these quantum approaches to student affairs practice. Living and working in a quantum, postmodern institution requires

> that student affairs professionals bring their talents to the table, make necessary changes in their practice, develop new capacities, challenge traditional ways of working and develop the new relationships needed to influence institutional leadership and transformation. To do so, we

need to develop new ways of relating, influencing change, learning, and leading. (p. 22)

The future of organizational functioning is wholeness, not separation. Brown (1972) foreshadowed this holistic approach to student affairs organizations and practice.

> It is time for student personnel workers to recognize that they too have been dealing with only a part of the student, and it is no more valid for them to expect effectiveness in dealing with the student's development, independent of his [sic] academic life, than it is for the professor to think a student's personal self does not affect his academic growth. (p. 38)

The debate about organizational effectiveness and structural ways to achieve high-quality student affairs practice has expressed itself in the reporting options for Vice Presidents for Student Affairs (VPSAs) and deans of students. (For ease in discussion, only the VPSA will be used in the examples.) In the extra-curricular model, student affairs is often organized as a stand alone or independent division (see Figure 4.1). The VPSA is equal to other institutional executive officers including those in development, finance, administration, and academics (although, as Sandeen [1991] notes, the academic vice president is often "first among equals"). The benefits of this direct reporting structure include (1) recognition of the importance of both student and academic affairs; (2) an independent budget and resource allocation; (3) opportunity to advocate for student affairs programs and policies

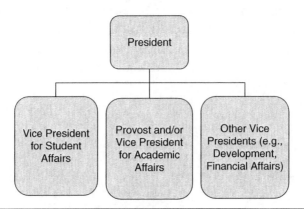

Figure 4.1 Student Affairs as an Independent Division

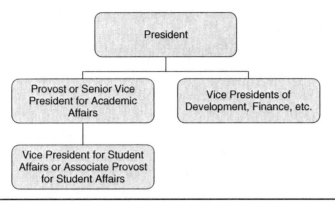

Figure 4.2 Student Affairs as an Entity of Academic Affairs

directly to the president; and (4) inclusion on the president's staff and, hence, institution-wide decision making.

At the DEEP institutions, ones that had higher than predicted student engagement and student success, student affairs as a detached and independent division was not the predominant model. In this study, only one institution had a model of student affairs where the VPSA reported to the president (NSSE, 2003e). Instead, the predominant organizational model was one where the VPSA reported to the provost or vice president for academic affairs (see Figure 4.2). Through this configuration, the intertwined academic and student affairs missions were reflected in the organizational structure.

The benefits of the model in which the VPSA reports to the Academic Vice President or provost include (1) more opportunities for collaboration between the student and academic affairs missions, (2) less competition between the academic and student affairs resource structures, and (3) potential buy-in by the academic officer into the student affairs mission. In discussing the role of the senior student affairs officer (called "chief student affairs officer" [CSAO] in his lexicon), Sandeen (1991) points to the importance of the senior student affairs-senior academic affairs officer relationship.

> The CSAO's relationship to the chief academic officer is almost as important as the relationship to the president. If the CSAO and the chief academic officer have widely differing views about education and the role of the university in its relations with students, the separation

between academic and student life will most likely be great . . . the goal of the CSAO-chief academic officer relationship should be . . . working together for the education of students, so that the college experience is viewed as a whole. (p. 27)

Features of the Extra-Curricular Model

The extra-curricular model embodies the following assumptions: (1) independent practice that may conflict with the academic mission; (2) programs, services, environmental management, and other interventions initiated by student affairs professionals; (3) infinite settings outside the classroom for student development and learning; and (4) an organizational structure that defines student affairs as detached from academic affairs.

Independent Practice That May Conflict With the Academic Mission. The student affairs field emerged when faculty members were prevailed upon by college and university presidents to take up the discipline responsibilities of student conduct. These positions eventually became Deans of Men and Deans of Women (Dungy & Gordon, 2011; Schwartz, 1997, 2002). The extra-curricular model was a departure from the earliest student personnel models that more adroitly blended student and academic affairs. The field then diverged into separate realms of student affairs and academic affairs with the faculty exercising detachment over areas in which they had earlier been fully engaged (Fenske, 1989). As the student affairs field became more professionalized, these two areas further disconnected from one another.

In the extra-curricular model, it is possible for student affairs professionals and academic affairs staff and faculty to have minimal to no interaction. Their goals and purposes differ leading some among the faculty to believe that student affairs programs and interventions are superfluous. But, nationally recognized tragedies (e.g., the Virginia Tech shootings) have shifted the thinking among many faculty, executive leaders, and others concerning the crucial role of student affairs staff during campus crises. These tragedies have also reinforced the need for early intervention with students who exhibit disturbing behavior. The presence of a vibrant student affairs program is now widely recognized as an essential element of a healthy campus life.

Student Engagement Initiated by Student Affairs Professionals. In the extra-curricular model, student affairs staff are responsible for the choices made about the services, programs, and environments molded to advance a student's education. While students serve as para- and semiprofessional staff members, the framework, procedures, and overall direction of the engagement achieved is managed by the full-time staff. The staffing patterns determined, policies enacted, and best practices employed in the extra-curricular model originate with professional staff. In this way, out-of-classroom activities, programs, and services, not academics or student initiative, are at the center of the effort in the extra-curricular model.

The limits and specific actions of the staff-emphasized approach to student affairs practice have been debated and refined over the years. Its essentials can be illustrated through several longstanding debates within the student affairs field. Should student club and organization advising be direct or indirect? Should students have the right to determine community standards or are there minimal standards, particularly in the residence halls (e.g., quiet hours, alcohol use), that should serve as a foundation upon which students add additional standards? If student affairs professionals are more mature, experienced, and knowledgeable about educational practice, should not they make decisions in the best interests of students? Student affairs professionals wrestle each day with questions about responsibilities to be shared (and not shared) with students, the limits of standards of practice, and nuances of their roles with students.

Infinite Settings Outside the Classroom for Student Development and Learning. A unique feature of the learning that occurs through student affairs practice is the potential for learning to occur through infinite opportunities. The learning and development that occurs through programs, services, environmental management, policy, and other means available to student affairs educators is not limited by time or location. All campus facilities and environments become opportunities for learning as student affairs educators hire student staff (e.g., campus center managers); add learning scenarios to seemingly mundane campus amenities (e.g., dining halls); and create developmental opportunities for student crises (e.g., student death). The 24/7 nature of student affairs means that occasions for learning and development are readily available.

Strengths and Weaknesses of the Extra-Curricular Model

The extra-curricular model, though perhaps out of date with today's emphasis on student and academic affairs collaboration (Cook & Lewis, 2007; Kezar, Hirsch, & Burack, 2002), served the field well in its time. Advantages accrued to student affairs as a result of the extra-curricular approach occurred because the model

1. Allows specialized expertise in the student affairs functional areas to be developed.
2. Encourages the use of budgets and resources discretely as a means to develop the department within student affairs divisions and departments.
3. Frees faculty to concentrate their efforts on teaching, research, and service.
4. Permits the expansion of programs, services, and policies that would, most likely, have remained underdeveloped if integrated closely with academic affairs.
5. Creates opportunities for institutions to expand learning, leadership, and developmental opportunities for students beyond academics.

Several areas of student affairs administration have thrived under the extra-curricular model including student activities and residence life (particularly in the areas of community building and social programming). Orientation, service learning, academic advising, and career development, areas more closely aligned with the academic mission, fit less well structurally and philosophically with the out-of-classroom models.

Extra-curricular involvement has been repeatedly related to retention, satisfaction with the institution, and academic gains (Flowers, 2004; Foubert & Grainger, 2006; Pascarella & Terenzini, 2005). Tinto's (1993, 2012) model of retention paid particular attention to students' extra-curricular lives in his discussion of social integration. The leadership development resulting from the volunteer and paid student leader opportunities as a result of the practices within the extra-curricular model has been substantial. Significant gains in student satisfaction with the institution and increased retention have long been associated with the learning and development associated with the out-of-classroom models. The gains resulting from the leadership skills, knowledge, and experience taught in out-of-classroom circumstances were and continue to be substantial. The extra-curricular model involves concentrated effort regarding community building, an essential aspect of campus life. Residence halls, clubs and organizations, commuter programs, and any affiliation building activities are a way to achieve this community.

Despite the successes of the extra-curricular model, particularly in the formative years of the student affairs field, several weaknesses illustrate the fact that this approach may need to be updated with more current models. These weaknesses include the (1) lack of student and academic affairs integration; (2) inability to achieve the whole person goal; (3) overreliance on an individually based approach; and (4) confusion about the purposes of college.

Lack of Student and Academic Affairs Integration. Brown challenged the out-of-classroom approach to student affairs practice when he stated, "Higher education took the wrong fork in the road when it thrust personnel maintenance upon staff with specialized duties"(1972, p. 37). The confusion resulting from the academic-student affairs split in educational functions resulted in debates about the importance of student affairs compared with academic affairs. Many complained that student affairs professionals were often treated as second-class citizens. Their mission, argued some, was as educationally valuable as— and, therefore, equal to – the academic mission of the curriculum and in-class efforts. The authors of *A Perspective on Student Affairs* (NASPA, 1989) challenged this "equal to" perspective.

> The Academic Mission of the Institution is Preeminent. . . . The work of student affairs should not compete with and cannot substitute for the academic experience. As a partner in the educational enterprise, student affairs enhances and supports the academic mission. (p. 12)

Although seen by some as relegating student affairs to a subordinate position, the 1989 *Perspective* called for collaboration and integration of the student affairs and academic missions, a sentiment advocated again in *The Student Learning Imperative* (ACPA, 1996) and other policy statements (Keeling, Wall, Underhile, & Dungy, 2008; Kuh & Ikenberry, 2009). Regardless of one's individual stance in this debate, it is clear that the extra-curricular model (and the co-curricular model described later in this chapter) does not fully integrate the learning that occurs on college campuses.

Inability to Achieve a Whole Student Philosophy Goal. The extra-curricular model is fundamentally flawed as an approach to working with students in part because the out-of-classroom venue is not amenable to all students. The model works extremely well for students at both ends of the disciplinary continuum: student leaders who are extremely involved or students who are frequent visitors to the disciplinary system. Both student groups receive a significant amount of time and attention from student affairs staff. But

> what about the more typical student who never sees a counselor, who never creates a disturbance in the residence hall, or who is never a campus leader? His [*sic*] contact with the student personnel staff is limited and his life style is affected very indirectly, if at all, by student personnel services or policies. (Brown, 1972, p. 37)

Surely the founders and early theorists of the student affairs field had a broader approach for the field in mind than the one embraced by the out-of-classroom centered models.

Overreliance on an Individually Based Approach. The predominantly one-on-one approach of the extra-curricular model precludes a staff member's ability to reach all students. Brown, as early as 1972, noted this weakness: "One of the major weaknesses of current student development programs and student affairs functions is that they directly affect a small minority of students and even indirectly have almost no impact on the academic aspects of student life" (p. 43). Recent technological interventions (e.g., websites, email) have mitigated the over-emphasis on too few students, but the flaw in the model remains. While all students may be influenced, at some point, by a program, policy, or approach to student development, a disproportionate amount of staff time is spent on too few students. This issue is more significant today in light of decreased budgets and increased need to "do more with less."

Confusion about College Purposes. Student affairs professionals working with students who are actively (and perhaps overly) involved in the extra-curricular life of the campus often challenge them to maintain a balance. Too often, the extra-curricular activities, leadership positions, and learning priorities can be, particularly for young students, more interesting and appealing than studying, taking examinations, and completing academic assignments. The extra-curricular model, with its emphasis on social and emotional development, inherently more interesting for many than intellectual development, is fundamentally prone to this type of misunderstanding. As such, students may lose perspective about the importance of their academic goals. When the extra-curricular becomes more important than the curricular, the essential purpose of college is lost. This is the case for students and student affairs professionals. Student affairs professionals, students, and faculty must collaborate closely about the ultimate goals of higher education to avoid this confusion.

The Co-Curricular Model

The co-curricular model, which further emphasizes the educational and developmental value of the out-of-classroom experience, was, for its time, an evolution beyond the extra-curricular model. The co-curricular model is distinguished from the extra-curricular model in the way that the former is parallel to the academic curriculum while the latter is outside of, supplemental, and basically unrelated to the educational effort of the academic curriculum. From this perspective, student affairs fulfills an important educational mission which is not "extra" but concurrent with the academic mission.

An example of this approach to student affairs work is as follows:

The senior student affairs staff at Eastern University had a retreat in late summer in preparation for the academic year. Staff were committed to providing educational experiences for students and the purpose of the retreat was to identify a series of opportunities for students for the upcoming year built around two or three themes. This work resulted in the following themes for the year: learning based on leadership development, experiences with diversity, and service to the community. Each of the unit heads in the division agreed to develop a series of programs and other experiences for students built on these themes. Examples of these experiences included a leadership training program for organization officers, a mentor program sponsored by the office of diversity programming, and a series of community service activities for residence hall students. Everyone agreed that these plans would contribute substantially to student growth in their out-of-class experiences for the upcoming year.

At the same time the senior academic affairs leaders had a retreat looking at areas of emphasis in faculty development for the upcoming year. They decided that the faculty development program for the year should emphasize pedagogical techniques that feature active learning and applications of classroom learning in practical settings. These leaders agreed that they would work with their department chairs and faculty so as to enhance these dimensions of the formal curriculum during the upcoming academic year and perhaps beyond.

Theoretical Foundations of the Co-Curricular Model

The theoretical foundations of the co-curricular model match those of the extra-curricular model: psychosocial student development, leadership theory, student involvement, and organizational theory. The difference between the models is how the theories are approached. Professionals following a co-curricular approach connect their activities to learning objectives and developmental goals. From this perspective, a professional student affairs staff member could point to the educational outcomes of the student affairs curriculum, a curriculum that parallels the academic.

Features of the Co-Curricular Model

Although student and academic affairs are separated in much the same way as the extra-curricular model, the introduction of the co-curricular model ushered the idea that student affairs professionals were and are educators. Armed with the assumption that student affairs initiatives are educational, the co-curriculum involved more than the management of necessary services. Programs, services, environmental management, and other student affairs initiatives became grounded in developmental, leadership, involvement, and organizational theories with an eye for crafting experiences from which students could learn. These educational experiences remained independent from, yet concurrent with, the academic efforts of the faculty, curriculum, and academic affairs.

Complementary, but Separate Missions. In this model the missions of academic and student affairs are distinct, but the units acknowledge the contributions of each other to the student experience. Student affairs is concerned with the out-of-class development of students and academic affairs focuses on what students learn in their classroom experiences. What students learn outside the formal curriculum is perceived to be important, but secondary, to what is learned inside the curriculum. This differed from some of the activities and programs of the extra-curriculum, which some in higher education felt had insufficient educational value.

Independent Work. Student affairs and academic affairs work independently of one another, but members of the various units communicate with one another on important issues. For example, a joint orientation committee plans the events and experiences for new students each fall. Members of the committee recognize that both academic and student affairs contribute to the orientation process, and time is reserved for each unit to offer experiences for students. But, the planning of an orientation schedule is more about avoiding scheduling conflicts, not collaborating to plan events designed to facilitate student learning from multiple perspectives.

Assessment Efforts. The co-curricular effort, as separate from academics, can be represented in the co-curricular model through assessment. Assessment efforts separate student and academic affairs into two categories. Independent procedures assess the academic experience of students in the classroom versus the student affairs experience out of the classroom. The learning goals in these two areas within the college may overlap but that would be by coincidence more than plan.

Organizational Configuration and Reporting Lines. The reporting lines in the co-curricular model may be similar to those of the extra-curricular model: academic affairs is administered under the Vice President for Academic Affairs or Provost and student affairs is administered by a Vice President for Student Affairs. Both report directly to the president with only collegial and minimal philosophical or educational coordination between the two (see Figure 4.1).

Contributions to Student Learning. Student affairs staff are committed to contributing to educational efforts, but in their own sphere of influence. The student affairs division may have a well-conceived strategic plan, which outlines its learning goals for students but this plan is not coordinated with any academic unit including the provost, deans, or other academic leadership. Rather than trying to collaborate with faculty or academic affairs staff, the student affairs professionals plan their student learning experiences on their own. An example of this is a community service program planned for residence hall students. Several residence hall staff members have solid connections with community leaders in the neighboring town. They begin to work with these leaders on various community service projects. These are successful and the students who participate learn a great deal from them. Residence life staff members do not consider contacting faculty in the sociology department to determine if they would have an interest in weaving such experiences into their courses and perhaps develop a service-learning program. The organizational culture does not work that way.

Boundaries Characterize the Work Environment. In spite of the acknowledgment of the contributions of various parts of the institution to student learning, boundaries demarcate where staff from the various units can deliver learning experiences. Faculty, for example, would not consider offering a residentially based program. They do not feel welcome taking a meal with students in the residence halls, even if they were invited to do so. Student affairs staff would not consider proposing to offer an experience for credit, even though they would be qualified to do so under the institution's faculty personnel policies. The formal curriculum and co-curriculum are defined, and the boundaries between the two are crossed only in rare situations.

Strengths and Weaknesses of the Co-curricular Model

As with all the models of student practice, the co-curricular model has strengths, which may make it an appropriate fit for some institutions. These strengths include learning outcomes and the educational mission, student affairs view as educators, and the potential for a lively campus life.

Learning Outcomes and the Educational Mission. The introduction of the co-curricular model ushered in the idea that student affairs professionals were more than administrators. They were educators who were obligated to set and maintain learning objectives for the activities and initiatives in which they were engaged. Student affairs professionals adhering to a co-curricular model saw these learning goals as separate from but as important as the academic learning objectives. Examples of learning objectives were often drawn from student development theory with an emphasis on the psychosocial aspects of student growth.

Student Affairs View as Educators. The co-curricular model coincided with the history of the student affairs field as having a distinctive educational mission. As such, student affairs professionals were educators who filled their educational mission through their roles as programmers, consultants, counselors, and administrators, among other roles (Brown, 1972).

Potential for a Lively Campus Life. The early students who organized activities, literary societies, and fraternities knew that a healthy campus and student lifestyle demanded more than academics. The co-curricular activities on a college campus have the potential to build strong communities, teach students important life skills, and create lively, interesting places to study and work.

The weaknesses of the co-curricular model mirror those of the extra-curricular approach: the full range of learning is unfulfilled, student and academic affairs collaboration is incomplete, and student frustration over the lack of integration is possible.

The Full Range of Learning Is Unfulfilled. When learning is separated into in- and out-of-classroom experiences, the integration and synthesis that occurs with a more coordinated approach is lost.

The Academic Community Fails to Come Together. When faculty go their way and student affairs go theirs, the community as a whole fails to coalesce. Rather than all taking part in a committed approach to the entire learning environment, the community is fractured and split.

Incomplete Collaboration between Academic and Student Affairs. When collaboration between academic and student affairs fails to occur, the synthesis possible within the learning environment is lost. More practically, however, this lack of coordination means that resources, notoriously underfunded, are wasted. Programs are duplicated, funds that could be saved through minor and major coordination efforts are expended, and equipment and other physical assets are not shared.

Student Frustration. An important weakness of the co-curricular model is the student frustration that is a byproduct of this institutional approach. Students, as described previously, do not draw tight boundaries between and among their learning experiences. They are less apt to demarcate the in- and out-of-classroom learning in the ways that administrators and faculty do. When students are faced with a model or organizational structure that is at odds with the way they experience and understand the institution, frustration can ensue. They may be left wondering why student affairs and academic affairs, part of one institution with overall learning objectives, cannot get along.

As early as 1972, student affairs scholars suggested that both the extra- and co-curricular approaches needed revision. Impatience with unnecessarily divided student and academic affairs can be found in the observation by Brown (1972), "In the past the threads of intellectual and student development ran parallel, but in more recent years the theorists have suggested that they should be intertwined" (p. 29).

Where Do These Out-of-Classroom Models Work Most Effectively?

Several institutional types lend themselves to an out-of-classroom traditional model. Campuses with a traditionally aged, predominantly residential population have student populations with the flexibility of time and accessibility to campus facilities to take full advantage of the out-of-classroom offerings. The campus culture of these institutions lends itself to student expectations about what occurs on college campuses. Students will arrive on the campus and in the residence halls ready to become involved in extra- and co-curricular activities.

A second institutional type that lends itself well to the out-of-classroom models includes campuses with traditional student activities and affairs approaches. Campuses that depend on a psychosocial rather than learning perspective will be staffed with professionals who will shape expectations about the importance of social activities, the relationship building potential of community development, and the emotional growth possible through out-of-classroom activities.

Several institutional types are less than congruent or relatively incongruent with an out-of-classroom model. Staff on campuses with significant commuter-based and/or nontraditionally aged populations may struggle to fit the out-of-classroom model with their student populations. Students who live off campus, either with family, in apartments, or apartment style campus-owned facilities, may be less involved with the discretionary activities, programs, and services organized by student affairs professionals than traditionally aged, residentially based college students. When students have off-campus obligations such as jobs and family and/or other off-campus interests, they may find it difficult to become involved in the full range of campus features that are available. Some of these students, given their other obligations, may find the out-of-classroom activities to be a poor fit given their current priorities. Levine and Cureton (1998) describe nontraditional students as more apt to want the services and programs at their institution to resemble a bank (specifically an ATM) rather than the "full service" approach adopted in the out-of-classroom models. The time and energy required of students taking advantage of the out-of-classroom models may not be available to commuters or nontraditional students.

Finally, institutions with a strong emphasis on academics may be inhospitable places for the out-of-classroom model of student affairs practice. Students at institutions with a strong academic mission by necessity must put their emphasis on studying. The challenge of academics in this environment may preclude involvement in out-of-classroom activities. In essence, students in these institutions enroll at the institution to study and engage in the academic mission. The out-of-classroom life of the campus is secondary and/or superfluous.

Conclusion

Engagement increases the odds that any student—educational and social background notwithstanding—will attain his or her educational and personal objectives, acquire the skills and competencies demanded by the challenges of the twenty-first century, and enjoy the intellectual and monetary advantages associated with the completion of the baccalaureate degree (Kuh, 2009, p. 698).

While the DEEP research discussed in this book found that there are many ways to achieve student engagement (Kuh, Kinzie, Schuh, Whitt, & Associates, 2005/2010), none of the institutions studied exhibited the extra-curricular or co-curricular models. In fact, a significant finding of the DEEP research was that faculty and administrators (including student affairs professionals) within these institutions took a holistic, collaborative approach to student engagement. The activities leading to student engagement and success were not sharply divided into in- and out-of-classroom realms. Rather, engagement was viewed as an institutional commitment in which all were involved. Assumptions about territory and role were reduced in favor of working collaboratively toward student success.

Student engagement has two key components that contribute to student success. The first is the amount of time and effort students put into their studies and other activities that lead to the experiences and outcomes that constitute student success. The second is the ways the institution allocates resources and organizes learning opportunities and services to induce students to participate in and benefit from such activities (Kuh, Kinzie, Schuh, Whitt, & Associates, 2005/2010). Notably, this definition does not split educationally purposeful activities into the in- and out-of-classroom realms.

Since the establishment of the colonial colleges in the United States, higher education has been a 24-hour-a-day operation. Students live on campus, eat in campus facilities, exercise in college-owned buildings, and study at all hours of the day and night in college-owned spaces. While the expectations of service have long been present, the assumption of learning goals underscoring these services has not always been assumed. One could argue that the introduction of the student learning approach to student affairs is the death knell for the extra-curricular model. If seamless learning is the goal, then the distinction between in- and out-of-classroom learning blurs. All campus environments are ripe for every possible type of student learning and development. Data from the DEEP research show that institutions with high engagement and graduation rates experience this blurring of in- and out-of-classroom learning. Faculty and student affairs staff see their roles as collaborative and serving a singular goal of student learning.

The connection between the extra- and co-curricular models and student learning, though perhaps obvious to some, is not without difficulties. A basic premise of the out-of-classroom models, at least as they have been practiced in the past, is the separation of social/emotional and cognitive learning. While learning in the social/emotional realm is certainly of value, the primary purpose of higher education is the academic (or cognitive development) mission. This difference between the primacy of cognitive development and secondary nature of social/emotional development has been the source of much discussion about second class citizenship in student affairs. Discussion about student learning has led to confusion about the need for student affairs practitioners to teach in a classroom setting and, conversely, for faculty to teach in an out-of-classroom setting.

With the tide of accepted practice moving away from the extra- and co-curricular approaches, why would an institution choose to employ this model? As with all approaches discussed in this book, the institution's context, history, and educational goals dictate the fit of any model to the particular setting.

Questions for Discussion

- What is the nature of the academic and student affairs missions? Are they separate entities? Is there a desire to integrate the academic and student affairs missions?
- What is the philosophy of the student affairs professionals regarding practice? Do they see themselves as educators, administrators, development specialists, or something else?
- What is the nature of the student body? Do they come to the institution expressly to develop leadership and other skills in an out-of-classroom context?
- How interested are the faculty in the out-of-classroom life of the students? How interested are student affairs professionals in the in-classroom life of students? Is there any room for collaboration between these two groups?
- Do any of the institutional characteristics (e.g., size, complexity, history) preclude close collaboration between academic and student affairs goals? Are the goals of both better achieved through a distinct separation of task and mission?

5

ADMINISTRATIVE-CENTERED TRADITIONAL MODELS

The Vice President for Student Affairs (VPSA) takes great pride in the Division of Student Affairs she built. Established on a firm foundation of organizational theory, management principles, and leadership theory, the Division of Student Affairs is an institutional example of administrative efficiency and effectiveness. While the educational background and training of the VPSA includes student development and counseling, her professional philosophy leans toward service to students. A veteran of the student affairs profession, the VPSA knows that the words "student development" do not sell well at the executive leadership level of her institution. Retention, fiscal responsibility, and strategic planning are management realities in her world.

The Administrative-Centered Perspective

The VPSA in the previous vignette represents one of the many possible approaches to student affairs practice. While some professionals argue for a student-centered approach, others argue that students are best served by creating an organizational and management structure that competently and proficiently organizes services, programs, policy, and other initiatives for students. Over the years, the student affairs field has jockeyed back and forth between administrative and developmental approaches to student affairs work.

Over time, the practice of student affairs administration has evolved with two approaches: One of service and the other of development. The former approach is concerned with the efficient delivery of programs and services to meet an array of student needs, whereas the latter is concerned

Table 5.1 Models of Student Affairs Practice

TRADITIONAL	INNOVATIVE
Out of Classroom-Centered	Student-Centered
Extra-curricular	Ethic of Care
Co-curricular	Student-Driven
Administrative-Centered	Student Agency
Functional Silos	Academic-Centered
Student Services	Academic-Student Affairs Collaboration
Learning-Centered	Academic-Driven
Competitive and Adversarial	
Seamless Learning	

with the purposeful design of programs and services to effect desired student outcomes. (Javinar, 2000, p. 86)

This chapter discusses administrative-centered approaches to student affairs practice (see Table 5.1). The two models discussed here, functional silos and student services, place the management and organizational perspective at the center of student affairs practice.

History and Assumptions of the Administrative-Centered Models

The student affairs field grew out of the twin purposes of student guidance (i.e., discipline and *in loco parentis*) and administrative need (Appleton, Briggs, & Rhatigan, 1978). The two approaches took divergent paths after the '60s, particularly as different institutions interpreted student affairs functions. Institutions adopting a guidance approach use counseling and human development as their foundation. Institutions adopting an administrative-centered approach use a management perspective as the logic for organizing programs and functions. Student development models and theories may be an aspect of the organizing philosophy, yet the predominant influences are administration, leadership, and management.

Student affairs folklore, right or wrong, supports the belief that institutional size, in particular, dictates whether the student affairs division staff takes an administrative-centered approach to student affairs practice. In other words, large institutions are more administratively oriented while smaller institutions are less bureau-cratic and more focused on the individual. We argue here that the administrative-centered models, similar to others discussed in this book, are not determined by institutional type but rather by the unique characteristics of the institution, historical approaches to student affairs practice at the specific institution, and leadership priorities of the administration. In other words, institutional character will determine the philosophical perspective driving the model of student affairs practice used. We purport that any model of student affairs practice needs to be congruent with the institutional mission. Therefore, some institutions are more suited to administrative-oriented student affairs practice while others are more suited to a development-oriented, learning-centered, or other orientation to student affairs practice.

Theoretical Foundations of the Administrative-Centered Models

The administrative-centered models grew out the professionalization of student affairs as a field of educational practice. As discussed in the founding documents (ACE, 1937, 1949), the functions of student affairs, from its earliest days, were varied and specialized.

Bureaucracy as the Foundation for Administrative-Centered Approaches. Administrators have a wide variety of organizational theories and models available to understand and guide their practice. Education organizational theorists place organizational theories into broad categories: organized anarchy, collegial, political, cultural, bureaucracy, new science, feminist, and spiritual (see Birnbaum, 1991; Manning, 2013). The administrative-oriented model uses the bureaucratic model as a guide for its organization.

The bureaucratic theory first advanced by Weber (1947) is, by far, the most prevalent theory of organizational structure in the Western world. Higher education organizations certainly use the bureaucratic model more than any other, although many (see Baldridge, Curtis, Ecker, & Riley, 1980; Cohen & March, 1986) hold that the political model is a more salient lens through which to understand colleges and universities. Every administrator, every student for that matter, with varying levels of success, knows how to negotiate the bureaucracy.

Students bemoan it as "red tape," administrators know how to "get things done," and the politically astute perform end runs around bureaucratic protocols. Although most organizational participants dislike bureaucracy, its logic provides a philosophy and organizational framework upon which student affairs work can be achieved. Bureaucracies embody particular tensions that exist within student affairs and administrative practice.

Specialization and Fragmentation versus Integration. Bureaucracies by definition are organizations where functions are specialized (Manning, 2013; Morgan, 1997). Offices are created to serve particular purposes. Job descriptions are written to delineate responsibilities of staff. As bureaucracies become more mature, their functions are increasingly specialized; some say "fossilized." This inherent specialization tendency of bureaucracy leads to red tape, which occurs when offices fail to coordinate their functions and send students from one place to another. When red tape abounds, services offered through various offices are not coordinated and communication is limited or nonexistent. Despite any intrinsic relationship among functions, offices perform as if they are discrete entities—separate silos, so to speak.

Although specialization is a major force within bureaucracies, integration of these specialized functions is equally important. Integration is largely achieved through coordination. Socialization, communication, cultural artifacts, standard operating procedures, and planning are ways coordination is achieved. In a classic bureaucracy, coordination is achieved through the chain of command and supervisory mechanisms, group and individual meetings, and communication structures that inform organizational members of each other's behavior (Blau, 1970/1973; Simon, 1957; Weber, 1947).

Student affairs has a unique history concerning coordination. In the field's original founding document, *The Student Personnel Point of View* (ACE, 1937), coordination was prominently discussed. In a publication limited in size, the authors dedicated a significant amount of words and pages to the importance of coordinating student services functions. Several original textbooks in the student affairs field, *Student Services: A Handbook for the Profession* (Delworth & Hanson, 1980, 1989) and *Student Affairs Functions in Higher Education* (Rentz & Saddlemire, 1988), delineated the student affairs functions by area and topic. As such, these early student affairs textbooks adopted a specialized approach to student affairs practice. The danger in this approach is the fragmentation that results when people consider their functional areas as separate, rather than related, areas of service for students. Through specialization, functions can become isolated and independent.

Public versus Private. The urge toward specialization and the delineation among different parts of the institution are not so different from the public/private split often sought within organizational life. The personal has always been associated with feminine characteristics and the public with masculine (Collins, 1986; Harding, 1987, 1991). Feminist theorists argue that women need to occupy the public domain as well as dismantle the barriers to thinking that the personal does not belong within the public. In fact, the rallying cry, "the personal is political," raised by feminists in the 1980s makes the point that a separation between public and private is arbitrary and inaccurate.

Student affairs educators have long interchanged the personal and public. They work with students on issues that are clearly private in nature: health, families, and relationships, among others. The University of Maine at Farmington, a DEEP project institution,

> has fostered an environment that actively supports the mixing of personal and work lives in healthy ways. Students encounter their professors on a regular basis in this small community; thus, they have many opportunities for informal conversations. These frequent contacts also help to reinforce students' identities in the minds of faculty. (NSSE, 2003g, p. 43)

The public/private split is one worthy of exploration and thought in student affairs, a profession long relegated to or celebrated as (depending on your perspective) feminine. The dominance of women in educational fields certainly is reflected in student affairs where, at least at the nonexecutive level of higher education administration, women outnumber men by a significant percentage. With the longstanding overlap of personal and public, it is not at all surprising that one way student affairs administrators managed this tension was to establish two models for practice: administrative and counseling/developmental.

Centralization versus Decentralization. In addition to the bureaucratic tendency to specialize and fragment, a structural tension in

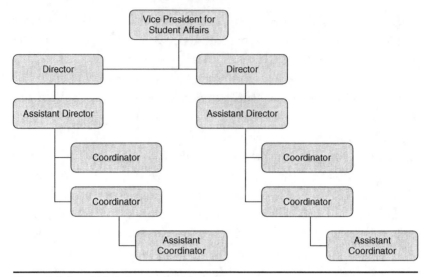

Figure 5.1 Pyramid Style Organizational Structure

bureaucratic structures is centralization versus decentralization. In theory, bureaucracies seek to centralize functions. If you imagine the standard pyramid style organizational chart, the impression given is that the person at the top is "in charge" (see Figure 5.1).

As the person to whom the entire division ultimately reports, one may have the impression that this "top" person is privy to all communication and knowledge available. This perception is often displayed on campus during a crisis (for example, an athletic scandal). Vice presidents experiencing this kind of crisis may be fired or forced to resign as trustees, students, parents, and local community members state that he or she "should have known what was going on in his or her institution." This widespread belief exists despite the fact that Blau (1970/1973, 1972) in classic studies of the bureaucratic structure found two interesting aspects of bureaucracies. The first is that information within bureaucracies becomes less, not more, reliable as the communication progresses up the hierarchy. Blau attributes this phenomenon to the fact that few are willing to report their mistakes to superiors. As the communication travels up the hierarchy, the negative aspects of the situation are weakened, leaving the report an unrealistically positive version of the original account. Second, despite the common folklore about "large bureaucracies" and the control inherent in them,

Blau also found that larger bureaucracies are more diffuse and less apt to be centrally controlled than smaller bureaucracies. This tendency is attributed to the fact that the positional leader (i.e., person at the top) cannot possibly comprehend all the activity, communication, and knowledge that abounds in a large organization. Instead, trusted staff are relied upon to know and do their jobs with minimal supervision and oversight. Corporate scandals (e.g., J.P. Morgan, HSBC, Enron) provide evidence that the assumptions about firm control in bureaucracies are unwarranted. Such beliefs can place organizational viability and leadership success in jeopardy.

The Functional Silos Model

The first use of the term "functional silos" in the student affairs literature is difficult to identify. Arguably, the 1996 *Student Learning Imperative* (ACPA) may have been the first document where the term gained currency among student affairs professionals. The document's authors used the term "functional silos" in the following context: "As with other units in a college or university, fragmented units that operate as 'functional silos': that is, meaningful collaboration with other units is a [*sic*] serendipitous" (p. 4).

For anyone living in a state or area where farms are prevalent, silos are familiar icons. You can see silos from miles away: They stand like sentinels over the landscape. As devices that store grain or silage, they are an ingenious way to increase the productivity of the farm. But what is readily apparent when you look at silos is that they are disconnected. They stand on their own, detached from other structures (and, therefore, other functions of the farm). They serve their one function, perhaps very well, but that one function is the extent of their usefulness. Silo is now a metaphor to depict disconnection and isolation from other campus offices. While some welcome this isolation as a superior way to conduct business (see vignette in the Features of Functional Silos section), others see the approach as an impediment to high quality student affairs practice. In the 1990s, student affairs, after approximately 50 years of existence as a field of education, heartily embraced the bureaucratic trend of increased specialization and silos. Despite periodic budget cuts and staff retrenchment, the overall number of student affairs positions on college campuses grew and specialized.

Features of the Functional Silos Model

The functional silos model entails the following characteristics: (1) allegiance to the specific functional area literature in lieu of the broad-spectrum student affairs literature; (2) autonomy by function and often by space and resources; (3) decentralization of supervision, professional development, and, oftentimes, goals; and (4) competition for resources and student attention among departments. The characteristics are underscored by the assumption that students require different programs, services, and environments that are best offered by distinct and separate offices. It is also assumed that services, programs, and policies can be well or adequately delivered without or with minimal division-level coordination. Several of the characteristics of the functional silos model are illustrated in the following vignette.

> *The director of residence life at a midsized public institution came into a student affairs division comprised of approximately eight other offices. His unit, residence life, was the largest auxiliary service of the division. In fact, as an auxiliary service, residence life was vastly different from the other student affairs functions. Because of the budgetary and programmatic differences between his area and the other offices, the director of residence life often felt out of place at division staff meetings. While there were some overlapping goals concerning student development, interventions exercised with the students, and coordination with discipline issues, the director still felt that his area entailed management and administrative issues of a different magnitude than other division functions. At a staff meeting, the director of residence life expressed his frustration at this situation by saying, "Sometimes I feel that I don't have to interact at all with the rest of you. My department is so different that it really stands on its own in terms of unique financial obligations to the institution, staff issues, and the need to serve students as customers." The director preferred the autonomy to determine his budget and make personnel decisions. He was frustrated by the divisional attempts to coordinate efforts across the various units.*

As this vignette indicates, there are power and resource implications to the functional silos model. A department can afford to be independent if resources support that self-determination. But, if a department shares or borrows resources, such independence and autonomy is ill advised. Even with independent resources, one wonders at the choice not to form a professional community with the other staff. In fact, the DEEP research found that the formation of silos adversely affected student engagement and success.

Allegiance to the Specific Functional Area Literature. With the evolution of student affairs into functions (e.g., residence life, career development, counseling, activities), the literature and scholarship in the field experienced a concurrent specialization. Blimling (2009) argued that the student affairs literature could be divided into four communities of practice: "(a) student learning, (b) student development, (c) student services, and (d) student administration. The first two of these communities come from an educational perspective and the second two come from a management perspective" (p. 713). One can easily see how the scholarship from these different communities would be embraced or not by professionals representing different areas of student affairs practice. In fact, professionally-enhancing arguments have been waged about the need to emphasize management over student development or student services over administration. Some authors (e.g., Bloland, Stamatakos, & Rogers, 1994) have decried the overemphasis on student development and argued for a broader approach to guide student affairs practice. In reality, as an interdisciplinary field, proficient and effective student affairs practice requires the use of a wide range of scholarship to inform practice. Within the specialized areas, however, there will always be the need for scholarship that applies specifically to that area. The challenge for the field is to craft foundational scholarship shared across the field and specialized scholarship that applies to particular areas.

Autonomy by Function, Space, and Resources. The struggle between more and less autonomy can be seen in the division of space and location of offices on any college campus. During the DEEP study, several institutions were observed to have a centralized "one stop shopping" configuration for their student affairs offices. Often located in a student center or central building, these offices were physically located to maximize student convenience. The central location was intended to mitigate "red tape" and run-around that often occurs within bureaucracies.

This centralized configuration, however, requires compromise. When offices share a common space, any one function may not have enough physical space to adequately serve students in the ways desired by the staff. Economies of scale may be acquired through sharing resources (e.g., clerical staff, budget) but those shared assets may not adequately meet the needs of individual offices. The functional silos model is characterized by a separate, as opposed to shared, configuration. Budgets, space, and resources are individually assigned to offices that are autonomous from other student affairs functions. The concept of shared resources is foreign to the functional silos approach.

Decentralization of Supervision, Professional Development, and Goals. In a similar pattern to the autonomy of function, space, and resources, supervision, professional development, and goals are decentralized in the functional silos model. The assumption with decentralization is that the staffing and management needs of the individual student affairs functions and offices are unique. For example, residence life has different needs from student activities, which has different needs from career development. The supervision would be different; different theories and approaches would necessitate unique professional development. A challenge for student affairs in the ensuing years will be to determine what are the theoretical and philosophical elements of the field that hold it together and what are those elements that are unique to each functional area.

Competition among Departments for Resources and Student Attention. A danger of the functional silos approach is the competition that can occur when different offices and functional areas compete with one another for space, staff, and other resources. If the functions are decentralized with minimal contact and interest shared among staff members, common values may be lost including student-centeredness, ethics, social justice, and selflessness. If these values are subsumed by the individual values of the functional area, the founding values of the field can become diffused and scattered. Leadership is an antidote to the potential for competition in the functional silos model. Central leadership emanating from a dean of students or vice president for student affairs can create momentum to keep the division from disintegrating into a series of individual offices that lack connection to the overall mission of the division.

Strengths and Weaknesses of the Functional Silos Model

The first, and most significant, strength of the functional silos model is the staff member expertise available to students. These professionals know their fields extremely well and often undertake the most cutting edge practice within their area. They are specialists with strong professional links to student affairs educators outside the institution who occupy similar silos. Because of this emphasis on expertise, students receive a high level of service and program delivery. This expertise also translates into high levels of professionalism.

Another strength that can quickly become a weakness is the presence of independent, stand-alone budgets often called "responsibility centered budgeting." The expression "every tub on its own bottom" describes this approach. This prevalent budget model is extremely well suited to the functional silos model. Every office, whether an auxiliary service or a general fund-based office, is responsible for its income and expenses. For the model to work, autonomy accompanied with professional expertise must be granted to the individual office.

A third strength of the functional silos model is the administrative and organizational clarity afforded by this model. Because of the adherence to specialization, division of labor and specialization of task are clear. This clarity, though, is more obvious to administrators than students because the former are familiar with the organizational principles upon which functional silos are built. Students, on the other hand, are not only unfamiliar with the bureaucratic assumptions, but they may use a completely different organizational logic (e.g., functions grouped as they are chronologically experienced in college, by related functions, or by location in the same building) than the logic employed by administrators. Students, therefore, become confused and perhaps frustrated when negotiating the system.

In addition to the strengths of the model, the functional silos model contains several weaknesses. The most significant one is that the model is administration-centered rather than student-centered. Since student affairs is basically and ultimately about serving students, this administrative-centered approach begs the question, who is student affairs ultimately there to serve?

A second weakness of the functional silos model is the professional isolation that may result from the distinctive specialization of the offices. This isolation can quickly turn into professional solitude and lack of community. With these elements, the potential for staff burnout increases. Some of this isolation and burnout may emanate from the homogeneity of theoretical perspective and approach. Any monocultural, singular approach is likely to be weaker than heterogeneous approaches where diversity of experience, approach, and theoretical perspective are emphasized.

A third weakness of the functional silos model is that the existence of stand-alone, independent units means that these offices can be eliminated more easily during budget cuts or shifts in approach. Because the offices are isolated and only loosely coupled to other campus offices, such changes can result in a quick eradication of the whole unit.

Finally, such monotheoretical emphasis as is present in the functional silos model can lead staff to exaggerate their self-importance (see residence life director vignette discussed in the Features of Functional Silos section). This situation can cause student affairs staff to lose perspective about the centrality of their area to the overall mission of student and academic affairs.

A private institution of 5,000 students, nonreligiously affiliated, has a long history of separate academic and student affairs units. Described as the "other side of the house," both sets of personnel are comfortable with the dichotomy that has evolved. While the student affairs units have adopted a learning approach over the past 15 years, spurred by association publications such as The Student Learning Imperative (ACPA, 1996) *and* Learning Reconsidered (ACPA & NASPA, 2004), *they function as a separate silo from the academic learning perspective. Occasionally, conflict arises within the institution over where offices that exist on the boundary between academic and student affairs (e.g., academic advising, career development) belong within the organization. Some argue that these offices clearly lie within the academic realm. Others argue that the offices are a student affairs function. Because this conflict is rarely resolved on a philosophical or administrative basis, offices switch back and forth between the provost and student affairs divisions. The decisions about where to locate these offices are often made on the strength or weakness of personalities (e.g., vice president, staff members).*

Student Services Model

A second administrative-centered student affairs model is the student services model where functions and services often are clustered together: financial aid, registrar, and admissions; orientation, academic advising, and admissions; academic advising, counseling, and students with disabilities services. These services and offices generally are not organized under student affairs but are, instead, associated with financial services, student accounts, and the bursar's offices. Although traditional student affairs functions such as student activities and residential life may take a student services approach, in this chapter, the classic student services offices are discussed.

Several assumptions underlie the student services model including beliefs about the purpose of student affairs, expectations about the standard of service, and necessity (or lack thereof) of a student development approach. The first assumption of the student services model is that the main purpose of student affairs is to deliver services, not provide a developmentally oriented education to students. In other words, proponents of the student services model do not assume that all administrators, staff, and faculty are involved in student development. From this assumption flows the belief that student services and the developmental/educational aspects of student affairs can be separate. As with any administrative-based organization, some functions provide services and convenience that support the goals of education, not a provision of the education itself. It is not that student development is absent as a goal of the campus. Rather, a developmental approach to the provision of services is not assumed.

A second assumption of the student services model is that students are better served and more satisfied when services are conveniently organized and provided. The convenience and high standard of quality is to be provided in part because students pay tuition for those services but, more important, because they are members of the campus community. This assumption is built on a perspective that suggests that students

> prefer a relationship (with the institution) like those they already enjoy with their bank, the telephone company, and the supermarket. . . . They want their colleges nearby and operating at the hours most useful to

them, preferably around the clock. They want convenience: easy, accessible parking (in the classroom would not be at all bad); no lines; and polite, helpful and efficient staff service. (Levine & Cureton, 1998, p. 50)

Features of the Student Services Model

The first characteristic of the student services model is that students access the services organized under this model on a periodic, rather than daily, basis. Students consume these services as the need arises. Second, institutions often use enrollment management, total quality management, and other customer-oriented management approaches from the corporate sector to promote a "one-stop-shopping" approach for the convenience of students. Third, in the student service model, individual relationships between students and administrators are not as crucial as the overall reputation of the office.

Periodic Rather than Daily Basis. In the student services model, students are viewed as customers or consumers who use the services, as needed. They often have an overall perspective on the quality of services throughout the institution (e.g., course registration is difficult) that leads to a generalized level of satisfaction or dissatisfaction with campus life. Starting in the 1990s, Total Quality Management (TQM) and techniques borrowed from Disney were approaches used to improve the quality of services offered on campus. The focus was customer satisfaction. The periodic nature of the service delivery does not make these services any less important than ones accessed every day. Each interaction with students, regardless of its source and intent, is an opportunity for student affairs professionals to encourage student growth and development.

"One-Stop-Shopping" Approach. If student services are to be efficiently and effectively delivered to students, their physical placement must be considered. Student affairs has long considered the effect of the environment on student learning. The early campus ecology movement (Banning, 1978) and the more recent campus environments literature (Strange & Banning, 2001) eloquently speak to the importance of matching physical considerations to learning and developmental goals. "Rather than putting student services on the perimeter of the campus, or in out of the way places, student services at DEEP

institutions were centrally located and easy to find" (Kuh, Kinzie, Schuh, Whitt, & Associates, 2005/2010, p. 314).

Reputation of the Office. Staff in student affairs offices built on a developmental model expect to build personal relationships with students. Student services offices, on the other hand, expect to remain in the public rather than private sphere of students' lives. That approach is illustrated in the following vignette.

> *John Jones, a student at Green Mountain University [a pseudonym], has student loans to cover the costs of college. Each semester, he visits the financial aid office to sign forms, process his loans, and apply the loan money to his bill. His family situation is complicated because his parents are divorced and pay for college separately. The family communication often is strained so he depends on the financial aid staff to help him understand the outstanding balance on his university bill and other aspects of his finances. Although he visits the office each semester, he has not formed a relationship with any one staff member. He feels comfortable with any of the staff available and is impressed with their level of professionalism and care. Their systems are organized in such a way that, even if he is talking with someone he has never interacted with before, the staff member is quickly apprised of his situation. The staff know their jobs and can help a wide variety of students who walk through the door. He has never had to wait for a particular staff member who is more familiar with his situation than another.*

Strengths and Weaknesses of the Student Services Model

The student services model contains several inherent strengths. The first is convenience for students. In fact, the model is premised on convenience. In the 1990s, this approach was highlighted in student affairs through the use of total quality management (TQM) as a way to promote excellence in service to the customer. Although many in student affairs took issue with the word "customer," the idea of maintaining a high quality of service is certainly a worthy goal.

A second strength of the student services model is that it creates the space for those who work on teaching, the primary mission of the institution, to be unimpeded by service demands. Faculty and student affairs educators both can get on with the business of education when tuition is collected, loans are processed, and registration is completed.

Related to this strength is the idea that the student services model and the functions entailed with this approach support the infrastructure of the institution: resources are generated, courses are filled, and students are admitted.

A third strength of the student services model is that these services are more readily coordinated with the goals and purposes of institution-wide initiatives such as enrollment management. The coordination necessary between offices that support the infrastructure of the institution creates an opportunity to trace student progress, track student achievement, and understand student attrition. Although traditional development approaches to student affairs play an important role in enrollment management, their more general educational goals and outcomes lack the precision of the student services approach.

The primary weakness of the student services model is obvious: lack of integration of various functions and services. When functions are delineated into specialized areas, the model does not provide an administrative or organizational structure for integration. Without this, offices are disconnected, miscommunication is common, and institutional goals are only partially met. In other words, services that students may think should logically be grouped together are, instead, separated into offices with little or no overlap. Various attempts (e.g., clustering offices by similar functional areas) to integrate student services functions have been attempted. An innovative model at Trenton State College (now the College of New Jersey) in the 1980s clustered student affairs functions by "individual" student services (e.g., counseling, health services, career services) and group student services (e.g., residence life, student activities, student center). This, like others, was an attempt to bring together student affairs staff with similar functions to better integrate their functions and more skillfully serve students.

A second weakness of the student services model and one related to the lack of integration is the lost opportunity for collaboration between academic and student affairs professionals. In recent years, student affairs practice has increased in complexity and pace. The demands of student affairs work increased to its current fever pitch. As the pace and complexity increased, opportunities for collaboration decreased. Collaboration has many benefits in the long run: better communication, greater creativity, improved staff relations, enriched learning experiences, and enhanced service to students. In the short run, however, collaboration is viewed as time consuming and unnecessary. When services and programs are separate, the opportunities for natural collaboration between and among offices are strained. Attempts to build collaboration to increase collegiality and familiarity with the services available can be artificial in the student services model. Innovative cross-office programs that serve students and professional development programs become "in addition to" the basic work performed by the individual unit. These lost opportunities for collaboration have a more long-lasting effect than immediately realized. The more innovative approaches of new science and quantum theory, when applied to leadership and management, identify collaboration as an essential step to high-quality management in the 21st century (Allen & Cherrey, 2000; Wheatley, 2010; Zohar, 1997). In organizations as complex as colleges and universities, leaders must have the ability to view the whole. Allen and Cherrey talk about "getting on the balcony" to achieve this wholeness perspective. This connection and attention to the whole was emphasized most notably at Alverno College, a DEEP project institution.

> Alverno non-teaching staff members also passionately endorse the emphasis on the whole. For example, the Student Services division promotes itself as "Partners in Learning in developing a community of learners." In fact, the Partners in Learning strategy resulted from efforts within the division to identify the ways in which Alverno's mission, curriculum, and students shaped their work. According to one staff member, "We see ourselves as an extension of the classroom. We're all important to student learning and we constantly build on the curriculum." For example, student services staff "help students translate their learning into different settings and call them to reflect on their experiences" outside the classroom as well as in. (NSSE, 2003a, p. 12)

If one emphasizes discrete, separate student services offices, wholeness and collaboration are elusive concepts. This de-emphasis on collaborative and holistic approaches will not serve students and the student affairs field in the future.

A final weakness of this model is the fact that maintenance of efficient bureaucratic procedures, often a priority, is not always achieved. This is the case with any service that is built on a use and service provision business-oriented model. The provision of any service is difficult to maintain and often degrades over time. Enlightened and sustained leadership is necessary for a high quality of service to be maintained.

Where Do These Administrative-Centered Models Work Most Effectively?

These models have the most saliency in several types of colleges and universities. Institutions with first-generation college students or others who need clear pathways for success (Kuh, Kinzie, Schuh, Whitt, & Associates, 2005/2010) are ones that would lend themselves very well to the administrative-centered models. First-generation students, for example, will most likely have the skills to succeed in college but less familiarity with the ways that the institution is organized. A well-organized division of student affairs fashioned on a student services or functional silos approach may provide a clear path for the student to follow on the way to success and graduation. Any institutional type that has a significant population of students with multiple demands, such as family and full-time positions, would benefit from an administrative-centered approach.

Institutions, for example, Ivy League institutions and specialized colleges or universities (e.g., engineering schools) that do not have a traditional student affairs mission, would likely find the administrative-centered models to be a good fit for their institution.

Another institutional type that would lend itself to the administrative-centered models would be one with complex processes for graduation, course requirements, and other administrative procedures. These institutions would by necessity place a priority on straightforward and well-organized administrative procedures to better serve students.

As with any model presented in this book, all offices in a student affairs division need not follow the same model. This is particularly the case for the student services model. While the functional silos model can be applied to any area of student affairs practice, the student services model fits some areas of student affairs practice better than others. One might be hard pressed to use this model in student activities, disciplinary affairs, and service learning. Several traditional areas within student affairs (e.g., residence life, career services), while usually adopting a developmental approach, could utilize the student services model and perspective. Some areas (e.g., financial aid, admissions) are particularly congruent with this approach.

Conclusion

One of the remarkable aspects of the 20 DEEP project schools was that the functional silos model was minimal. Walls of specialization did not separate the various offices. Instead, there was seamlessness among the services, programs, and functions at these institutions. This was certainly the case within student affairs divisions, but the seamlessness also extended to the academic/student affairs connections.

> The collaborative spirit and positive attitude that characterize DEEP campuses are evident in the quality of working relationships enjoyed by academic and student affairs which operate on many other campuses as functional silos, a situation which is all too common in higher education. (Kuh, Kinzie, Schuh, Whitt, & Associates, 2005/2010, p. 172)

This "blurring" effect mimics the approach students take to services, programs, and functions. Rarely do students make distinctions between academic and student life, tenured faculty members and graduate assistants, and offices in one division and another. Instead, to students, college life is one big seamless whole where classes are taken, help obtained, and programs attended by a variety of offices identified as part of the university or college, not a specific part of that institution. At the DEEP project institutions, collaboration is the means to the seamlessness that students experience. Administrators and faculty must know their colleagues, institutional tasks, and the relationship between institutional mission and the function being performed to enact the seamlessness felt by the students.

> Almost all staff and faculty [at George Mason University] we spoke with mentioned that a supportive environment was created based on the collaboration of various units on campus. Few work in silos. The Office of Academic Student Affairs is an example of this type of collaboration, which combines the functions of these two areas that are usually distinct

> on campuses. . . . The Academic Advising Center is based on collabo-
> ration with department faculty, the Career Center, Orientation, and a
> variety of other offices. There is also a notion of a seamless handoff with
> academic advising. (NSSE, 2003b, p. 38)

Collaboration dismantles silos or does not allow them to emerge
in the first place. An administrator at the University of Kansas commented, "If students are going to have good access to services, then
the people who run those services have to have access to each other"
(NSSE, 2003d, pp. 41–42).

A quality of the student services model that emerged from the
DEEP study was the use of student employees as essential members
of the college staff. University of Maine at Farmington was easily the
exemplar of this approach.

> Student services . . . employs students. . . . They have close contact with
> faculty, staff and supervisors, and obtain significant responsibilities over
> the course of their college career. Funding for student clubs is largely
> coordinated and monitored by student employees. The wellness program
> (aerobics classes, etc.) at the student fitness center also is coordinated
> and—for the most part—taught by students. Students also serve on a
> number of University committees. One example is particularly strik-
> ing: We heard from a young man who was asked by an administrator
> to spearhead the construction of a new Education facility according to
> "green" standards. The student has taken it upon himself to become an
> advocate for the project by educating himself about the green move-
> ment and the realities of the project budget. "I thought I was going to
> have to push a boulder up a hill. Instead, it's been positive. I felt like a
> professional. I had to know my stuff. The President is pretty serious.
> She made sure I knew my stuff," he explained. It was on the basis of this
> student's initiative—involving significant research which he then had
> to present before faculty and administrators—that the University made
> a commitment to "green" buildings in planning for new construction.
> (NSSE, 2003e, pp. 28–29)

In addition to Farmington, Gonzaga University in Spokane, Washington amply uses student staff as a way to teach leadership as well
as provide staff support in an institutional climate of scare resources.

Student life and student services offices not only hire students to augment full-time staff, these students are essential to ensuring the delivery of quality services to peers. Often, student staff members' responsibilities are on par with entry-level full-time staff. (NSSE, 2003c, p. 31)

The lack of a holistic perspective and overlooked collaborative approach of the administrative-centered models encourages competitive rather than collaborative approaches to student affairs. The two administrative-centered models discussed in this chapter and critiqued in *The Student Learning Imperative* (ACPA, 1996) emphasize a nonintegrated, decentralized approach that does not serve students or the learning goals of the campus as well as other choices. When only the VPSA has a bird's eye view on the division, directors may be apt to adopt a decentralized approach where competition rather than cooperation is the standard operating procedure. Students cannot help but be served inadequately when competition as opposed to cooperation and decentralization as opposed to integration are the norms. Unhealthy competition may occur about the funding that must be acquired, the degree to which students are served, and the number of staff positions obtained. At its worst, competition breeds empire building and myopia. Directors argue for their individual offices rather than maintain a view that takes the good of the entire division and institution into account. With an emphasis on decentralization and discrete operations, unit directors may feel that they need not interact with other directors within their division.

Since the mid-1990s, the emphasis in student affairs has been less on administrative-centered models and more on learning-centered approaches. While the administrative-centered approach is not as current as in the formative days of the student affairs field, these models, depending on institutional mission, retain their currency. As student affairs administrators, particularly senior student affairs officers, make decisions about the ways to organize a division of student affairs, the strengths and weaknesses of the models discussed in this chapter can be considered. Perhaps it is possible to take the strengths of these models (e.g., quality of service to students, expertise present in staff) and weave them into models that more adequately reflect the current learning-centered approaches to student affairs practice.

Questions for Discussion

- What officers and programs warrant an administrative-centered approach? Which offices and programs do not?
- How can architecture and campus environments be managed to provide the best service to students?
- What management principles can be used to most effectively serve students?
- How can a student success perspective be built into the administrative-centered models?
- In what ways can collaboration and cooperation be built into seemingly disparate services?

6

LEARNING-CENTERED
TRADITIONAL MODELS

One of the foundational elements of contemporary student affairs practice is student learning. While learning has been an emphasis of student affairs practice for decades, directly or indirectly at least since the publication of the *Student Personnel Point of View* in 1937 (American Council on Education), the release of *The Student Learning Imperative* (American College Personnel Association, 1996) stimulated consideration and implementation of strategies that were designed to enhance the learning dimension of the student experience. Student affairs practice has been conceptualized to encourage and stimulate student learning (see, for example, Kuh, 1999; Magolda, 1999), and measuring student learning has become an important dimension of student affairs practice (Kuh, Kinzie, Schuh, Whitt, & Associates, 2005/2010; Schuh & Associates, 2009).

The following description of two students' experiences is designed to illustrate different approaches to two learning-centered models: seamless learning model and competitive and adversarial model (see Table 6.1).

They occur at the same university but result in quite different experiences for the students.

Sam and Alex were best friends in high school but chose different post secondary institutions after graduating from high school. Sam selected Mid Central University (MCU), a large, public residential university with a broad curriculum and many opportunities for students to get involved in the life of the university. Alex went to Eastern Continental University (ECU), also a large, public residential university. Sam was unclear about selecting a major and

Table 6.1 Models of Student Affairs Practice

TRADITIONAL	INNOVATIVE
<u>Out of Classroom-Centered</u>	<u>Student-Centered</u>
Extra-curricular	Ethic of Care
Co-curricular	Student-Driven
<u>Administrative-Centered</u>	Student Agency
Functional Silos	<u>Academic-Centered</u>
Student Services	Academic-Student Affairs Collaboration
<u>Learning-Centered</u>	Academic-Driven
Competitive and Adversarial	
Seamless Learning	

chose MCU because of its broad curriculum. Alex, on the other hand, wanted to study sociology, a strength of ECU. While they both lived in campus residence halls, Alex elected to participate in a learning community while pursuing the major in sociology. Sam lived in a residence hall that did not have learning communities and deferred selecting a major until after completing some general education courses.

Sociology majors who participate in the sociology learning community are expected to have a sociology major for a roommate, and Alex did, rooming with Charlie. Upon arriving on campus, they immediately began to participate in activities sponsored by the learning community. Among these experiences were a first year seminar for sociology majors taught jointly by a faculty member from the sociology department, a faculty member from the English department, and the associate dean of students who had been a sociology major as an undergraduate at another university. They had part-time jobs as student assistants in the sociology department and volunteered to read to first grade students at the local elementary school twice a week. In addition, sociology learning community participants took three classes together and were involved in a study group that met three times a week to review assignments, prepare for tests, and discuss material covered in lectures. If things went well, Alex very likely could become a student teaching assistant as a junior or senior, an experience that would position him for graduate school, a potential path for sociology majors after graduation.

Professor Clarkson from the sociology department met with the students from the sociology learning community every other week in the residence hall floor lounge to answer questions that the students might have and also to provide suggestions for the students as they navigated through their first year.

The students also invited Professor Clarkson to have lunch with them after Monday morning's lecture. Support for the meal program was provided by the ECU residence department, which had a program whereby students could invite faculty members to share a meal with them on an occasional basis. Professor Clarkson also served as the temporary academic adviser for the learning community students, who could select a permanent adviser after completing their first year. Max, a senior major in sociology who planned to pursue a master's degree after graduating in spring, led the learning community activities and lived on the floor with the students though a resident assistant also lived on the floor. The learning community consisted of 15 students, all first year, who lived together on the same residence hall floor with Alex and Charlie.

Sam's experience was different than that of Alex. As an undeclared student, Sam was advised by a staff member from the MCU advising center. This person served as Sam's academic adviser until Sam selected a major. Sam was enrolled in courses that would meet the MCU general education requirements and by the end of the fall term was leaning toward a major in Political Science with a possible career in public service, possibly as an environmental lawyer. Sam's adviser helped in narrowing career options but it was up to Sam to work with the adviser in doing so. One of the courses Sam took was a first year seminar that was designed to help "undeclared students" sort out their academic interests taught by a faculty member from the history department and a member of the career planning staff.

Sam's roommate was a chemistry major and as the semester unfolded spent more and more time with laboratory activities. As luck would have it, they did not have any overlap in their curriculum so while they were serious students, their class preparation took them in different directions. When they had a free moment, which was not often, they enjoyed grabbing a cup of coffee at a snack bar in the Student Union and comparing the rigors of their coursework.

Activities in the residence hall were organized by the floor resident assistant (RA) and members of the resident student government and ranged from intramural sports competition to collecting items for a food drive around Thanksgiving. Sam was elected as floor president and was quite involved in organizing floor activities and emerged as a leader in the residence hall. Sam needed a part time job to help defray expenses and took a job in town with a clothing store that was listed by the Part-Time Job Service in the Office of Career Services. Sam also decided to get help from the campus English lab because writing had been challenging for him in high school and he did not want to fall behind in this important course. Sam was very busy and enjoyed various forms of involvement that became available.

Right after Thanksgiving break Sam's resident assistant posted a notice on the floor bulletin board indicating that applications for resident assistant positions for the next academic year would be taken at the beginning of the spring term. In a private conversation the RA expressed the opinion that Sam had been an excellent leader and had very good interpersonal skills that could lead to success as an RA. Sam was delighted at the conversation and filed an application to become an RA, which, after a series of interviews, led to an offer of a position. Sam was thrilled and accepted the offer. The position would help with defraying some college expenses and also provide an opportunity to develop leadership skills, long an interest of Sam's.

Both Sam and Alex had very successful fall terms and the spring also was going quite well until Sam encountered a problem. At MCU no classes were held on Friday afternoon so that fields trips could be scheduled for various courses as well as training workshops such as leadership development programs offered by the Student Activities Center or seminars on how to become an intramural sports official by the Campus Recreation Department.

Reaching out beyond the campus has been an important feature of the didactic approach of the University and midway through the term Sam's instructor for a political science course in state government arranged for a trip for the class to meet with the governor and legislative leaders at the state capital, a short 45 miles from campus. The state leaders were going to talk about the complexities of contemporary political leadership. Their focus was on the competing interests in the state for increased funding in a static revenue environment. All members of the class were expected to attend and short of illness or a true emergency, no excuses for missing the field trip were accepted.

At about the same time the trip was scheduled, Sam learned that a preservice training program for all newly selected resident assistants was planned for the same afternoon as the field trip. The training activity was to begin on Friday afternoon and continue all Saturday at a lodge MCU operated off campus. As was the case with the field trip, all newly elected RAs were expected to attend and missing part of it was not acceptable. So, Sam was in quite a dilemma—miss class and be penalized by having a grade lowered, or miss the training program and possibly lose a highly coveted job? What to do?

History and Assumptions of the Learning-Centered Models

Guiding the work of the student affairs staff likely will be a student development approach, narrowly defined. But the selection of an approach will often be left to the individual department, so residence life might choose Chickering's theory of psychosocial development (Chickering & Reisser, 1993) while judicial affairs might select Kohlberg's (1969) theory of moral development or Gilligan's (1982) theory of moral development in women. While having professional practice guided by a theory of student development can be quite helpful in program planning and working with students, it is frequently difficult to disentangle students' experiences (for an in-depth discussion of student development theories, see Renn & Reason, 2013). Accordingly, parceling students' experiences into distinct, unrelated parts fails to recognize the holistic nature of the student experience.

The previous example is a collage of experiences of students who attended DEEP schools. Among the elements of the example are the following experiences that were common to many DEEP institutions:

1. Interdisciplinary courses, team taught by faculty members,
2. Faculty interacting with students outside of class, focusing on coursework,
3. Learning communities,
4. Undergraduate research assistantships,
5. Internships and service learning,
6. Academic clubs, and
7. Social interactions between faculty and students.

Both MCU and ECU are committed to providing robust educational experiences for undergraduates, both inside and outside the classroom. But as the example illustrates, at MCU student affairs and academic affairs operate independently of one another, while at ECU collaboration is expected and practiced between the two divisions. The next sections of this chapter describe each approach in detail.

The Competitive and Adversarial Model

This learning-centered model, in effect, places student affairs-related activities and experiences in competition with classroom activities.

Adversarial suggests that the two elements of the university, those responsible for out-of-class activities and those with responsibility for classroom and other for-credit experiences, plan and execute their programs and other aspects of their domains without paying much, if any, attention to what their colleagues are doing. It also suggests that academic and student affairs units are concerned with what students learn and how they grow and develop, but that neither reaches out to the other to create coordinated, complementary learning experiences for students.

An important dimension of this model could be unintended, yet real, competition for students' attention and time. This competition is not just manifested in scheduling problems. Experiences, opportunities, and activities are planned without regard to what other units are doing or how they might collaborate and complement each other. This may result in duplication of effort in some cases, while in others students may be forced to choose between equally worthy opportunities. To drill down a bit further, for example, similar programs being offered by units within student affairs or units within academic affairs can illustrate competition. Leadership development programs, for example, could be offered by residence life, student activities, or Greek life. Volunteer programs in the community might be offered by units in student affairs as well as by academic departments. Without question staff and faculty are committed to an enriching student experience, but they tend to go about their work independently of one another, and in the end they very well can compete for the attention and time of students.

The adversarial dimension of this model is illustrated by Sam's experience. Sam was supposed to participate in a training experience for newly selected resident assistants while at the same time participating in a required experience for a political science course. Sam is really stuck and one would hope that in an actual situation, some way to ameliorate the problem could be found. Those planning the training workshop looked at the structure of classes and saw that nothing was in the way of regularly scheduled courses for the Friday afternoon in question, and the faculty member who planned the field trip assumed that since Friday afternoons were set aside for field experiences, there would be no problem with planning a trip to the state capital. The result was a mess that was left to Sam to resolve.

Theoretical Foundations of the Competitive and Adversarial Model

A number of factors have contributed to the evolution of student affairs as a profession (see Rhatigan, 2009). Rhatigan concluded that the end of World War II "transformed student personnel administration" (p. 11) through the expansion of existing programs and services and the addition of new ones. Specialization and narrowness of focus increasingly have been features of higher education and it is no wonder that the various units found in a division of student affairs often have mimicked this pattern. While student affairs functions began informally perhaps when avuncular faculty members provided advice to homesick students, the appointment of the first dean, at Harvard University in the latter part of the 19th century (Nuss, 2003; Rhatigan, 2009), marks the formal beginning of student affairs work. As the formal academic dimension has become more specialized over the years, so, too, has student affairs. Even though a few academic departments were organized in the second half of the 1700s (Hecht, Higgerson, Gmelch, & Tucker, 1999), it was more than a century later that this organizational structure was common. Student affairs followed a similar pattern of specialization triggered, according to Rhatigan (2009), by significant enrollment growth after World War II. Such areas of student affairs practice as placement, counseling services, residence hall programs, student activities, and others emerged. And, as faculty chose to divest themselves of certain academic support functions, such areas as academic advising and the registrar's functions became part of the student affairs portfolio at many institutions of higher education.

Growth was an important ingredient in the increasing specialization in higher education. Institutions of higher education, particularly state universities, have become larger and more specialized over the years, against the recommendation of Astin (1977, cited by Kuh, Kinzie, Schuh, Whitt, & Associates, 2005/2010) that undergraduate enrollments should not be greater than 15,000. For example, in fall, 1996, 350 institutions had an enrollment of 10,000 or more (The *Chronicle* 1999–2000 Almanac) but by fall, 2010, the number of institutions with an enrollment of more than 10,000 was 594 (U.S. Department of Education, 2011, Table 248). This means that an additional 244 institutions approached a level of enrollment in just 15 years that would make them less desirable using Astin's perspective. And, the largest 120 institutions in the U.S. in 2010 ranged in enrollment from 27,692 to over 300,000 (U.S. Department of Education, 2011, Table 249). Why? To accommodate an increasingly larger percentage of the population that seeks postsecondary education, it is easier and cheaper to accommodate enrollments through enrollment growth rather than by founding new institutions.

One consequence of increasingly large undergraduate enrollments and more specialized units is that communication between the various elements of a university (e.g., academic departments and student affairs units) becomes increasingly difficult as institutions grow. Similarly, communication between individuals becomes more difficult because as institutions grow in size, individuals simply will know an increasingly smaller percentage of the faculty and staff.

One cannot expect institutions to get smaller, particularly in the face of increasingly larger percentages of high school graduates attending college in the future. "Total enrollment in postsecondary degree-granting institutions is expected to increase 15 percent between fall 2010, the last year of actual data, and fall 2021" (Hussar & Bailey, 2013, p. 19). In the face of growing enrollments, the increasing tendency is for departments and units to specialize. This growth leads to "compartmentalization and fragmentation, often resulting in what is popularly described as *'functional silos'* or *'mine shafts'*" (emphasis added) (Schroeder, 1999a, p. 137). Insularity, according to Schroeder, is the likely result of these developments and insularity leads to the following observation by Whitt, "For many years, reformers have charged that colleges and universities have become too divided by organizational structure, disciplinary priorities, and competing missions to educate students effectively" (2011, p. 483).

The fundamental difference between this model and the functional silos model discussed in Chapter 5 is that "Competitive, Adversarial Model" focuses on student learning rather than on organizational structures and unit functions. Remember that in Chapter 5 the "Functional Silos Model" is administratively focused rather than centered on student learning. The "Competitive, Adversarial Model" presented in this chapter contains many of the features of the "Functional Silos

Model" but the focus on what students learn is a fundamental difference. We present a number of features of the "Competitive, Adversarial Model" in the next section of this chapter and we trust that as the
model is contrasted with that presented in Chapter 5, the differences
will become obvious.

Young (1996) wrote of the philosophical tensions between the student personnel point of view and a philosophy of practice. In the case
of the example of the RA training workshop competing with the field
trip for Sam's time, the philosophy of practice conceptualizes the student experience as individualistic and segregated. One consequence of
this approach is that student affairs practitioners work hard at providing the very best experiences and services possible for students, within
the framework of their departments. The coordinator of residence life,
in the example, tries to develop the best leadership development program possible, without really thinking about how the program could
be linked to leadership development offered by the political science
department. Or, to use another example, the volunteer coordinator
develops an outstanding program for students at the local youth shel-
ter, but does not realize that the sociology department may be trying
to do the same thing with service learning courses.

This does not mean that administrative actions are guided by a
lack of interest in working together, or an unwillingness to cooperate.
Rather, individuals strive to do the best they can within their sphere of
influence, and since reaching out to develop collaborative relationships
is not the "MCU way," the culture evolves to the point where specialization frames departmental approaches to student growth. Once in
motion, this model results in increasing specialization, greater attention to improvement within the silo, and focusing on doing one's narrow definition of work better. The consequence of this approach is that
opportunities are missed, frequently.

Features of the Competitive and Adversarial Model

The features of this model including the organizational structure,
independent staff development, distinctive missions, independence of
work, separate locus of learning, and segmented organizational boundaries illustrate the lack of communication and collaboration between
the academic and student affairs staffs.

Organizational Structure. The competitive adversarial model typically has student affairs and academic affairs reporting to independent vice presidents as illustrated by Figure 6.1.

In this depiction the senior officers for academic and student affairs report to the president and any coordination of their work is left to the president. The president may from time to time suggest that the two vice presidents and their units work together toward an institutional goal such as developing strategies designed to improve the institution's graduation rate, but the details are left to them to resolve. Even with a goal as important as improving graduation rates, it is entirely possible in this model that academic and student affairs staffs work independently of one another in strengthening programs designed to raise the graduation rate.

At very large institutions, the units that are included in student affairs, which are depicted in Figure 6.2, can be so expansive and complex that they may or may not choose to collaborate with other units in student affairs.

Leadership development was cited as an example earlier in this chapter. If the residence life department provides housing for 5,000 students, for example, and there are 30 Greek letter organizations on campus, it might appear to be simpler to leaders in both units to organize their own leadership development programs. After all, isn't serving as president of a Greek letter organization different than serving as president of a residence hall? In some respects it is, but in other ways it is not. The competitive adversarial model would let the units develop their own programs and not be overly concerned about how economies of scale could be realized.

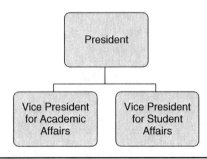

Figure 6.1 The Competitive and Adversarial Approach to Organizing Student Affairs

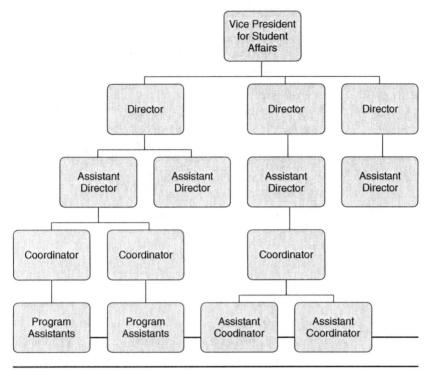

Figure 6.2 Organization of Student Affairs Using the Competitive and Adversarial Approach

Independent Staff Development. Staff development is another activity that might be done independently, that is, on a unit-by-unit basis. The thinking that goes into offering staff development programs without collaborating with other student affairs units has to do with size, complexity, and expertise. "What we do in our department is different than the other units in student affairs, so we prefer to offer our own training programs" goes this line of thinking.

Distinctive Missions. The missions of academic affairs and student affairs are crafted in this model as if neither unit is aware of the contributions that the units can make to each other. Student affairs staff members conceptualize their contributions to student learning as occurring outside the classroom or laboratory and they do not think about the cognitive development of students. The cognitive development of students is left to the faculty and classrooms. Student affairs provides distinctive learning experiences for students that may or may not complement other campus experiences. That is, what students learn from their out-of-class experiences is a consequence of a specific experience as opposed to a series of experiences linked to other occurrences on campus. Communications skills workshops, for example, may be provided in the residence halls, student activities, and Greek affairs without regard to what students learn through courses offered in academic departments such as the speech department or honors program. In this illustration, four units could be engaged in communications skills workshops independently of one another.

Independence of Work. As the leadership training example suggests, the work of the various units on campus is conducted separately of one another. This leads to overlapping and duplicative efforts. The approach tends to be quite inefficient because more than one unit may be devoting resources to similar student experiences when they could work together to provide a more robust, less costly set of experiences for students.

Loci of Learning. In the adversarial and competitive model, the location where student experience occurs is important. That is, certain forms of learning are conceptualized in certain places. For example, it is assumed that psychosocial development results from out-of-class experiences. Cognitive development is left to formal, academic experiences, usually within a classroom, laboratory, or library. Rather than thinking that various types of student learning could occur virtually anywhere at any time, certain kinds of learning are assumed to occur only in certain places. Some forms of learning are reserved for the formal curriculum, and other forms of learning are in the territory of the out-of-class experience. An example of this could be that the residence life staff members decide to organize a tutoring program for students who are enrolled in the math course that most first year students take. At the same time, the supplemental instruction program offers a program for first year students who are taking the entry-level math course. Neither office thinks to contact the other to determine if they could collaborate on such a program. The staff members, instead, work in their own silos.

Organizational Boundaries. Student life is conceptualized as occurring in segments, and staff members from student affairs do not think to work with academic affairs staff on common issues. Similarly, academic affairs staff members see what occurs outside the classroom as not much more than being social in nature. Divisional staff within the institution work independently of one another. The consequence can be something like this example:

> Academic orientation is planned independently of orientation to living in the residence halls. Receptions for students to meet faculty members in their major areas of study are planned in the late afternoon by academic departments at the same time a residence hall volleyball tournament is scheduled. Communication about avoiding scheduling conflicts is not even considered, and student participation in both experiences is diluted.

Strengths and Weaknesses of the Competitive and Adversarial Model

One might assume that this model lends itself to large, complex institutions. While that certainly can be the case, it also can be found at smaller institutions where student affairs and academic affairs function independently of one another. It is entirely possible that senior officers and their key associates have never experienced a situation where a blended, linked approach to student learning was employed. They simply function in their own sphere of responsibility without considering what could be gained by being more closely linked with their counterparts who also are interested in the student learning experience.

The obvious strength of the model is its expertise-based approach to the student experience. That is, the person or persons who are the most capable organize and deliver experiences and activities to and for students. For example, if one is interested in providing leadership development experiences for resident assistants, there is a person on the residence life staff who has that expertise. The consequence is that the institution places the responsibility for various student experiences, such as orientation, staff development, leadership development, or community service in the hands of experts. The resulting quality of the student experience has the potential to be very high.

The model reflects one of the properties of a loosely coupled institution (Weick, 1976); the consequence of which is that if new initiatives are unsuccessful in a department or unit, the larger organization is affected only marginally or perhaps not all. Therefore, if a new experience is added to residence hall orientation, say an afternoon where students provide service to the local community, any potential failure or negative consequences are slight and contained within the residence halls.

But the primary strength of the model in some respects turns out to be a weakness. Since every unit delivers its own programs and experiences, competition, as was the case for Sam, for student time can become a serious problem. Little coordination occurs and students have to pick and choose between attractive experiences that are scheduled at the same time. The problem is more than a simple one of conflicting time demands. The overlap in expertise required results in duplication of staffing and effort expended in the development of student learning experiences. Quite obviously, this approach has the potential to be very expensive. Several of us once served as consultants to an institution that had a high number of programs and experiences planned by and made available to students. The senior student affairs officer lamented that the institution was in search of participants and audiences since every student seemed to be engaged to developing programs and few were available to simply attend those programs.

Seamless Learning Model

This model reflects the adopted institutional philosophy that student learning has the potential to result from virtually all student experiences. Structures are in place so that academic and student affairs leaders are aware of developments in each division of the institution, and ideas for working together on issues related to student learning are suggested routinely. Alex, as mentioned in the previous example, attends such an institution, Eastern Continental University (ECU). Adopting a seamless learning approach to organizing the student experience requires hard work and a deliberate commitment. A good example of how a commitment to seamless learning could be illustrated is ECU's approach to learning communities. The following scenario might be how this occurred.

A decade ago senior members of the student affairs at Eastern Continental University were considering various ideas to enrich the quality of residential life. Residence life staff and others in the division had believed for a year or so that the quality of residential life was not what it could be. After discussion at the Vice President for Student Affairs cabinet meeting, the decision was made to consider different initiatives. The residence life staff members who instigated the discussion were instructed to develop two to four proposals that would have the potential to improve the quality of the student experience.

The organizational structure of the division was such that a senior member of the Provost's staff, the Associate Provost for Student Learning, regularly attended the division's meetings. Similarly, the Assistant Vice President for Student Life attended the Provost's staff meetings. In developing quality of residential life enhancement proposals, the residence life staff asked the Associate Provost to participate in the discussions and the development of the proposals. Two proposals that emerged were the development of learning communities and a plan by which students could invite faculty members to join them for meals in the residence halls at no cost to the faculty member.

A joint meeting of the senior staff in student affairs with senior staff in academic affairs was called to consider the proposals. After carefully considering the advantages and disadvantages of the proposals, the learning communities proposal was adopted but the meal program was postponed for budgetary reasons. Two years later the meal program was put in place as an element of the learning communities program. From this group the Vice President for Student Affairs and the Provost appointed the core of an implementation task force that would identify how the details of the learning communities project would be addressed.

History and Assumptions of the Seamless Learning Model

Brown (1972) questioned the co-curricular approach that was in vogue at the time of his writing, but it took a number of years before documents emerged that recognized the connectedness of the student experience. Bowen's volume (1977) included the following observation: "Education, or the teaching-learning function, is defined to embrace not only the formal academic curricula, classes and laboratories but also those influences upon students flowing from the many and varied experience of campus life" (p. 33). Bowen identified a number of historical documents related to this concept (i.e., that higher education ought to be concerned with the whole student experience). The Study Group on the Conditions of Excellence in American Higher Education (1984) emphasized, "perhaps the most important for purposes of improving undergraduate education—is *student involvement*" (p. 17, emphasis in original). The National Association of Student Personnel Administrators (1989) in its document *Points of View* asserted, "Out-of-class social and physical environments are rarely neutral; they help or detract from students' social and intellectual development" (p. 13). These works and those of others (e.g., Astin, 1993; Kuh, Schuh, Whitt, & Associates, 1991; Tinto, 1993) led to the paper *The Student Learning Imperative* (American College Personnel Association, 1996) that contributed to the current emphasis on student learning, irrespective of whether this learning occurs in a classroom, residence hall, or somewhere else, on or off campus. Subsequent work (e.g., Schuh & Whitt, 1999; Kuh, Kinzie, Schuh, Whitt, & Associates, 2005/2010) has provided additional ideas on the extent to which institutions can create partnerships and conditions that facilitate student learning.

The Student Learning Imperative (ACPA, 1996) indicates that the mission of a student affairs division committed to student learning "complements the institution's mission, with the enhancement of student learning and personal development being the primary goal of student affairs programs and services" (p. 119). The document authors added another characteristic of the learning-oriented student affairs division: collaboration with other staff within the institution as a means to encourage student learning and personal development.

Kuh (1996) added to *The Student Learning Imperative* by advocating that colleges and universities should strive to create seamless learning environments. In this case seamless refers to "what was once believed to be separate, distinct parts (e.g., in-class and out-of-class, academic and nonacademic, curricular and co-curricular, or on-campus and off-campus experiences) are now of one piece, bound together so as to appear whole or continuous" (p. 136). Instead of working in silos, to provide the best possible experiences for students regardless of what was occurring elsewhere on campus, student affairs professionals and faculty need to break out of their silos and develop integrated, complementary experiences for students. This philosophy suggests that the whole of the student experience is greater than the sum of its parts and that no persons or units possess sufficient expertise that other units or people cannot add value by working with them. Instead, the student experience is best conceived of as an ongoing developmental process that begins when a student applies for admission and ends, in a formal sense, at graduation.

We argue that while institutions can have a marginal effect on the characteristics of the students who enroll due to such factors as institutional location, finances, or mission, they can have a powerful effect on the experiences students have while they are enrolled. We know that some experiences are likely to affect student persistence to graduation in positive ways, as was pointed out in Project DEEP (Kuh, Kinzie, Schuh, Whitt, & Associates, 2005/2010). The research purpose of Project DEEP was to identify what institutions that had higher than predicted scores on the NSSE and higher than predicted graduation rates were doing to achieve those two measures of success. A commitment to seamless learning was an important factor in how student affairs interacted and collaborated with academic affairs to provide a robust environment in which students learned. The seamless learning model's organization described in the next section can help facilitate the learning environments of institutions.

Organizational Structure. The seamless learning model is depicted in Figure 6.3.

This model has the senior student affairs officer reporting to the senior academic officer. We found this organizational approach implemented at several DEEP institutions with great success because the senior academic officer served as a strong advocate for blending learning

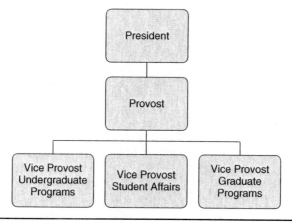

Figure 6.3 A Seamless Learning Approach to Organizing Student Affairs

that occurred both inside and outside the classroom. To be successful, the senior academic officer has to be interested in out-of-class learning and recognize the stiff learning curve to be mastered in order to be conversant in the subtleties and nuances of student affairs practice. It also meant that the academic officer could articulate the value of out-of-class learning to the institution's president and governing board. For the seamless learning model to be successful much more needs to be accomplished than simply drawing up an organizational chart, as will be pointed out later in this section.

Another organizational approach to this model is depicted in Figure 6.4.

In this approach, a staff member coordinates and organizes student learning activities on behalf of both academic and student affairs, and reports to both vice presidents. The vice presidents report independently to the president and have their own portfolios of units. The

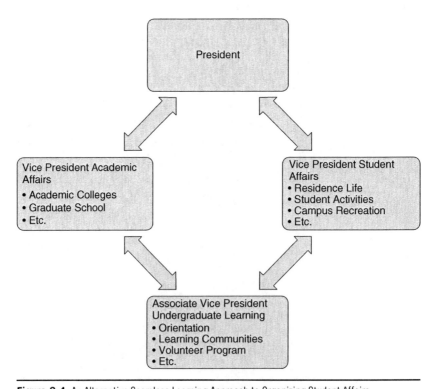

Figure 6.4 An Alternative Seamless Learning Approach to Organizing Student Affairs

challenge in this approach is to find a person who is conversant in both academic and student affairs, has sufficient credibility to work effectively with faculty and student affairs staff, and can articulate the value of collaborative efforts. The person most likely would be a faculty member who holds tenure and, most likely, the rank of professor. An effective person in this role would have quite a history of involvement with undergraduates, perhaps as a student organization advisor or an associate dean who coordinates student services in an academic college. An appreciation of how experiences outside the classroom contribute to an undergraduate's education would be a prerequisite for this role. While people who have such a blend of credentials are not easy to identify, it is possible and we include this approach as an alternative to having the senior student affairs officer report to the senior academic affairs officer.

Features of the Seamless Learning Model

The features of this model are such that academic and student affairs work together to contribute to the student experience: missions designed to support student learning, shared initiatives, wide-ranging contributions of staff to student learning, blurred in- and out-of-classroom experiences, and indistinguishable boundaries.

Missions Designed to Support Student Learning. In the seamless learning model, the institution is dedicated to providing a robust, enriched learning experience for students. The missions of both academic and student affairs are dedicated to contributing to this total learning experience to which the institution is committed.

Shared Initiatives. Representatives from academic and student affairs recognize that student learning is what the institution is dedicated to and they work together to devise ways to enhance student learning. An example is the approach to orientation. Before planning any programs, the members of the orientation committee with representatives from academic and student affairs work together to identify the learning outcomes for orientation. After a thorough study regarding the potential for learning, programs are planned with these outcomes in mind. Some programs are planned jointly between academic and student affairs staffs while others are planned primarily by one group or the other.

The orientation committee closely monitors the planning of the experiences, including those of student affairs, and keeps a master calendar so that the various experiences can be linked to the desired student learning outcomes. Recall the example of the volleyball tournament and departmental receptions conflicting during orientation under the competitive model. Using a seamless learning approach, the volleyball matches might be scheduled on an afternoon on the lawn adjacent to an academic building where open houses are held simultaneously and the afternoon could conclude with a student-faculty picnic.

Everyone Contributes to Student Learning. The seamless learning model is undergirded by the assumption that every member of the institution can contribute to learning. This means that everyone's ideas are worth considering, and that the value of one's contributions is not linked to one's formal institutional role. The cafeteria staff member may have an idea on how to enrich student-faculty conversations in the dining hall. A member of the grounds crew might know how to use the lawns for picnics or other forms of student-faculty interaction.

In- and Out-of-Classroom Learning is Blurred. The potential for student learning is recognized regardless of what students and faculty are doing at any point in time. While students are expected to learn in class, it also means that experiences can be developed for them to learn outside of class. As institutional priorities change or evolve, what may have been in the territory of the out-of-class experiences of students may be infused into the curriculum or vice versa. The driving force for what students learn is an unwavering commitment to achieving the mission and goals of the institution. Various units dedicate themselves to devising ways that they can work together so that students have the best learning experiences possible.

Boundaries Are Indistinguishable. Whereas in the other models it was easy to identify the boundaries between various units on campus and what students learned in- or out-of-class, boundaries are difficult to identify on campuses that adopt the seamless learning model. To be sure, students receive formal credit for their academic work, but that work might occur in class, outside of class on campus, or in the local community. Members of the various units collaborate to provide the best learning experiences possible, driven by the mission of the institution and the learning experiences desired for students. Academic and student affairs work together on such experiences as service learning, tutoring, leadership development, and internships.

Strengths and Weaknesses of the Seamless Learning Model

As was suggested with the competitive, adversarial model, the seamless learning approach is not necessarily determined by institutional size. While it is true that smaller, less complicated institutions may find it easier to implement the seamless learning model, if senior officers are not interested in collaborating to develop a learning-rich environment, even a small college can take a competitive adversarial approach to student learning. In some respects, senior officers have to go out of their way to develop the seamless learning approach as the foundation for student affairs.

The clear strength of this approach is the integrated, coordinated approach taken to the student experience. In the best of circumstances one might find, as we did at one of the DEEP institutions, that faculty members did not know what we meant when queried about student learning outside the classroom. When we clarified our question about in- and out-of-classroom learning, their response was, "Oh, that. We really don't differentiate between what goes on inside or outside the classroom. We're engaged with students all the time outside the classroom. Tonight, for example, we're going to a lecture on campus with students from one of the residence halls."

This model has the potential to be efficient, focused on accomplishing institutional goals regarding the student experience, and able to allow students to maximize their experiences. By that we mean that students need not choose between experiences as Sam did, but rather are offered a blended approach to their experiences, as was the case for Alex.

This model suggests that senior officers in academic and student affairs share a common interest in student learning no matter where it occurs. In other words, they are willing to cede elements of authority and responsibility to each other and their staffs. It also means that the members of their units (meaning student affairs practitioners and faculty) recognize the challenges and skills that each other brings to the student experience. A student affairs staff member, for example, will understand the challenges faculty members face regarding promotion and tenure while a faculty member will appreciate the difficulties student affairs staff members encounter as they strive to create healthy learning environments for students.

The model also can have challenges with respect to sustainability. By that we mean that as newly appointed senior officers come on the scene they will be as interested in the blended student experience as their predecessors were. In some respects the model is fragile in that it depends on institutional members who continue to work together over time. Newcomers are oriented to the institution's core values so that they sustain the commitment to seamless learning. We found this at one DEEP institution where the recruitment process for new faculty was an in-depth experience for the prospective faculty member. Upon completing the interview, the candidate understood the institutional values in terms of seamless student learning and faculty-student interaction.

Where Do These Learning-Centered Models Work Most Effectively?

Although it is difficult to generalize about the effectiveness of any model out of context, the learning-centered models have the potential to work well across a wide range of institutions. The competitive and adversarial model, as the only negative perspective in the book, is not recommended for any institutional type. The seamless learning model is particularly recommended for several different types of campuses. Colleges or universities with close interaction among faculty and staff would very likely be institutions that use a seamless learning model. Programs, policies, environmental management, and services can each be arranged so that students obtain the impression that everyone on campus is invested in student learning and that boundless opportunities for learning exist throughout the institution. A second institutional type where the seamless learning model is likely to be found is one with an active student body seeking engagement, learning, and development across a wide range of settings. These institutions may be ones with a history of active student interest in various types of learning opportunities. Finally, institutions with commuter, nontraditional, and other populations less connected to the institution may find value in the seamless learning model. The integrated learning perspective may be easier to access by students who have limited on campus time to discover learning opportunities outside of their routine actions.

Conclusion

This chapter was designed to discuss two models of student affairs practice that focus on student learning. While they have the same general goal, that is, trying to identify services, programs, and activities that contribute to student learning, the approaches taken are dramatically different. In one case the division of student affairs operates very independently of the rest of the institution. In the second approach, units from the division of student affairs collaborate regularly with academic affairs to provide the best experiences possible for students. Our obvious bias is toward the second model, since, in our judgment, this approach has the potential to provide the most robust student experience. Our study of the 20 DEEP institutions leads us to draw this conclusion, since we saw literally hundreds of examples of student and academic affairs collaboration to develop learning experiences for students. We think this approach provides excellent promise for increasing the robustness of the student learning experience on contemporary college campuses.

Questions for Discussion

- How can a campus with separate and disconnected learning experiences be transformed to one with a seamless approach to learning and development?
- What are the institutional characteristics that impeded the change to a learning-centered institution? What characteristics enhance this change?
- How can students be involved in shaping a campus to be more learning-focused?
- What theories within the student affairs literature provide guidance regarding a learning-centered approach?
- How can campuses, if embroiled in a competitive and adversarial model, use faculty allies to change the model?
- What prevalent assumptions and attitudes exist within student affairs and academic affairs that present barriers to transforming a competitive and adversarial model?

PART III

INNOVATIVE
MODELS OF
STUDENT
AFFAIRS
PRACTICE

7

STUDENT-CENTERED
INNOVATIVE MODELS

Students have always been at the center of the student affairs profession. Beginning with The *Student Personnel Point of View*, 1937 (ACE, 1937), the profession claimed as its central purpose the education of the whole student. This emphasis intensified as student affairs accepted chief responsibility for responding to the needs of new nontraditional students brought into higher education through the GI Bill. The adoption of the philosophy of student development afforded the profession the authority of being a strong voice for students in the academy. Student development theory has furthered the view that students are at the center of the academy.

History and Assumptions of the Student-Centered Models

Early approaches to student affairs practice such as those described in Chapter 3 emphasize the responsibility that student affairs has taken for student needs in the out-of-classroom environment, or extra-curriculum. This approach makes the social, emotional, spiritual, and psychological needs of students preeminent. However, because these needs are typically separated from curricular activities, the approach has been criticized as having limited utility in promoting student learning. As we studied the educationally effective colleges and universities in the DEEP project, we saw evidence of student-centered approaches in student affairs divisions that attended to the historical emphasis on out-of-the-classroom, but enhanced student engagement and success (see Table 7.1).

Table 7.1 Models of Student Affairs Practice

TRADITIONAL	INNOVATIVE
Out of Classroom-Centered	**Student-Centered**
Extra-curricular	**Ethic of Care**
Co-curricular	**Student-Driven**
Administrative-Centered	**Student Agency**
Functional Silos	Academic-Centered
Student Services	Academic-Student Affairs Collaboration
Learning-Centered	Academic-Driven
Competitive and Adversarial	
Seamless Learning	

Some institutions developed intrusive developmental and learning support services to respond to student needs, while others elevated students to important roles in campus governance and employed them as paraprofessionals. At a few institutions students were empowered to lead campus initiatives with limited intervention from administrators. The whole person philosophy sparked the development of these student-centered models, but this idea is expanded on in ways that more intentionally promote student learning and success.

In this chapter, we outline three innovative approaches to student affairs that retain the view of students at the center of the enterprise, but do so in novel ways to enhance student success. We first describe the student-centered ethic of care model, then the student-driven model, and conclude with the student agency model. Several vignettes are used to introduce the concepts and add context for understanding the models. We then outline the strengths and weaknesses of each approach and consider the relationship between these student affairs models and student success.

Ethic of Care Model

The first model discussed in this chapter is a student-centered ethic of care. Although each model in this chapter places students at the forefront of student affairs practice, this one focuses on care and relationships.

Theoretical Foundations of the Ethic of Care Model

Gilligan's (1982) ethic of care and Nel Noddings's (1984) expansion of this concept provide theoretical underpinnings of this model's approach marked by a fundamental response to student needs; services geared toward the goal of facilitating student success; integrated services, policies, and programs; and practice centered on an ethic of care.

In early 2000, Adams University [a pseudonym] faced significant challenges related to student retention. First year student retention rates had dropped for four years in a row, and student survey data indicated overall dissatisfaction with the quality of advising, infrequent use of academic support services such as tutoring, and a perception that the institution did little to help students succeed academically. A task force was assembled and charged with determining a plan for improving the situation for students.

The task force report identified recommendations based on student development theory and influential documents like The Student Learning Imperative *and* Making Quality Count; *they detailed a plan titled "Student Success Initiatives." The crux of the plan was the integration of services to more effectively meet the needs of students, particularly in their first year of college. The vice president of student affairs and the provost were put in charge of realizing the vision of the plan.*

One of the first initiatives realized from the plan was the establishment of the Student Success Center. Although services such as advising and tutoring were previously available to students, they were housed in several offices across different divisions. The creation of the Student Success Center integrated services such as tutoring, academic advising, computer instruction, academic skill development, testing and placement, and career exploration. Broadly, the Center serves individual needs of students as they persist toward an undergraduate degree and develop into lifelong learners. Specific initiatives for first year students, including a first year peer mentoring program and an interactive computer simulation to help students assess their writing, were developed. Most important, the Center afforded the institution the opportunity to more clearly articulate a shared vision and philosophy for student success.

Although the Student Success Center was intended to provide essential services in one convenient location, student affairs units also recognized that to adequately address student advising and general academic support needs, it was necessary to conduct additional outreach. To this end, the Career Development

Center sponsored a variety of outreach programs in the residence halls including "Suite Talk," a program that engaged students in their residence hall suites in conversations about setting educational goals, career advising, developing resumes, and securing internships. The Center also collaborated with dining services to offer an etiquette series to help seniors gain experience interviewing over a meal. Center staff set as their goal to conduct one workshop a month in student space.

This depiction of the Student Success Center development and enhancement of student support services represents many characteristics of a student-centered ethic of care model. In this model students' needs are preeminent. "Caring involves stepping out of one's own personal frame of reference into the other's. When we care, we consider the other's point of view, his [*sic*] objective needs, and what he expects of us" (Noddings, 1984, p. 24). Whether developmental in an affirmative sense (e.g., orientation leadership training) or reactive (e.g., disciplinary action), the ethic of care model places students' needs at the center. This commitment to care exists even when student affairs educators understand how time consuming working through an individual student's issues can be.

In 1982, Carol Gilligan wrote a classic work about women's psychological and moral development. *In a Different Voice* has stood the test of time as a significant work in human development. Generations of student affairs educators have used her theories to understand psychological development, which is based on an ethic of care rather than an ethic of justice. Gilligan's work offered several assumptions that proved to be groundbreaking. The first was that the previously assumed "neutral" theories of psychological and moral development were actually gender-related. Prior to Gilligan, the prevailing theories of human development (e.g., Kohlberg, Freud, Perry) were crafted from research on male subjects but generalized to men and women. Gilligan redefined women's development, previously considered at a lower level than male development, as different, not deficient.

The second assumption posited by Gilligan grew from an extension of Chodorow's theories about the role of relationship in the lives of women. "Female identity formation takes place in a context of ongoing relationship since mothers tend to experience their daughters as more like, and more continuous with, themselves" (Gilligan, 1982, p. 7). The theory formed was that women's development occurred in the context of relationship and connection; men's development occurred in the context of autonomy and separation. Since Gilligan's 1982 work, theory about an ethic of care has been debated, refined, and expanded. But, the impact of this early work cannot be underestimated.

Additional influences on the ethic of care approach to student affairs practice include Schlossberg's (1989) concepts of marginality and mattering and Rendón's (1994) developmental process of validation. Schlossberg emphasized that students need to feel like they matter before they can get involved in or invested in their education. Educators therefore, must provide personal attention and support to demonstrate to students that they are cared about, and that someone else will empathize with their failures and successes. Validation is particularly relevant for understanding students who may enter college uncertain about their academic ability or capacity for success in college. Expressions of validation, including positive reinforcement to take advantage of learning support services; encouragement to get involved in campus organizations; and words of praise for achievements delivered by faculty, student affairs educators, and staff help students develop confidence in their capacity to learn, increase feelings of self-worth, and reassure students that they have something to offer to the academic community. As a field already marked by care and connection, student affairs practice has been strongly influenced by the expressions of care explicated by Noddings, Gilligan, Schlossberg, and Rendón.

Features of the Ethic of Care Model

The ethic of care model acknowledges that some students come to college inadequately prepared to perform at academically acceptable levels, may lack the belief in their capacity, or do not have the necessary social skills or capital to succeed in college. The model emphasizes that colleges and universities have a moral and educational obligation to provide the academic, personal, and social support students need to succeed. Notably, at the educationally effective colleges in the DEEP project, this is not about lowering academic standards or "coddling." Instead, the institutions provide the resources and skill development opportunities students need to improve their performance and the reinforcement students need to meet achievement standards.

The ethic of care model focuses attention on students most in need of support. For example, most institutions pay far more attention to new, first-time, first year students than they do to transfer students. As a result, transfers often do not know enough about the available resources, services, and institutional features. Equally problematic, they have little in common with the academic and social experiences of their first year peers and cannot easily connect with other transfer students. Thus, they often feel disconnected. However, DEEP colleges and universities with an ethic of care model address this challenge with events that welcome and introduce transfer students to the institution. For example, at one institution, about half of the annual incoming class is transfer students. Separate orientation programs and support services are tailored to their needs. Specially designated sections of the semester-long "Introduction to the University" class review university policies, requirements, procedures, and campus resources. Career Services reaches out to and informs transfer students about internship opportunities and, if they are undeclared, about majors. The campus retention committee, representing student and academic affairs, examines transfer student data to ensure that adequate services are provided.

Student affairs divisions organized on the ethic of care model develop services and programs with the goal of facilitating student success and maximizing student development outcomes. When services are linked and safety nets established, fewer students fall through the cracks. These initiatives are even more effective when student and academic affairs collaborate on these efforts.

Strengths and Weaknesses of the Ethic of Care Model

A strength of the ethic of care model is clearly the level of service available to students. In this case, "service" is not the same concept as discussed in Chapter 4 in the student services model. While the student services model is based on administrative expediency and procedure, the ethic of care model premises service provision on the ability of the student affairs educator to devote time to students in need, assist the student in the most sensitive and compassionate means possible, and create a climate in which every member of the community is valued. This model is highly individualized in that care must be tailored to support each student, but also entails a broader professional commitment to ensuring that all students know, through programs, recognition, and interactions, that they genuinely matter and that the institution is committed to helping them achieve.

A second strength of the ethic of care model is the environment created by an atmosphere of care. When professionals earn a reputation for caring, trust seeps through the college environment. Community building proceeds in an easier manner as students obtain the emotional support necessary to form healthy relationships, engage in constructive risk taking, and pursue developmental tasks that lead to engagement and involvement. The receipt of positive messages from faculty, student affairs staff, and peers helps confirm that a student belongs at and is valued by the academic community. Such feelings are particularly salient for historically underrepresented students who may be more likely to question the extent to which their participation is valued and success supported by an institution.

The major weakness of the ethic of care model is glaringly obvious: It is highly time consuming. With budget constraints, increased psychological and emotional needs of students, and the sheer volume of student affairs work growing each year, the labor intensive nature of the ethic of care model may not be possible on many campuses. Another weakness of the ethic of care model is a possibility of treating students in a childlike manner. With a model framed nearly exclusively by care, one must be careful to avoid parental and overly protective approaches to student affairs work. The prevalent models of care often are fashioned on conceptions of proper parenting. Obviously, student affairs educators are not parents but the field has a long history of in loco parentis and paternalism. Any professional using this model must be vigilant so that care does not turn into coddling.

Student-Driven Model

The second student-centered model discussed is the student-driven model. Assumptions of this model include trust in students' ability to manage college functions, understanding of the potential of the college environment to teach student leadership, and belief in empowered students.

At Superior University (SU) [a pseudonym], about half of the 3,000 enrolled students live on or within walking distance of campus and almost all are working more than 20 hours a week while enrolled full time. Most entered the university directly out of a high school in the region, and very few are of non-traditional age. Many of the students at SU qualify for Federal Work-Study and most are paying their own way through college. These students work on average up to 30 hours a week to afford education and living expenses. Few are working just to earn spending money. However, despite the fact that SU students are spending a significant portion of their time working, they are satisfied with the quality of their college experience, and even indicate levels of involvement in co-curricular life on par with other small, residential institutions where students are working five or fewer hours. In addition, the university has a respectable retention and graduation rate.

The campus has always been committed to involving students in the campus community. University regulations prescribe that all policy committees (with the exception of personnel committees) have a minimum of 20% student representation. Many faculty members, particularly those in small departments, rely on advanced undergraduates to help with departmental programming, tutoring, and teaching assistance. A joint initiative between the provost's and student life offices formalized the significance of students working on campus when discretionary funds were used to create more meaningful learning experiences through campus employment. Faculty and administrative offices applied for the funds by submitting position descriptions. A university committee periodically reviews these positions to ensure that they provide students educationally relevant work experience. As a result, undergraduates serve as research assistants, campus photographers, landscapers, and directors of community service and fitness programs. Currently the SU students are employed on campus in jobs that at many institutions are staffed by full-time employees.

The high involvement of students as employees yields significant benefits for all students. A large number of students show up for campus events, including major concerts, parties, lectures, and poetry readings. The Friday night coffeehouse featuring SU student talent draws a few hundred students each week. Most of this programming is created and delivered by students with student affairs professionals providing considerable support to student leadership development. For example, residence life professionals developed a training program to teach resident assistants and student leaders in campus activities how to collaborate on events, maximize resources, develop interactive educational programming, and promote programs. In addition, SU students and student affairs professionals, particularly financial aid and career service center staff, work closely with interested faculty members involved in local community service. The collaborative goal is to increase student participation in existing community initiatives. These initiatives expanded after SU took full advantage of funds through the Community Service Federal Work-Study program, in which students with awards are employed in community service organizations. This effort also increased the number of student coordinators of campus-community partnerships.

In this vignette, student involvement and leadership are core operating principles. In the student-driven model, the focus is on developing students' capacity as peer educators and leaders and valuing students as integral members of the college or university community. Students drive campus activities and are involved at high levels in co-curricular life. The institution has organized itself through institutional policy mandating student membership on committees, in the allocation of discretionary funds, and through employment for significant numbers of students. These initiatives promote meaningful involvement of students across various levels of the institution.

Theoretical Foundations of the Student-Driven Model

In the mid-1800s, U.S. colleges were profoundly transformed by the actions of undergraduate students. Students established activities, including literary societies and fraternities, which added new vitality to campus life. According to Rudolph (1990), "the vigor of the extra-curriculum was proof that the undergraduates had succeeded in assuming significant authority over college life" (p. 156). The history of U.S. higher education attests to the fact that these early organizations quickly became an expected part of campus life (Horowitz, 1987). The student-driven model is a continuation of student authority in and responsibility for campus life.

Student Involvement Theory. Astin's (1977, 1984, 1993) involvement theory is a guiding framework for the student-driven model for student affairs practice. This theory proposes that the amount of physical and psychological energy that a student devotes to the academic experience is positively related to the impact of college on the student. Essentially, how students spend their time during campus affects what they gain from their education.

Pascarella and Terenzini (1991) summarized Astin's student involvement theory as simply "*Students learn by becoming involved*" (p. 50, emphasis in original). Astin's (1984) theory includes elements of the Freudian notion of cathexis (the investment of psychological energy), and the learning theory concept of time-on-task. Involvement theory is grounded in five basic postulates: (1) involvement requires the investment of psychological and physical energy in "objects" (for example, tasks, people, activities); (2) involvement is a continuous concept, and different students will invest varying amounts of energy in different objects; (3) involvement has both quantitative and qualitative features; (4) the amount of learning or development is directly proportional to the quality and quantity of involvement; and (5) "the educational effectiveness of any policy or practice is related to its capacity to induce student involvement" (p. 298).

Although most student affairs units actively support the concept of student involvement, the student-driven model takes involvement a step beyond to something more akin to student investment. The student-driven model strategically and purposefully builds student involvement in salient campus activities. The student-driven model capitalizes on student talent and leadership. Using talented students in paraprofessional roles has long been encouraged in student affairs (Winston & Ender, 1988). But in the student-driven model, paraprofessionals are effectively used in a variety of settings customarily reserved for full-time student affairs professionals. These areas include academic advising, tutoring, counseling, health education, career development and placement, admissions, drug and alcohol education, community service and volunteer coordination, and recreation programs. Campuses with this model hire or involve students voluntarily in building design and planning, program management and delivery, and committee leadership. The student-driven model relies on students' talents and investment in the institution. Through meaningful campus work experiences, students become vested members of the campus community. They take the initiative and responsibility to positively contribute to campus and community life as well as assume greater responsibility for the quality of the undergraduate program.

The student-driven model exemplifies the crux of the involvement theory in that the more a student is involved in the college or university experience, the more positive outcomes accrue (Astin, 1984, 1993; Pascarella & Terenzini, 1991, 2005). Through involvement, students benefit from positive interactions with their peers as well as frequent, meaningful interactions with faculty and other adults on campus.

Student Engagement. Growing from student involvement theory is the second concept related to the student-driven model: student engagement. Student engagement has two key components. The first is the amount of time and effort students put into educationally productive activities set up by the institution that lead to the desirable learning outcomes. The second element is the intentional ways that the institution allocates resources and organizes learning opportunities and services to induce students to participate in and benefit from such activities (Kuh, Kinzie, Schuh, Whitt, & Associates, 2005/2010). Student engagement, therefore, is a joint effort between the student and the institution. Students must be prepared to be actively involved and engaged in campus life. But, institutions must marshal their resources, shape their environment and facilities, determine their policies, and plan their services and programs in ways that encourage student involvement. Neither party, nor student, nor institution can achieve the learning potential of student engagement separately (Kuh, Kinzie, Schuh, Whitt, & Associates, 2005/2010).

A major principle of student engagement is fulfilled in the student-driven model in that the institution channels students' energies into the activities that research shows contribute to student learning and development. In the institution profiled in the previous vignette, campus leaders intentionally decreased the number of students working off-campus by increasing the number and quality of campus jobs. Since research finds that students who work on campus are more likely to persist (Pascarella & Terenzini, 2005), meaningful campus work experiences have significant educational benefits. Students gain opportunities to apply what they are learning to practical, real-life situations that prepare them for employment after graduation. Therefore, campus employment opportunities were strategically used to increase student engagement and success.

Mattering. Schlossberg's "Marginality and Mattering" (1989) lends additional theoretical strength to the student-driven model. Schlossberg theorized that the more students feel that their efforts are needed and appreciated, the more they feel like they matter. Mattering is expressed by faculty and administrators and felt by students when students are invited to lend their expertise to efforts, paid or volunteer, that acknowledge their talents. When their sense of responsibility and achievement is engaged and perspectives valued, mattering occurs. Although Schlossberg saw mattering as a precursor to students' involvement, when students know that they matter within a community, involvement and engagement in college life are sustained.

Retention and Integration. Congruent with the concept of student involvement, student engagement, and mattering, Tinto's (1993) theory of integration suggests that involvement in the institution—both academic and social—is critical for student success and persistence. The theory explains that students are influenced by interactions with the structures and members of the academic and social systems of the institution. The more students are integrated into the institution, the more likely they will remain enrolled. This theory is enacted through the student-driven model when students identify strongly with the culture, purposes, and goals of the institution. The student-driven model cultivates students' identification with the institution and such identification leads to increased student retention (Tinto, 1993).

Strengths and Weaknesses of the Student-Driven Model

The primary strength of the student-driven model is that it enriches student learning outside the classroom. Students who formed the early literary societies and fraternities recognized the potential of out-of-classroom learning. In fact, the literary societies were founded because of student disappointment with the in-class academic experience (Rudolph, 1990). More recently, as Newton, Ender, and Gardner (2010) espouse, the benefit of being a peer educator or paraprofessional includes learning new skills, gaining relevant experience, and contributing to the academic community. In addition, peer educators are valuable for an academic institution because they are experienced with the campus, can relate to the situations of other students, and are effective. It is not only the students directly involved as peer educators, with out-of-classroom experiences, or with campus employment, who benefit from gains in involvement and student engagement. A finding of the DEEP study, certainly reflected in decades of student affairs work, was that students are better able to draw their peers into educationally purposeful activities. Although student affairs educators provide the structure, encouragement, and supervision required for successful student involvement, this highly involved and deeply implicated strategy of paraprofessional involvement yields tremendous gains for all students.

A second benefit of the student-driven model is that while students' high levels of institutional investment advantages students in terms of leadership experience and meaningful connections, the institution also benefits in increased retention rates and an enriched quality of student life. The student-driven model yields strong student ownership of university programming and services. In this model, students' contributions to campus life are recognized and highly valued by campus leaders. As one student affairs professional at a DEEP school stated, "'The university needs students to operate'. Another described . . . [the institution] as a 'nonprofit organization—its success depends on volunteers'" (Kuh, Kinzie, Schuh, Whitt, & Associates, 2005/2010, pp. 149–150).

This model also offers a way for an under-resourced institution to reframe a financial necessity into an educationally empowering experience. Not only do paraprofessionals and peer educators stretch precious institutional resources further to reach more students, but these campus employees greatly benefit from the experience. For example, tutors usually learn as much or more about the respective subject than those they tutor (Pascarella & Terenzini, 1991, 2005).

Paraprofessionals enable expanded services otherwise not available on a resource-limited campus. More important, their involvement encourages community affiliation. Student-driven models cultivate a strong sense of identification between the student and the institution. The student gains a belief that they matter. Through the paraprofessionals' involvement as leaders and campus staff members, their peers benefit from the caring, mattering environment created. This learning climate fosters student retention and satisfaction as well as a rich educational experience.

Faculty members and administrators also benefit from working with paraprofessionals. For example, at one DEEP institution, upper-division student preceptors were paired with faculty members teaching in the first year curriculum. The preceptors were responsible for co-creating the course and assignments with the faculty member, coordinating co-curricular learning experiences, and mentoring new students. The faculty in these courses learned from preceptors how undergraduates today respond to class assignments and activities as well as how to modify policies to encourage a desired effect on student behavior. Most important, perhaps, preceptors provided new ideas about how to improve the course and faculty members' teaching. Indeed, faculty at many DEEP schools told us that working with a preceptor or peer tutor renewed and deepened their enthusiasm for teaching.

Involvement theory (Astin, 1990), student engagement (Kuh, Kinzie, Schuh, Whitt, & Associates, 2005/2010), and mattering and marginality (Schlossberg, 1989) are foundational theories for the student-driven model, a model that works well in college settings with traditional students as the majority population. However, the model does not as easily adapt to the realities of college students and institutions today. For example, students historically underrepresented in higher education in general and at specific institutions might find it hard to get involved to the degree expected of the student-driven model. The power of tradition among the student body at some institutions may squelch the involvement of students who may not see themselves reflected in the activities and programming events. While the most traditional form of the student-driven model contains these faults, one can easily see how adaptations of the model can increase its relevance and applicability to current students. Although students today represent a wider range of ages, economic backgrounds, educational preparation, and other diverse characteristics than ever before, the model has great salience for student affairs educators who use the principles of the model yet adopt its traditional application. The DEEP research shows that all students, to varying degrees, desire a rich learning experience. Although the traditional approaches to leadership involvement may not fit all who student affairs educators wish to reach, the student-driven model, with adaptations, has the potential to shape a learning climate that touches all students to a certain extent. In fact, this abundance of learning opportunities was another characteristic of the DEEP project schools and a reason for the higher than predicted student engagement.

Employing students as paraprofessionals has its challenges. As Frigault, Maloney, and Trevino (1986) suggest, student affairs divisions implementing a paraprofessional program must be aware of the increased demands it will place on the staff. Paraprofessionals provide additional staff resources, but they also increase staff responsibilities with respect to training and supervision. Benedict, Casper, Larson, Littlepage, and Panke (2000) noted challenges associated with peer paraprofessional programs, including the loss of students during the training process, lack of fit between students' academic life and office pressures, danger of asking too much of these students, limitations on their time schedule due to class conflicts, time and money necessary to do these programs well, and competition between nonpaid and paid positions.

In the end, the challenge associated with adopting a student-driven model is not one of recognizing and utilizing student talents. It is one of effectively and efficiently managing the approach so that student success is enhanced. The commitment to deliberately and strategically employing paraprofessionals and peer educators through the adoption of a student-driven model entails, to some extent, relinquishing some control and power. Student affairs divisions considering this approach must decide how willing they are to bestow this level of trust and confidence in their students.

Student Agency Model

The third model discussed in this chapter on student-centered innovative student affairs models is the student agency model. This model advances several steps beyond the student-driven model such that students are completely responsible for student life and perform as full, equal partners with faculty and staff in these efforts.

Warren College [a pseudonym] is a small, mostly residential campus community with a clear sense of purpose, coherent values, and a collegial atmosphere. Students, faculty, and staff share a philosophical obligation to make the college an intense, empowering educational experience as well as to further ideals of civic engagement and social responsibility. An unusual and functional egalitarianism and a special level of caring and community are distinctive qualities of the college. From the first week on campus, almost all students get involved in something. The institution instills in its students a sense of collective responsibility for operating important areas of the campus. Students tutor peers at the writing center, plan major events, enforce the honor code, serve on institutional committees and task forces, and hold approximately 700 leadership roles in clubs and organizations.

The institution's honor code is a focal point for socializing students to the Warren culture. Students talk about the Honor Code Rule with respect. A senior said, "Warren gives you the freedom to make mistakes and learn from them. You're accountable to your peers and you learn to trust each other." Equally important, students hold each other accountable.

Some of the important lessons students learn are not from books or classroom discussions but from being held accountable and taking responsibility for their actions. New students hear about it long before they matriculate. After they arrive, upper-division students inform newcomers what is acceptable and what is not. The honor code orienteers (HCOs) oversee new students' introduction to the code. They facilitate discussions of Honor Code issues and serve as resources for students and faculty.

It's nearing the end of the fall term and the Warren First Year Core Council, a committee of students, faculty, and student affairs administrators, are meeting to finalize decisions on the proposals for next year's first year seminar topics as well as to discuss new students' orientation to the Honor Code. The committee is co-chaired by the director of First Year Experience and a junior. The junior convenes the meeting and the group quickly decides on topics based mostly on input from students. Students then champion the adoption of a theme for the first year experience to integrate the activities associated with the course and co-curricular activities. A sophomore and a student affairs staff member agree to co-chair the subcommittee to develop components of the theme. Next, the committee discusses ways that the HCOs can have a greater role in helping students develop community standards for their residence hall floors.

Theoretical Foundations of the Student Agency Model

Bandura (2001) defined the concept of personal agency as the capacity to exercise control over the nature and quality of one's life. To be an agent is to intentionally make things happen by one's actions. The core features of agency enable students to play a role in their self development and learning. The word "agency" is thoroughly and vigorously discussed in sociological theory. Giddens (1979), in particular, is a proponent of agency and its relationship to structure and power. According to Giddens, "'action' or agency . . . does not refer to a series of discrete acts combined together, but to *a continuous flow of conduct*" (1979, p. 55, emphasis in original). Most relevant to the student agency model is the idea that human beings are conscious agents of their actions. Human agents—or in other words, students—monitor and rationalize their activities to make intentional, aware choices. This approach is in stark contrast to paternalistic approaches, which consider students as either irrational actors who sometimes make unintentional and ill-informed choices or actors not to be trusted to make their own choices. Theories of agency, on the contrary, state that all humans have some degree of consciousness about the choices they make.

Features of the Student Agency Model

When students are acknowledged as knowing, aware actors, they become empowered, active, and invested in their education. Student empowerment occurs when a climate is created and mechanisms enacted through which students want to be responsible for their education. They are agents of their learning process. Student affairs practice in a student agency model utilizes a hands-off, rather than hands-on, approach to student success. Extremely high expectations communicated prior to admission through a process of anticipatory socialization set the tone that students are responsible for the educational climate. In fact, when student agents are left on their own (without influence from professional staff), they are empowered by the ability to come to their own intentionally driven actions. Initiative results from their ability to make personal/group conclusions on what goals and decisions are important (R. Jeep, personal communication, April 2005). Because faculty and administrators create structures that empower rather than limit, students take ownership for and become invested in creating, learning, and sharing knowledge.

Rather than planning and implementing activities based on individual student needs as in the ethic of care model, the student agency model requires student affairs professionals to empower students as a whole to take initiative. For instance, using this model, student affairs units create policies and structures to facilitate student involvement. They provide training and support to student leaders to enable their efforts. But in the end, the activities, decisions, and programs are the responsibility of students.

The previous vignette provides a glimpse of how Warren College cultivates student empowerment through its egalitarian philosophy and belief in highly involved student participation. The belief in students' capacity as human empowered agents is a core assumption of the student agency model. Student initiative is encouraged and high expectations for student participation in decision making and governance are set and fostered. Vastly different from the models for practice where administrators are central, students are the primary agents of the learning process. Student affairs administrators have important roles to play, but it is helpful to think of these roles more as guides or facilitators, not the central actors. The student agency model is the student-centered model that likely feels most unfamiliar to the student affairs field. Student affairs professionals who are accustomed to exerting control over programs and for directing students will find that there is little tolerance for intrusive administrators in this model.

The student agency model is predominantly found in colleges and universities, or within student affairs units, with missions and philosophies rooted in the liberal arts. The model works well in institutions that are iconoclastic, innovative, or experimental. These institutions or units expect students to assume as much responsibility as possible for their education and recognize that a student agency approach to student affairs is central to this goal.

Although the principles of student agency were fostered to some degree at all of the educationally effective colleges in the DEEP project, several student affairs units extensively employed this approach to facilitate student engagement and success. In these instances, academic and co-curricular programs are organized to foster substantial student commitment and accountability. For example, at one DEEP school, students are required to take charge of their learning by contributing to course development. Faculty list course proposals on the specified bulletin boards in the library building; students add their ideas and comment on those suggested by faculty. As such, the shape of the final course is a collaborative effort of students and faculty who are all considered "co-learners" in the educational process. Students are expected to advise deans and faculty about the overall shape, scope, and content of the curriculum.

Shared governance and student involvement in decision making are other central features of the student agency model. Campus governance structures and processes depend on student participation and leadership. Although most student affairs divisions involve students on committees, in a student agency approach, administrators go beyond simply seeking student input and views. In contrast, significant aspects of the institutional governance process in the student agency model are the students' responsibility. Governance is a true collaboration among equal students, faculty, and administrators. A student leader at a DEEP school that embraced this philosophy told us,

> "The committee I was on was selecting an architect. I didn't like the designs of one of the firms and we spent two hours talking about my concerns." Another student concurred . . . "They see us as equals. My vote counted just as much as the faculty's." Yet another stated, "They know this is our school and they want to know how we want the university to be run." (Kuh, Kinzie, Schuh, Whitt, & Associates, 2005/2010, p. 169)

In return for taking responsibility, the learning environment is extremely rich.

There were several additional examples of student agency at DEEP institutions. At the University of Kansas, over the years the Student Senate has been responsible for initiating a number of major programs including the Center for Community Outreach (CCO) and the Multicultural Resource Center—both of which would not be in existence had it not been for student initiative and a "take charge" attitude. During various student interviews, students commented on the encouragement they received from administrators and faculty to "take initiative" and be responsible for various aspects of their undergraduate experience. This, in turn, results in a great deal of "student empowerment" that leads to higher levels of involvement in a range of institutional activities (NSSE, 2004c, p. 31).

At Evergreen State University in Washington, one of the founding values was innovation and the rejection of its opposite—"standardization." This way the College could stay free of the usual (and too often ineffective) academic routines in favor of working collegially, helping students take responsibility for their own education, and affording students the freedom to grow with the minimum of intellectual prescription or restraint. Instead, they have developed an effective pedagogy marked by individual responsibility for learning coupled with attention and nurturance by the faculty. This innovation and freedom is matched in the approach to student affairs practice where students are full partners, not merely advisors or observers. Evergreen is, perhaps, the most notable example of the student agency model (NSSE, 2004b).

The notion of giving students voice and choice in their educational life has roots in the work of John Dewey (1916, 1940) and the progressive movement in education. Dewey advocated that education should encourage students to function as members of a community, actively pursuing interests in cooperation with others. This process of self-directed learning guided by educators best prepares students for the demands of responsible membership within a democratic community.

Student empowerment took on greater significance in education through the influential work of Paulo Freire (1985, 1990), who believed that education has the potential to empower students by instilling in them "critical consciousness," or the ability to perceive social, political, and economic oppression and to take action against the oppressive elements of society. Students empower themselves by taking responsibility for their own learning (actively engaging as teachers as well as students), by increasing their understanding of the communities in which they live, and by understanding how they as individuals are affected by current and potential policies and structures. Student empowerment models are grounded in social transformation and pluralism. These models often frame awareness programs and other social justice activities to promote awareness of oppression and social justice. Educators using a student agency model must be willing to challenge deeply held assumptions about power, social justice, and other conventions about education.

Although educational philosophies of empowerment typically focus on social purposes of empowerment, including working toward democracy and social transformation, Lightfoot (1986) defined empowerment as "the opportunity a person has for autonomy, responsibility, choice, and authority" (p. 9). This view attaches a personal emphasis on the development of an individual's sense of agency in education. In keeping with the goals of democracy and community involvement, the student agency model is closely aligned with the principles of social action and service learning. As students complete service-learning projects with a deeper sense of meaning about what they are learning, they also see more clearly and appreciate the connections between the university and community.

Strengths and Weaknesses of the Student Agency Model

To empower students is to give them a share in the movement and direction of the educational enterprise. When students perceive that they are responsible for the quality of their educational experience, they are likely to feel invested in their learning and success. A student at one of the DEEP schools stated it plainly: "*Students are so empowered here to be engaged. We truly have ownership of our lives and so we just assume we'll be in charge of things. It's amazing how motivated that makes you to take on responsibility and succeed*" (Kuh, Kinzie, Schuh, Whitt, & Associates, 2005/2010, p. 2, emphasis in original). Student affairs professionals who are able to increase student involvement in decision making as well as provide students the opportunity to initiate and carry out new ideas create enhanced learning opportunities for students.

Education from a position of student agency teaches students about their rights and their responsibilities. This balance not only teaches them how to make decisions and choices that affect their lives but also fosters independence. Engaging students in their own learning by having them be active in and contribute to the campus community enables them to develop autonomy and personal responsibility.

Similar to the student-driven model, the student agency model also relies on student workers, paraprofessionals, or peer educators, to provide a wide range of student services. However, in a student agency model, this involvement is focused on students' contributions as educators. For example, students at DEEP schools with a student agency model serve in important roles as tutors and peer educators. At one institution, tutors must obtain certification from the College Reading and Learning Association, maintain a cumulative and major grade point average (GPA) of 3.0, and work a certain number of hours per semester. By investing in quality tutoring and peer education training and offering students academic credit for this training, these institutions have legitimized peer teaching as a vehicle for sharing responsibility for student learning. Another institution employs student mentors to assist students with research. Juniors and seniors, the primary investigators on the research project, mentor first year students. The faculty member overseeing the research project in turn mentors the advanced student. This collaborative model increases the number of students who can participate in a meaningful way in research and connects faculty with both advanced and beginning students.

The often task-oriented perspective of the student affairs field creates an uncomfortable fit with the student agency model. Certainly, more than one student affairs educator has bemoaned the inefficiency of leaving program and service planning and execution to student initiative. But, student initiative is what student agency model proponents desire. In this model, programs and services may be inefficient and a bit messy. Students may fulfill their urge to reinvent the system each year or every couple of years. Administrators may find themselves revisiting issues that they would rather put behind them as resolved. This continual making and remaking is central to student agency work. Student affairs educators working within this model must have high tolerances for ambiguity and reiteration.

In the student agency model, students are expected to examine situations critically and make thoughtful, well-informed decisions. However, as more than one student affairs administrator at DEEP schools with this model told us, "'students struggle with the tension between freedom and responsibility and with the absence of clearly defined limits sometimes they screw up'" (Kuh, Kinzie, Schuh, Whitt, & Associates, 2005/2010, p. 123). Indeed, the student agency perspective views students making mistakes as an important part of their learning.

Where Do These Student-Centered Models Work Most Effectively?

Student-centered models work best, in our view, at small, private, not-for-profit baccalaureate institutions that are quite selective in their admissions processes. For student-centered models to work, the students must be confident, independent, and willing to assume significant responsibilities.

Even though students may be paid for some of the activities in which they are engaged, such as resident assistants, the fact is that student-centered models require a great deal of student time. If students must work while they are enrolled, they will not have the time to serve on committees, task forces, or organization executive boards. The institution must, therefore, have a robust financial aid program, recruit students who do not need financial assistance, or determine some other way of keeping costs contained.

Student-centered models, in our view, will not achieve their desired results when the student population largely consists of part-time students, returning adult learners, or students with significant work responsibilities. Even if they have an interest in participating heavily in the life of the institutions, these students very well may not have the time. In an environment that has little margin for error, the student-driven approaches are not advised. Regardless of how well students perform, they will make mistakes and if the external environment, in particular, is not forgiving, it is likely that student affairs staff will spend a great deal of time apologizing for mistakes made by students who plan and deliver services, programs, activities, and other experiences for their peers. These circumstances must be turned into positive learning experiences by willing student affairs staff members.

The student agency model would, most likely, be incongruent on campuses with high involvement of external stakeholders such as parents and legislators. These external participants in campus life often expect a level of professionalism and service not afforded by the student agency model. This type of education (often featuring trial by error or tolerance of learning through mistakes) would, most likely, not appear to be efficient to these important constituents. In a consumer environment, where highly polished and crisply delivered services and programs are expected, the student agency model would fall short.

Conclusion

Often in student affairs, our efforts are invisible if, through pro-action, problems are averted and students thrive in intentionally designed environments. In the student agency model, mistakes and errors readily occur. The inherent messiness of this model is evident for all to see. Therefore, how might one assess educational progress and achievement in the student agency model? How is educational success measured in the student agency model? Engagement and process are key elements in determining success in the student agency model. The power of the student agency model was indicated at several DEEP institutions in their success regarding higher than predicted student engagement and graduation rates.

Certainly, the student-driven models are not appropriate for all schools, nor are they an easy approach to adopt in student affairs. In fact, there may be very few schools or student affairs units able to carry out this model effectively. But, as an innovative approach focusing on student empowerment and initiative, perhaps more colleges and universities and the field of student affairs could benefit from a consideration of its principles and philosophy.

Questions for Discussion

- What are the institutional characteristics that impede the adoption of a student-centered model? What characteristics enhance this change?
- Are there specific units in a typical student affairs division that lend themselves to a student-centered model? Are there units that do not? Why?
- How can students be involved in shaping a campus to be more student-centered?
- What theories within the student affairs literature provide guidance regarding a student-centered approach?
- How can a campus use faculty allies to adopt a student-centered model?
- What prevalent assumptions and attitudes exist within student affairs and academic affairs that present barriers to adopting a student-centered model?

8

Academic-Centered Innovative Models

Collaboration between academic and student affairs has received considerable encouragement since the publication of *Powerful Partnerships* (AAHE, ACPA, & NASPA, 1998). The partnership has been furthered through the proliferation of learning communities, service learning, first year experience programs, and other initiatives dependent on cooperation between student and academic affairs (Sandeen, 2004). Evidence of the necessity for collaboration is required to address contemporary campus challenges such as building inclusive communities and constrained resources (Kezar & Lester, 2009). Although improved institutional effectiveness and administrative functioning are often behind the formation of student and academic affairs partnerships (Kezar & Lester, 2009; Martin & Murphy, 2000; Schroeder, 1999a), the most significant rationale for such collaboration is enhancing student learning and success (Garland & Grace, 1993; Schroeder, 1999b; Schuh, 1999).

Indeed, the rich histories and traditions of student and academic affairs offer complementary strengths to support student learning and development (Price, 1999). A focus on student success creates even more impetus for collaboration. Recent research examining the outcomes for students participating in academic and student affairs partnership programs at 18 institutions demonstrated that programs arising from collaboration between academic and student affairs units play an important role in helping institutions achieve desired outcomes for students and in fostering student learning and success (Nesheim et al., 2007). According to Guarasci (2001), absent an alliance between academic and student affairs, an institution is only minimally supporting student success.

Colleges and universities that exemplify linked academic and student affairs divisions place student learning at the center of their joint enterprise and create institutional coherence about student success. Unlike the learning-centered models described in Chapter 6 in which academic affairs and student affairs stake out separate domains concerning their contributions to student success, the more innovative and collaborative models discovered at several DEEP schools emphasize the educational mission, acknowledge their mutual territory, and combine efforts to engender student engagement and success.

Educationally effective models for student affairs practice that emphasize academic-centeredness and collaboration are in step with the educational mission, and work to promote student learning outcomes (see Table 8.1).

At several DEEP institutions, student affairs staff work in partnership with academic affairs and other institutional support structures to an impressive degree (Kinzie & Kuh, 2004; Kuh, Kinzie, Schuh, Whitt, & Associates, 2005/2010). In this chapter, two innovative approaches to student affairs practice that emphasize collaboration with the academic mission and a strong orientation to academics are described. The first model, academic-student affairs collaboration, features a tightly coupled student affairs-academic affairs structure and an operational philosophy discussed extensively in student affairs literature.

Table 8.1 Models of Student Affairs Practice

TRADITIONAL	INNOVATIVE
Out of Classroom-Centered	Student-Centered
Extra-curricular	Ethic of Care
Co-curricular	Student-Driven
	Student Agency
Administrative-Centered	
Functional Silos	**Academic-Centered**
Student Services	**Academic-Student Affairs Collaboration**
	Academic-Driven
Learning-Centered	
Competitive and Adversarial	
Seamless Learning	

This model emphasizes seamless collaboration between student and academic affairs. The second approach, academic-driven, is organized around the academic core and wholeheartedly privileges academic experiences over more traditional co-curricular activities common to student affairs. In this second model, student affairs is highly responsive to the rigors of the curriculum, providing structural support in an intense academic environment. These two models were more likely to be found at the selective institutions studied in the DEEP project. However, because the features of these models were exemplified at most of the DEEP project schools, it is likely that they are strongly associated with student success.

Academic-Student Affairs Collaboration Model

The director of student leadership programs at Manchester University [a pseudonym] is reviewing new senior capstone experience proposals for one of her main committee assignments on the Council for Liberal Education. The proposals were submitted by academic departments for the purpose of enhancing the integration of co-curricular and applied learning experiences in the required senior culminating course. The director, who championed this revision, created a rubric for committee members to evaluate the degree to which co-curricular experiences are knit into the proposed seminars. Co-curricular leadership has always been a highlight of the student experience at Manchester, and the infusion of applied leadership experiences in the capstone course has created a rich learning experience for seniors.

Earlier this fall the director worked with a small group of faculty and student affairs staff to design approaches to assess student learning outcomes, such as learning independently, working effectively with others, and contributing to the welfare of others. She's also been working with faculty members in business and sociology to increase the theoretical links between student activities programming related to service and leadership. Assessment data show that student learning is enhanced through the combined theoretical and applied structure.

Over the past 10 years, student affairs has been more intentional about enhancing the connections between programming and the academic mission of the institution. For example, residence life staff and faculty worked jointly to develop theme floors in the residence halls to increase the promotion of educational mission objectives concerning multiculturalism, the arts, and service. Faculty members' involvement in programming conducted through the student activities and residence life has also increased. The director of student leadership understands that her work is best achieved through working collaboratively with faculty and staff on the Council for Liberal Education and in other aspects of campus life. Although she still does a significant amount of leadership programming in student affairs, she recognizes that her work is more educationally effective when it is closely tied to the academic mission.

She observed in an interview with the student newspaper, "Now I see that my work is about finding opportunities for collaboration with other academic departments and faculty. It requires me to fully understand academic culture and to orient my work around the educational mission of the institution. At first I worried that I was giving up territory, but now I see that more can be accomplished in the name of student learning when student and academic affairs work together."

This depiction of student affairs work through the perspective of the director of student leadership at Manchester University is typical of the academic-student affairs collaboration model of student affairs practice. This model emphasizes significant interactions between student and academic affairs staff around the common purpose of enhanced student learning. Student affairs and academic affairs maintain most of their distinct functions, but capitalize on the strengths of their standpoints. For example, the director of student leadership used her extensive knowledge of leadership development during the creation of an applied leadership experience in the senior capstone course. In similar fashion, faculty members joined residence life staff in the creation of academic enrichment programming on theme floors to increase the educational potential of the residence halls.

In this model, student affairs professionals and faculty members appreciate each other's respective strengths and join together to facilitate the educational mission. Although separate spheres of expertise are respected, the aim is to blur the boundaries between the domains. For example, in the opening vignette, the collaboration among those within the council on liberal education is a reflection of seamless learning, in which the enhancement of student learning and creation of effective learning environments is a shared responsibility. This perspective is advanced through a committee that includes a balanced representation of faculty and student affairs professionals.

Powerful partnerships result when the contributions and talents of academic and student affairs are combined to promote student success. The relationship between student and academic affairs is reciprocal in that they are regularly involved in each other's primary areas. At several DEEP project schools, a shared focus on student success fostered this involvement and partnership. For example, one of the DEEP schools combined orientation, advising, learning communities, and academic support functions into a university college unit in academic affairs. The vice president for student affairs within this institution expressed the importance of maintaining an unwavering focus on student success as the goal, even after student advising programs were moved from student affairs to academic affairs: "'I gave up designs about territory long ago. Yes, one might look at this move as a loss for student affairs, but now we are better partners working to support students'" (Kuh, Kinzie, Schuh, Whitt, & Associates, 2005/2010, p. 167). The vice president's collaborative mindset was central to ensuring an effective university college program.

Theoretical Foundations of the Academic–Student Affairs Collaboration Model

In recent years, the call for student and academic affairs collaboration has been connected to advanced discussions about the key role student affairs professionals play in the student learning process. The leading student affairs professional associations including the ACPA and the NASPA advocated the importance of collaboration between student affairs and academic affairs and proposed models for creating a learning environment on campus. *The Student Learning Imperative*, published by ACPA in 1996, championed a joint commitment to student learning. However, in the early 1990s, the collaboration was perceived to be rather one sided, with the major emphasis being to involve faculty in student affairs programming, and with little reciprocal involvement of student affairs in the academic arena. In addition, Bourassa and Kruger (2001) indicated there was little evidence of a comparable movement among academic affairs organizations. Despite this initial lack of correspondence, over the next several years the collaboration evolved to a more complex, campus-wide perspective requiring parallel commitments by faculty and student affairs staff.

Although the focus on student learning and simultaneous emphasis on collaboration with academic affairs captured the attention of student affairs since 1994, Roberts (1998) posited that student learning as a cooperative effort among campus community members actually began much earlier with the ACE's *Student Personnel Point of View, 1937.* The statement was intended as a philosophy to be adopted by faculty *and* administrators. It specified that institutions should encourage the cooperation of all campus members, including faculty, administrators, and students, in an effort to create effective learning environments. Despite this early focus on collaboration, the emphasis was soon undermined with the creation of *The Student Personnel Point of View, 1949* revision that distinguished separate roles for student affairs staff and faculty, and effectively established functional areas in student affairs (Roberts, 1998). The *Student Learning Imperative* (ACPA, 1996) and other national position statements advocating institutional partnerships in effect renewed the philosophy of the original *Student Personnel Point of View, 1937* by advocating for true student and academic affairs collaboration.

Research on the impact of college on students provides further support for the academic-student affairs collaboration model. When student and academic affairs join their efforts, students have increased opportunities for learning since in- and out-of-classroom activities are structured to build upon each other (Kezar, 2003b; Nesheim et al., 2007; Schroeder & Hurst, 1996; Whitt et al., 2008). Given that student learning is enhanced through mutually reinforcing educational experiences in and out of the classroom (Pascarella & Terenzini, 2005), it seems that the academic-student affairs collaboration model is more likely to produce powerful learning environments and student success. A focus on learning in separate student and academic spheres diminishes these gains.

The guiding philosophy of the academic-student affairs collaboration model is the belief that student learning transcends administrative hierarchies and functional area boundaries. True collaboration between student and academic affairs is based in a tightly coupled system in which units deepen their understanding of the other's culture as well as appreciate the other's talents to create effective learning environments. Successful collaborative ventures are based in a trust that cooperation will not reduce the importance of, or result in a loss of territory for, either collaborator. Instead, the collaboration creates improved environments for all members of the campus community, particularly students.

Features of the Academic-Student Affairs Collaboration Model

The academic-student affairs collaboration model emphasizes the shared relationship between all campus entities as well as the importance of developing a mutual agenda concerning student success. Features include student affairs as a partner in the learning enterprise, student and academic affairs as tightly coupled, the presence of structural bridges linking student and academic affairs, and a shared educational mission and language concerning student learning and success.

Student Affairs as a Partner in the Learning Enterprise. The ability to collaborate depends on the belief that all parties are equally vital to the enterprise of student learning. For example, at one DEEP school with a strong academic-student affairs collaboration model, faculty, administrators, and students used the words "collaboration" and "partnerships" to describe the relationship among campus community members. This perspective reflected a shared vision held by senior academic and student affairs leaders of what the institution can and should be in relationship to the undergraduate experience. Most important, this approach works because the student affairs professionals understand that their fundamental mission is the intellectual mission of the university. Also important, student life programs and policies emphasize intellectual growth and challenge, often considered the domain of faculty. As a result, collaboration with academic affairs is a high priority and a guiding operating principle.

In contrast to the rhetoric portraying student affairs as secondary to the educational mission—or worse, inferior to academic affairs—the dialogue in the academic-student affairs collaboration model depicts student affairs as a full partner in the learning enterprise. Student affairs practitioners see themselves making significant contributions to student learning both in and out of the classroom. The emphasis on the educational mission and partnership with faculty also enables a creative and challenging work environment for student affairs professionals. Much like the director of student leadership in the opening vignette, student affairs staff members find novel opportunities to connect their work to the academic enterprise. Moreover, because student success can only be accomplished through the work of multiple functional areas, the educational role of student affairs is ensured.

Student and Academic Affairs as Tightly Coupled. Organizational theorists refer to the relationships between parts of organizations as "couplings." Coupling refers to the degree to which one component of the system influences, and is influenced by, other components. Weick (1976) is the theorist most closely identified with coupling in educational organizations. His definition is based on the number of variables shared between two separate entities. Coupling may be "tight" or "loose" according to the importance and commonality of variables. Two parts of a system are said to be tightly coupled if they have a great influence on each other. At educationally effective colleges and universities with a strong collaborative model, student and academic affairs are tightly coupled.

The units share the common purpose of fostering student learning and unite around the educational mission. For the collaborative model to be effective, key players in student and academic affairs must be frequently brought together. Collaborative relationships develop and are enhanced through personal contacts. More importantly, student and academic affairs staff must have the capacity to influence each other. For example, at one DEEP school, faculty members concerned about first year students' infrequent experiences with active and collaborative learning recognized that it was not enough to focus on improvements to teaching in the first year seminar. Instead, they formed a committee of student affairs staff, faculty, students, and librarians to implement an enriched first year program. The committee was encouraged by support from the dean of students and dean of the college, who pooled resources to create innovative curricular and co-curricular programming. Student affairs staff refined the programmatic aspects of the reconfigured program, including linking resident assistants and the first year seminar, introducing the program to new students at orientation, and supporting experiential activities. The success of this initiative demonstrates the benefits of tight coupling between student and academic affairs.

Structural Bridges Link Student and Academic Affairs. The importance of tight coupling in the collaboration model implies high levels of interaction between student affairs and academic affairs. For this to occur, structures must be in place to facilitate linkages among units. For example, at some DEEP institutions, student and academic affairs functional areas were restructured to share reporting lines. At one DEEP school, the vice president for student affairs reports directly to the provost and serves on the tenure committee. This ensures that students' out-of-class experiences are represented by student affairs during meetings of the academic deans. This, in turn, resulted in increased awareness of the educational value of faculty involvement in student affairs programs as well as a higher degree of faculty participation across the board.

At another DEEP institution, reporting lines were modified only in the areas in which collaboration between student affairs and academic affairs was most important. For example, because the university desired a strong partnership around community service and service learning, the community service center in student affairs was reconfigured to jointly report to the provost and vice president for student affairs. This structural change can result in clearer philosophical and pedagogical goals, stronger program delivery, increased institutional support, and enhanced student learning. Although some DEEP institutions altered organizational structures to achieve collaboration, other DEEP institutions maintained distinct reporting lines for student and academic affairs and used institutional committees with balanced representation of faculty and student affairs staff as the connection between the two areas. Successful collaboration requires several structural links to bridge the typical organizational boundaries and barriers between academic and student affairs.

Shared Educational Mission and Language Concerning Student Learning and Success. The academic-student affairs collaboration model is effective when the student affairs mission statement fully complements and coincides with the institution's academic mission. Student affairs units that embrace the academic mission and delineate learning outcomes consistent with the institutional educational philosophy are working in concert, rather than at cross purposes, with academic affairs. At one DEEP school with a strong academic-student affairs collaboration model, selection criteria for resident assistants include an understanding of the university mission. They are expected to convey this educational philosophy to new students as well as perform corresponding programming goals.

Common goals between academic and student affairs open opportunities to develop a shared language around student success. Using language related to the educational mission, student affairs staff members could more effectively expand practices that advance this mission, particularly in terms of student learning outcomes. At some DEEP institutions, position titles and office names were changed to reflect this mission commitment. For example, at one DEEP school, the vice president of student affairs title was changed to vice provost for student success. Another DEEP school's senior student affairs officer was renamed provost for undergraduate studies and campus life. At educationally effective colleges and universities adhering to an academic-student affairs collaboration model, the educational mission was communicated in language representing the educational core. The value of educationally enriching learning experiences for students was continually emphasized.

Strengths and Weaknesses of the Academic–Student Affairs Collaboration Model

Shared responsibility for student success is a common feature of the DEEP schools (Kuh, Kinzie, Schuh, Whitt, & Associates, 2005/2010). However, institutions with an academic-student affairs collaboration model shared responsibility for the educational mission to an impressive degree. As such, this interdependence significantly shaped a high-quality learning environment for undergraduates. In contrast to those at institutions where academic and student affairs compete for students' attention (see Chapter 4), student affairs professionals at academic-student affairs collaboration model institutions reported a high degree of satisfaction with their work. This was particularly true if they believed in and understood the integral relationship of student affairs to the educational mission. Other benefits of the model include a team-oriented environment in which creativity is encouraged, increased coherence in the undergraduate program, and the opportunity for student and academic affairs to share costs and resources.

Although the strengths of this model outweigh the weaknesses in terms of engendering student success, some challenges exist. Several DEEP schools with this model found that student affairs offices assumed a greater burden of the responsibility to partner with academic affairs. In such cases, student affairs staff must attend to opportunities for collaboration and are more likely to invite collaboration than be invited by academic affairs. A DEEP school transitioning to an academic-student affairs collaboration model experienced challenges when creating living-learning communities because some student affairs staff members did not understand that faculty involvement and a partnered academic-student affairs focus warranted a transformed operations philosophy (see Chapter 9 for a complete discussion of this topic). The tension around this initiative exposed the larger issue of lack of understanding and appreciation for differences in student affairs and academic cultures. Magolda (2005) provides some cautions with regard to partnerships, including investigating how the collaboration fits with the partners' views about teaching and learning.

Not all partnerships are virtuous. When student and academic affairs partners do not view themselves as equally vital to student learning, collaborations are lopsided and unfair. One DEEP school with a nascent academic-student affairs collaboration model crafted a limited role for student affairs staff members in their learning communities. The student affairs staff simply envisioned their role as planning the logistics of the experiential trips for the course, including scheduling the vans and arranging lunches. Although these tasks were vital to the success of learning communities and highlight the administrative strong suit of student affairs professionals, they failed to exercise the full educational talents of the staff members. In addition, if partnerships exist around only a few activities or worse, such activities represent only an isolated component of students' experiences, and they could be viewed as little more than diversions from the academic program.

When partnerships are reciprocal and organized around a common educational mission, collaborative models for student affairs practice create improved opportunities for student learning. With an integrated in- and out-of-classroom experience, students spend more time with educators in learning experiences that build upon each other. This integration is educationally and personally beneficial to students because their undergraduate experience is more holistic and coherent. The coherence inherent in the academic-student affairs collaboration model can address the longstanding problem of fragmentation in undergraduate education.

An additional strength of the academic-student affairs collaboration model is the opportunity to extend resources. For example, at one DEEP school, both student and academic affairs fund the center for service learning. Parallel budget lines make the center more affordable to both units as well as strengthen the commitment of student and academic affairs for the center's success. The center received external funding in part due to its strong academic and student learning outcomes perspective. At a second DEEP institution, the director of student leadership and a faculty member were coprincipal investigators on a grant to study the educational outcomes of experiential learning. At a third school, the dean of students and a faculty member obtained a grant to evaluate the success of a science-learning community. These projects not only brought additional resources to the institution, but more importantly reinforced the value of student and academic affairs collaboration.

Academic-Driven Model

Late on a Friday afternoon in one of the group study rooms in the library, senior international studies major, Latrease; sociology major juniors Raja, Derek, and Trina; and Dr. Chisholm, a tenured faculty member in the political science department, are meeting to map out the remaining details for the upcoming summit on poverty. The major speakers confirmed their participation, and the planning team is filling out the program with experiential activities and presummit events. They've adopted a global focus for the summit, including a campus display using World Bank statistics on poverty and a panel on global debt facing developing countries. They incorporated a series of local speakers and community service events to engage students in the local dimensions of poverty. Dr. Chisholm, who is involved in the regional chapter of Habitat for Humanity, and Latrease, who volunteers at the community food bank, are taking most of the responsibility for coordinating service events and other experiential activities. Trina reports that three student organizations and the office of multicultural affairs have signed on as cosponsors. The summit promises to be a significant campus event. Students have been organizing on the topic of poverty since the beginning of the school year when the author of the book, The Working Poor, *came to the campus for convocation. The committee hopes to reinvigorate the heated discussions started in first year seminar courses. The students become particularly engaged in conversations about socioeconomic status issues among college students. Raja adjourns the meeting at 6 p.m. so that he and Trina have time to get dinner before they meet up with their sociology study group at the local coffeehouse. Dr. Chisholm and Latrease discuss her graduate school plans as they walk to the student center to check out the space reserved for the summit breakout sessions.*

This vignette provides a glimpse of the rich educational programming that occurs at Suffolk College [a pseudonym]. Students take responsibility for the development of intellectually stimulating programs as well as tackle challenging issues in complex ways. They connect their community service initiatives to entities beyond the campus and work with faculty and administrators to integrate campus activities with their academic work. Students and faculty frequently discuss ideas from courses outside of class, and faculty members are highly involved with students in all aspects of campus life. This high level of engagement creates a vibrant intellectual community. What is noticeably absent from this illustration is any mention of student affairs. Although the director of student activities and the international program office, both in the division of student affairs, are involved in specific aspects of the poverty summit, this event, like many events at Suffolk, is being coordinated primarily by students and faculty.

Suffolk College is an academically intense learning environment. The institution is well known for its rigorous undergraduate program that appeals to academically motivated students, most of whom aspire to graduate or professional school. Students are dedicated to their coursework and devote significant time and energy to studying. But they appreciate the opportunity to explore ideas and participate in social action outside the classroom, and take responsibility for campus programming that enriches the learning community. Classroom experiences, field experiences and internships, international experiences, and diversity are woven into a tapestry that provides robust educational opportunities for Suffolk students.

Although student affairs is almost invisible in the opening vignette, there are many ways that it is directly involved in events like the poverty summit and, more broadly, in creating an intellectually vibrant learning environment. Student affairs staff members worked with students and faculty to assess the need for more group meeting space in the library. Student affairs staff members took the lead in creating enriched study rooms, with the addition of write-on boards and flexible furniture designs. They also worked with library staff to determine study space reservations, extend hours, and support the operation of a student-run juice and coffee bar in the library. The space quickly became a favorite meeting spot of students who were completing group assignments and conducting committee meetings. Student affairs professionals support the academic mission through work with faculty and students to facilitate discussion and reflection sessions in conjunction with community service projects. Furthermore, student affairs is directly involved in guiding and advising students who plan major events. Notably, the student affairs staff is lean. They expend little energy on sponsoring co-curricular programs and residence hall programs the majority of which are left to the resident assistants and floor council members.

The student affairs division at Suffolk employs an academic-driven model of student affairs practice. In this model, student affairs is involved in providing structural support to make rigorous academics work for students. Student affairs professionals help balance, but not distract from, the intensity of the academic environment and facilitate rich educational programming. According to the dean of students at a DEEP school with this model, "The intenseness of your academics is what makes you belong in this community. . . . The culture . . . is built around academic rigor" (NSSE, 2003f, p. 12). In response, student affairs is in tune with the academic culture and is organized to support and enrich the academic community. In such a pressure cooker-like educational environment, student affairs also plays a role in helping students relax and recreate. For example, residence hall programming frequently focuses on intramurals and organized study breaks. In this model it is important to keep in mind that involvement in an intense educational mission, and activities that extend academic experiences, trumps participation in traditional co- or extra-curricular activities that are not directly related to the academic mission.

Theoretical Foundations of the Academic-Driven Model

In the earliest colleges in U.S. higher education, a president and a few faculty and staff members administered all the tasks required to maintain the institution's existence (Caple, 1996; Rudolph, 1990). The president and faculty members were primarily concerned with academic matters, though they also performed some roles traditionally associated with counseling and guidance and student conduct. Faculty were involved in all aspects of students' lives. Although faculty and students co-created campus life, the primary focus was classroom learning. This early college structure, which was in place through the 1890s, is the foundation of the academic-driven model for student affairs.

As college enrollments expanded, more students with diverse interests attended college, institutions transformed into complex research institutions, faculty attention shifted to research, and a division of labor was needed. The "scientific study of the student" promoted by William Rainey Harper created specialized student affairs (Caple, 1996). These developments put forth a dualistic structure, with academic affairs being concerned about the classroom and student affairs charged with campus life outside of the classroom. (This fragmentation, specialization, and dual structure are discussed in Chapter 4.) As described earlier in the academic-student affairs collaboration model section, *The Student Personnel Point of View* (ACE, 1937, 1949) articulated a strong student affairs commitment to focus on academic and intellectual development. Although early statements of student affairs philosophy reinforce a commitment to the educational role of student affairs, Brown (1972) plainly confirmed that student affairs should join with faculty to invigorate the curriculum and eliminate the extra-curricular.

The academic-driven model for student affairs practice also draws from liberal arts education and liberal arts colleges. Liberal arts education is about strengthening the mind across varied topics to make it stronger and more able to grasp ideas and perform intellectual work. Exercising the mind across multiple academic areas in a liberal arts curriculum, the pursuit of self-initiated inquiry, and interaction with faculty are typical features of liberal arts education (Michalak & Robert, 1981). A liberal arts education is available at many institutional types, but liberal arts colleges are perhaps the most pure form. At their core, liberal arts colleges seek to develop intimate learning environments where extensive interaction between faculty and students and among students themselves fosters a community of serious discourse. Small class sizes, an emphasis on individualized instruction, active participation in the campus community, and faculty dedicated to teaching undergraduates represent the foundation of learning at these institutions (Hersh, 1999). These characteristics are the ideal conditions for the academic-driven model for student affairs practice.

Features of the Academic-Driven Model

Like the academic-student affairs collaboration model, the academic-driven model emphasizes shared responsibility for student success. However, features of the academic-driven model place a strong emphasis on the educational mission, creating an intellectual environment, and the role that student affairs plays in supporting and sustaining these goals.

The Academic-Driven Model and the Liberal Arts Mission. The academic-driven model is more likely to be found at small, liberal arts colleges or institutions that provide high-quality liberal arts education. In addition, comprehensive academic programs at larger institutions, such as residential colleges, honors colleges, and living-learning or interdisciplinary programs, may also demand an academic-driven model for student affairs practice. At institutions with an academic-driven model for student affairs, expectations about high levels of academic challenge are knit into the fabric of the history and culture of the institution and reinforced via a well-integrated core curriculum. The hallmark of small liberal arts colleges is that they are, on average, more academically challenging than other types of institutions. Student and academic affairs administrators interact more frequently in these institutions, and as a result, are more likely to work cooperatively on initiatives related to the educational mission (Hirt, Amelink, & Schneiter, 2004). These characteristics support an academic-driven model.

Student Learning and Educational Enrichment Are Key Objectives for Student Affairs. Students' personal development remains a primary concern for student affairs in the academic-driven model. But, an equally important emphasis is placed on the role student affairs plays in directly supporting student learning and enriching the intellectual community. Student success and academic rigor are of primary importance. As a result, student affairs professionals tend to:

1. Understand and inquire about students' studies and educational goals.
2. Encourage and support an academic environment that emphasizes studying and spending time on academic work.
3. Participate in the academic community by attending events, taking part in intellectual discourse, and facilitating the integration of in- and out-of-class learning and experiences.
4. Work alongside faculty and students to develop programming for a rich intellectual community.
5. Complement the academic experience through enriched programming and recreational and relaxing opportunities appropriate in an intense academic environment.

By understanding and inquiring about students' academic needs and goals, student affairs professionals in the academic-driven model are more likely to be proactive in identifying and addressing student learning needs. For example, at one DEEP school with an academic-driven model, the student affairs staff is keenly aware of the assignments in the rigorous first year seminar and other courses that challenge new students. Programming in the residence halls is responsive to students' academic needs and student affairs staff foster the development of environments that are conducive to studying and that support time spent on academic work. Equally important, student affairs staff members in an academic-driven model are present for campus academic events. They are likely to participate in events like the poverty summit described in the opening vignette. Participation is symbolically important because it communicates appreciation for the academic mission as well as contributes to student affairs practitioners' capacity to address students' needs.

Student and Academic Affairs Share Reporting Lines. Similar to the academic-student affairs collaboration model described earlier, the senior student affairs officer in an academic-driven model likely reports to the senior academic officer and works closely with academic deans and vice presidents. Campus units related to academic support may even be within the scope of student affairs. Although it is common for student affairs to report directly to the provost or dean of the college in small liberal arts colleges, larger DEEP institutions with an academic-driven model frequently had similar reporting lines. For example, student affairs staff members at a DEEP school with several residential colleges reported to both student and academic affairs. This model ensures that attention is paid to the development of a rich intellectual environment within the residential colleges.

Academic-Driven Models Influenced by an Intense Academic Student Culture. Students at DEEP schools with an academic-driven model of student affairs pull all-nighters and eschew partying to stay in and do homework at least one weekend night. This academic focus allows them to keep up with the level of intensity required to complete the heavy reading load and assignments necessary for the integration of diverse ideas. A student at one DEEP school with an academic-driven model described her college as having an environment that is "friendly" to studying. This is largely due to the academic orientation of students; however, it was furthered by the redesign of campus facilities based on student input. A variety of study options were created for students in libraries, near faculty offices, in residence halls, and in the student center. Library study space was designed as if it was a living room, and comfortable chairs in the student center improved the use of these spaces for studying. Furthermore, "amazing" food, lots of natural light, and a coffee bar brought more students and faculty into the student center to study and engage in dialogue.

Students at institutions with an academic-driven model share in the promotion of the focus on the educational mission. For example, juniors and seniors primarily run residence halls at one DEEP school. Although four full-time live-in staff members provide professional leadership for more than 15 living units housing 1,000 students, a staff of junior and senior resident assistants provides considerable leadership. The resident assistants' primary programming thrust is a series of programs called dialogues. Each resident assistant leads six dialogue programs per year, including such examples as the war on terror as it relates to civil liberties, international diversity compared with domestic diversity, and balancing greed with making a living. However, students did not view a heavy calendar of residentially based programming as a necessary ingredient for a successful residence hall experience. Rather, students view residence hall living as a complementary experience; that is, it is one of many important out-of-class experiences for students at the college.

Strengths and Weaknesses of the Academic-Driven Model

The academic-driven model has several strengths, the first of which is that organizing student affairs around promoting the educational mission clarifies the role of student affairs in undergraduate education. This model is aligned with the growing academic importance of student affairs in the enhancement of student learning. The academic-driven model provides unique opportunities for student affairs professionals to showcase their talents as educators. Student affairs professionals at DEEP schools with academic-driven models were likely to be teaching and serving in roles that contribute directly to the educational mission. Finally, in an era of diminishing resources and greater focus on increasing student-learning outcomes, organizing student affairs around the academic mission can be cost effective. Pooling resources and reducing compartmentalization makes for a focused effort concerning student success.

On the other hand, the prominence of the educational mission in student affairs work exposes several weaknesses of this model. Similar to findings reported by Hirt, Amelink, & Schneiter (2004), some student affairs administrators at DEEP schools with an academic-driven model reported that faculty did not seem to understand or appreciate what the field and its associated theories and practices contributed to undergraduate education. In response, student affairs staff at one DEEP institution presented a program demonstrating the relationship between student development theory and effective pedagogy at the annual faculty development workshop. Student affairs staff members received additional requests to present this to academic departments, leading to an increase in student affairs staff members' perceptions that faculty appreciated their work.

The academic-driven model is dependent on high levels of meaningful faculty-student interaction outside of the classroom. However, when this element is threatened—as it was at a DEEP institution that elevated expectations for faculty research in faculty hiring, promotion, and tenure review—the academic-driven model for student affairs practice is endangered. Increasing research productivity strained the long history of student-faculty interaction through campus programming and reduced student-faculty out-of-class interaction to collaborate on programs and to discuss ideas. Students, student affairs professionals, and faculty were all concerned about the impact of this shift on the quality of intellectual life on campus. In response, approaches to address the concerns were devised. But this new emphasis will require constant monitoring to ensure that the quality of student-faculty interaction does not diminish and that faculty are not overworked in attempts to meet both goals.

Where Do These Academic-Centered Models Work Most Effectively?

Academic-centered models work best, in our view, at small, private, not-for-profit baccalaureate institutions that are highly selective in their admissions process and at public institutions that are highly selective. This model will thrive only in circumstances where students are confident and independent, and have extraordinarily strong academic backgrounds upon which their college experience builds. Upon matriculation, students at these institutions already have plans for further education, in either graduate or professional school.

The model also requires student affairs staff who are willing to play a supportive role to the academic mission of the institution. As a consequence, these practitioners understand that the academic rigors of the institution mean that students will not be willing or able to participate in many of the typical experiences that one will find on many college campuses. For example, these institutions may not have Greek letter organizations, or if they do, these organizations do not have the full-blown array of activities that are found on most campuses with Greek and other socially oriented organizations.

Academic-centered models, in our view, will not achieve their desired results at most institutions, particularly ones without the requisite emphasis on a rigorous academic program. Rather than enumerating them, we prefer simply to assert that the number of institutions where these models will work is small. Students in need of remediation, who attend part-time, and who are returning adults will not thrive in one of these models. And importantly, student affairs educators who do not understand the clear preeminence of the academic mission at these institutions will not thrive professionally.

Conclusion

The academic-student affairs collaboration and academic-driven models are bolstered by increased emphasis on improving undergraduate education (Chickering & Gamson, 1987; Pascarella & Terenzini, 2005; Sandeen, 2004). Support for these models can be found in the research on student engagement that reinforces the importance of high-quality learning environments in which students and faculty enjoy high levels of interaction and students are frequently involved in educationally enriched activities (Kuh, 2001a; Pascarella & Terenzini, 2005; Schroeder, 1999b). These models offer innovative approaches for student affairs to make meaningful contributions to student engagement and success.

These innovative models help foster an environment described by Barr and Tagg (1995) as aligned with the learning paradigm. These models emphasize the creation of "environments and experiences that bring students to discover and construct knowledge for themselves, to make students members of communities of learners that make discoveries and solve problems . . . and . . . to create a series of ever more powerful learning environments" (p. 15). The potential for these models to create rich academic environments and robust learning experiences in and outside the classroom demonstrates their value to student success.

According to Sandeen (2004), student affairs professionals "should be expected to contribute significantly to the broadened student learning experiences on their campus" (p. 31). When student affairs professionals view their role as making a contribution to student learning, they are more likely to organize around student success. For example, residence hall directors at DEEP schools sought out opportunities to increase the educational potential of the residence halls by creating environments that supported student study time. If campus community members see the classroom and the laboratory as the exclusive domain for student learning, adopting this perspective can be challenging. Faculty members and administrators with a narrow interpretation of the term "educator" exacerbate the challenge of this approach. In addition, because new student affairs professionals are primarily trained at research institutions, they may be unaware of student affairs models with a strong academic focus that require them to work collaboratively with all campus constituents.

The academic-student affairs collaboration and academic-driven models share the perspective that student affairs is an integral component of the academic program in undergraduate education. The models are underscored with the belief that student affairs makes a significant contribution to student learning and success. The models share a common history and philosophy but differ on the degree to which the educational mission is at the core of their work. Whereas the essence of the academic-student affairs collaboration model is on the quality of the partnership between student and academic affairs and the nexus for this collaboration is student learning, the intense focus on supporting the educational mission featured in the academic-driven model can downplay student affairs contributions to student learning.

Both models illustrate the value of making student learning the center of the student affairs enterprise. However, the academic-student affairs collaboration model is more clearly an expression of the partnership theme in student affairs, while the academic-driven model is more likely a practical response to a robust undergraduate environment. These models have prompted some administrative reshuffling, so that student affairs reports to the provost or chief academic affairs office. Such arrangements are likely to enhance student learning, particularly when there is a genuine commitment from the provost, academic deans, and faculty to an enriched view of undergraduate education.

Although these models have their strengths and weaknesses, their features have profound implications for student affairs practice in an era focused on demonstrating contributions to learning and increasing student success.

Questions for Discussion

- What theories within the student affairs literature provide guidance regarding an academic-student affairs collaboration approach?
- What prevalent assumptions and attitudes exist within student affairs that present barriers to adopting an academic-student affairs collaboration model? What barriers exist within academic affairs?
- What institutional characteristics impede the adoption of an academic-driven model? What characteristics enhance this change?
- Are there specific units in a typical student affairs division that lend themselves to an academic-driven model? Are there units that do not? Why?
- How can students be involved in shaping a campus to be more academic-driven?

PART IV

CHANGING AND TRANSFORMING YOUR STUDENT AFFAIRS DIVISION

9

CATALYSTS AND TOOLS
FOR CHANGE

Over the last 20 years, student affairs divisions have experienced increased pressure to transform their practice to reflect a learning-centered approach. Beginning with *The Student Learning Imperative* (ACPA, 1996), student affairs professionals have altered their practice from service provision and programming to initiatives that focus on the holistic student experience, take a student-centered approach, and partner with curricular missions. Programs with this transformed perspective include residential learning communities, career development efforts aligned with academic majors, and student conduct programs focused on restorative justice principles. National initiatives such as the National Survey of Student Engagement (NSSE) have furthered efforts to increase interest in student and academic affairs collaborations, deploy resources to maximize student engagement and success, and align policy regarding teaching and learning. The emphasis on accountability to stakeholders including boards of trustees, parents, legislators, and the general public has been an additional catalyst for change in the ways student affairs is organized. Ever-increasing tuition rates have exacerbated this need for accountability.

The purpose of this chapter is to discuss change approaches that are useful as student affairs professionals transform student affairs divisions toward innovative models of student affairs practice. Theoretical and practice implications for organizational change in student affairs divisions and departments are included in the discussion. Organizational change and transformation, student engagement, student success, and fit to institutional mission are underlying values to the approaches suggested here.

Circumstances Warranting Change from One Model to Another

A number of signs point to the fact that a student affairs division or department needs transformation. One is if the division is not meeting its or institutional goals. Assessment is necessary to determine whether or not the goals and purposes of the division are being met. In the current climate of higher education, a division of student affairs cannot be successful without a well-established assessment program. Another sign signaling the need for transformation is the arrival of new professional staff or, in particular, a new senior student affairs officer (SSAO). New staff come with fresh ideas that point to opportunities and weaknesses in an established model for practice. They have experience from other institutions employing different models and ways of practicing.

Another circumstance that points to the need for a change in the model of student affairs practice is staff or leadership's desire to sustain a successful student affairs division. Changing from a traditional model (e.g., extra-curricular model) to an innovative one (e.g., academic-student affairs collaboration) opens opportunities across all areas of student affairs practice. The desire to avoid stagnation can be a catalyst for change. An additional, although hardly final, circumstance warranting change to a new model of practice is the desire to stay contemporary with institutional needs. This circumstance includes the effort to build sustainable student affairs divisions in terms of budget, staffing, and other resources. Building a sustainable division that lasts through turbulent and difficult times means building capacity within staff, resources, and budget. Identifying approaches that sustain student affairs divisions is essential if the division is to remain contemporary in its approach to providing learning experiences for students.

What We Know about Change and Sustainability

Whether change is planned or unplanned, a division must have an intact idea of its place within the institution and the larger world of higher education. From an institutional perspective, is the division seen as a central learning partner in students' education? Are their services viewed as integral to the intellectual efforts at the institution? What is the role of the division in the institutional change and strategic planning efforts? A division of student affairs contemplating change must also assess its position from an external-institutional perspective. Are the divisional policies and practices in keeping with the initiatives taking place in the national higher education scene? How do important stakeholders outside the institution view the divisional practices?

Budget cuts, outdated organizational structures, new leadership, and a basic desire for change are good reasons to alter an existing student affairs model of practice.

Before any change within the division can take place, an assessment of the institutional and divisional climate and openness for change must occur. Through this assessment, the possibility of planned and unplanned changes can occur. Planned changes are what they appear to be: changes that occur as a result of deliberate action on the part of leaders within the division. Unplanned change occurs through a development (e.g., crisis, budget cut) that occurs outside the purview of the department and without the ability to gather resources or undertake activities to strategize about the change. In the context of this discussion, we will talk about planned and unplanned changes from three vantage points: (a) inside higher education but outside the institution, (b) inside the institution but outside the division of student affairs, and (c) inside the student affairs division. We identify a few factors from each set to illustrate how student affairs can be affected by a myriad of factors over which they have little or no control.

Change Factors inside Higher Education Affecting Student Affairs

Factors external to higher education can take at least two forms—the dramatic or the gradual. An example of the dramatic is the September 11, 2001 tragedies that touched nearly every U.S. citizen as well as many others around the world. These tragedies led to two wars with a number of consequences for institutions of higher education, among them was increased programs for veterans (see Hamrick & Rumann, 2012). Other factors external to higher education may be less dramatic in nature but can have significant effects. For example, state support has been on an inexorable decline over the past number of years. The *Digest of Education Statistics* (Snyder & Dillow, 2012, Table 366) reported that as a percentage of budgets, state support for four-year public institutions has declined from 23.9% to 20.6% from 2005–2006 through 2009–2010. For two-year public institutions the decline has been greater, from 30% to 24.9%. On a year-by-year basis it may be difficult to notice this trend, but when one steps back and looks at the long-term consequences of the trend, typically higher tuition for students, the results can be dramatic. Consider the following conclusion by Baum and Ma (2012, p. 15): "Average published tuition and fees at public four-year colleges and universities increased by 31% beyond the rate of inflation over the five years from 2002–2003 to 2007–2008, and by another 27% between 2007–2008 and 2012–2013."

Demographic Shifts. Without question, the growth of the population of the United States is shifting to the South and West. While the percentage of high school graduates is projected to grow in the United States by 4.7% from 2008–2009 to 2021–2022, several states are projected to decline by more than 10% (for example, Vermont, Michigan, and Ohio). Other states are projected to experience growth by more than 10% (for example, Texas, Colorado, and Nebraska) (Hussar & Bailey, 2013). Consequently, student affairs officers in some states will need to plan for growth by expanding services and perhaps facilities while in other states planning will move in the opposite, meaning a contraction of staff and perhaps closing facilities.

Catastrophes and Disasters. No one looks forward to planning for a catastrophe or disaster, but failure to have plans in place can exacerbate the situation. Health emergencies, floods, tornadoes, blizzards, or other natural disasters can have a significant impact on the role of student affairs. For example, an outbreak of a disease (Schuh, 1983) can refocus the work of student affairs literally overnight. A weather event hitting multiple campuses can have dramatic implications for student affairs (Sanchez, 2013). Institutions can recover from disasters but the nature of student affairs will change dramatically, at least in the short run, as personal emergencies are addressed, longer-term problems are resolved, and the institution returns to its routine.

National and Global Financial Collapse. The events surrounding the real estate meltdown and national recession in the latter part of the first decade of this century had significant repercussions for higher education. As the real estate market went into severe decline in many states, state government revenues also declined. State appropriations to public, degree granting institutions declined in current dollars from over $68 billion in 2007–2008 to over $62.4 billion in 2009–2010 (Snyder & Dillow, 2012, Table 366) while at the same time enrollment increased. The story differs, however, from state to state. For example appropriations during this time period rose in some states such as Colorado, Connecticut, and Missouri but declined in others including Florida, Nevada, and California (Snyder & Dillow, 2012, Table 369). At the same time that appropriations were declining, enrollment at public institutions grew from 13,490,780 in 2007 to 14,810,642 in 2009 (Snyder & Dillow, 2012, Table 198). This represents an increase of nearly 1.5 million students while appropriations were declining by nearly six billion dollars. In the six states cited previously (Colorado, Connecticut, Missouri, Florida, Nevada, and California), enrollment in public degree granting institutions increased from fall 2007 to fall 2009 (Snyder & Dillow, 2012, Table 217). There is no relationship, at least according to this information, between appropriations and enrollment. That is, enrollment increases do not necessarily result in increases in state appropriations.

National Reports. National reports written by agencies or organizations external to higher education also can have an influence. An obvious example is *A Test of Leadership: Charting the Future of U.S. Higher Education* (commonly called the *Spellings Commission Report*) (U.S. Department of Education, 2006) that included a number of recommendations for institutions of higher education, some of which (such as managing costs, providing increased financial aid, and measuring student learning) had direct implications for student affairs. Divisions of student affairs had to take the report's recommendations into account in their long range planning.

Government Initiatives. One other potential influence on higher education and student affairs can be governmental initiatives, either federal or state. Examples are directives to enroll more students, increase graduation rates, or attract more students to certain majors or areas of study such as science, technology, engineering, and mathematics (STEM). Whether these initiatives are federally or state based, they can have an effect on student affairs and the experiences, programs, and services available to students. President Obama's initiative to

strengthen community colleges, make higher education more affordable, and link attainment in higher education to the skills needed for
the workforce is an example of a federal initiative affecting student
affairs.

Change Factors inside the Institution Affecting Student Affairs

Just as there are factors external to higher education, a number of factors internal to higher education institutions can affect how student
affairs programs, experiences, and services are delivered on campus.

Change in Senior Leadership. It is no secret that senior student affairs
officers serve at the pleasure of the institution's senior executive officer,
often termed the president or chancellor (we use "president" in this
book for ease of discussion). In the DEEP study, when asked about
the catalysts for change in institutional practice regarding student
engagement and success, new executive leadership was often cited as
an incentive for new initiatives.

A new president may or may not have served as the chief executive
at another institution before arriving on campus. Most commonly, but
not always, the incoming president will have experience as a senior
academic officer. Rarely does this person have more than limited exposure to the work of student affairs. Moreover, the president may or may
not have an interest in student affairs practice other than the view that
these professionals provide necessary services for students. That is, the
president may conceptualize the division of student affairs as a collection of service units that do things "for" students, such as providing
housing or recreational activities. On the other hand, the president
may be committed to an integrated learning experience that conceptualizes student affairs as a full partner with curricular programs in the
education of students. This approach suggests a very different conceptual role for student affairs on campus.

While the president may not have much more than anecdotal experience with student affairs, this officer may want to reorganize the
institution, an action that has substantial implications for a student
affairs division. Often the reorganization means a change in senior
leadership in student affairs, realignment regarding reporting relationships, and/or reassignment of oversight for student affairs from the

president's office to the office of the senior academic officer. If such is the case, then the approach taken to delivering the service, programs, and activities of student affairs may change.

A catalyst for change to consider is the increased knowledge about student affairs that a new or continuing president may gain over the years. It is extremely common for a president to become involved in an issue on campus (e.g., crisis, athletic scandal, fund raising effort for a new student center) that results in increased knowledge of student affairs organizations and functions. A role of the senior student affairs officer is to encourage the acquisition of knowledge about student affairs by the president. This process of "managing up" is a significant aspect of the SSAO's position and an attempt to best position the division of student affairs in the overall institutional context.

While the president position was most often cited as a catalyst for change in the DEEP study, a change in the provost or senior academic officer could change the institutional and divisional philosophy, organizational structure, and reporting lines. Student affairs professionals can take advantage of leadership transitions to make changes that may have been thwarted or minimized by earlier executives. Although these windows of opportunity do not remain open very long, astute professionals know how to take advantage of them when present.

Change in Mission and Vision. A change in senior leadership also may mean that the institution's mission and vision evolves. The change could be minor or significantly new. The hiring authority (e.g., Board of Trustees) may have brought a new president on board with the charge of increasing enrollment, introducing new graduate or professional programs, developing online education opportunities, or building branch campuses. Regardless, any of these initiatives brings changes in student affairs as manifested by new or expanded programs, facilities, or both. These initiatives also cause shifts in students served and curriculum delivered. Any change in institutional mission must be accompanied by a concomitant adjustment in the mission and vision of the division of student affairs. Both missions must be revisited to maintain congruence and connection.

Change in Organizational Structure. As suggested previously, a new president often brings ideas about new organizational structures. Will the vice president for student affairs report to the president or the senior academic officer? Sandeen and Barr (2006, p. 48) point out, rightly so in our view, "the most important issue for student affairs is not where it is placed in the organizational chart, but how effective its leadership is on the campus." We also assert that a change in organizational structure can bring new emphasis in terms of the purposes of student affairs. A change in organizational structure, for example, the incorporation of financial aid and admissions into student affairs, may warrant a switch to a student services model, at least in those departments. The incorporation of an academic advising center into student affairs may drive a shift from functional silos to academic-student affairs collaboration. An emphasis on academic excellence may warrant a change from any model to an academic-driven approach.

Change in the Strategic Plan. Strategic plans can have a significant influence on student affairs. Ellis (2010, p. 7) defined strategic planning as "the process of determining what a student affairs division intends to be and how it will get there." A major change in an institution's strategic plan, such as the expansion of online learning programs, may result in student affairs having to realign its strategic plan so that its initiatives, programs, and services will support the larger plan of the institution. This may result in adding staff and programs in some areas while reducing staff and programs in other areas. Different approaches to financing student affairs could ensue. Regardless of the changes, it is incumbent on senior leaders in student affairs to make sure that the division's plan is consistent with that of the larger institution.

Enrollment Challenges. Enrollment can be a challenge for student affairs; some situations may entail having too many students while in others there may be too few. Hussar and Bailey (2013) pointed out that between 2010 and 2021 enrollment in public elementary and secondary schools in 40 states is projected to grow while in 10 states and the District of Columbia, enrollments are projected to decline. By region growth will be largest (projected increase by 13%) in the West and smallest in both the Northeast and Midwest (projected increase by 2%). How might enrollment challenges affect student affairs and the models with which their practice is organized? If there are too few new high school graduates, does that mean that more courses will be offered online or that degree completion programs will be developed for "adult" learners? If the state's or region's graduating high school numbers are static or in decline, will more students have to be recruited from outside the geographic region to sustain the institution's enrollment? In other states experiencing potentially significant enrollment increases, residence hall capacity may have to be expanded and more student affairs educators hired. Enrollment changes, therefore, will have implications for student affairs that may result in an expansion or contraction of programs and staff than currently is in place.

Financial Difficulties. We have already noted that state support of public higher education has declined. It is also important to point out that in a period of decreasing equity prices and corporate earnings, institutional endowment support of higher education institutions also has been affected. This means that as endowment income has declined, the institution has had to look to other sources of income to balance its budget. For example, in 1999–2000, private, not-for-profit institutions relied on tuition for 24.6% of their income. By 2009–2010, the percentage had increased to 33.4% (Snyder & Dillow, 2012, Table 370). Income from investment return was 31.3% in 1999–2000 but this percentage had declined to 16.9% by 2009–2010 (Table 370). Most telling was that in the midst of a significant stock market decline, in 2008–2009 the percentage of income for private, not-for-profit institutions that came from tuition was 77.8%; investment return was -92.9% (Table 370). The implications are obvious. In a period of time when investment return was high, tuition increases could be limited but the opposite was true when investment return was modest or in the case of 2008–2009, negative. It is possible that student affairs staff may need to be reduced, programs contracted, or other "economies" identified. Rarely do student affairs educators at private not-for-profit institutions serve as investment managers but they will experience the outcomes of their institutions' investment results.

Curriculum Changes. Institutional changes in the curriculum (e.g., the revision of general education requirements, establishment of a diversity requirement, elimination of a college or school), whether incremental or major, can drive change within a division of student affairs. These curricular shifts can modify the type of student attracted to the institution, shift the priorities of the faculty, and/or alter the needs of students in terms of facilities used (e.g., library), schedules employed (e.g., summer semester), and effort demanded (e.g., availability of student employees). The institutional mission is in large part determined by the academic nature (e.g., rigorous, non-rigorous) of the curriculum. If purposes of student affairs divisions are to be congruent with that institution mission, than they must adapt to changes in the curriculum. These changes can be yet another catalyst for change from one model of student affairs practice to another.

Change need not be dramatic to have an effect. Current institutional processes such as strategic planning, program review, grant writing, leadership retreats, budgeting, and financial planning can all be catalysts for change in the short- or long-term. Several standard processes within higher education institutions provide opportunities for change within student affairs divisions.

Change Factors Internal to Student Affairs

Similar to the ways that external and internal changes to an institution can be catalysts for change, similar changes outside and inside of divisions of student affairs can create opportunities for change.

Divisional Leadership. When a new SSAO is appointed, a honeymoon period in the first 6 to 12 months can provide the space to make necessary changes from one model of student affairs practice to another. Although fraught with difficulties because of unfamiliarity with the institution and the division, SSAOs can use the acceptance afforded during these first few months to make changes that would be more difficult to enact at later dates. Professional staff are expecting, often hoping for, change when a new SSAO is hired. Although change is always difficult and often mightily resisted, the expectation for change exists in those first few months all the same. A new SSAO with an eye for updating an existing traditional model to an innovative one can lay the groundwork for the transition before arriving on campus. The campus interview is not too early for the senior administrator to shape expectations about possible changes to come. The level of acceptance or resistance to change through these activities can be a good gauge regarding fit to the institution.

Mission and Philosophy. Several times throughout this text we emphasized the importance of congruence between divisional and institutional missions. Any division within an institution, academic or nonacademic, should take available opportunities to align with the institutional mission. Institutional missions are often vague; division missions and purposes use the institutional mission as a guide but delineate how and why faculty and staff achieve that mission. The mission and philosophy of a division may be reviewed routinely, yet not often substantially changed.

The division mission and philosophy should be familiar to all who work within student affairs. The fit of that division mission to the institutional goals should be clearly articulated and unmistakably understood. Although multiple goals will certainly be present in the complex organization of any student affairs division, the presence of competing or contradictory goals, either within the division or with the larger institutional mission, is a signal that additional work on the formation and articulation of the mission is necessary.

Organizational Structure. Change in organizational structure has been likened to "rearranging the deck chairs on the Titanic." Hopefully, any reorganization of reporting lines and staff responsibilities will result in increased effectiveness and enhanced achievement of goals regarding student engagement and success. Organizational structure changes should be undertaken with an eye for the model of student affairs practice desired within the division. If the model chosen is academic-driven, then organizational choices regarding career services, academic advising, residence life, and other curriculum-oriented approaches will ensue. If a student services model is the preferred option, then organizational choices will involve groupings by how services are consumed by the students enrolled in the institution. Just as there is no one way to practice student affairs, there is no one way to organize the departments within the division. But, the structure must support the foundational assumptions of the model upon which divisional practice is based.

Strategic Planning. Philosopher Yogi Berra, so it is attributed, stated the obvious, "If you don't know where you are going, you will end up somewhere else." Strategic planning, both at institutional and divisional levels, is a means to determine where you are going and how you are going to get there. In addition to these important functions, strategic planning is an opportunity for divisional assumptions, priorities, and ways of operating to be expressed. Without the activities of strategic planning, divisional departments within student affairs may become disjointed. A possible model of practice that occurs in the absence of planning is the functional silos model where individual department rather than divisional priorities are stressed.

Program Review. Periodic program review is an excellent opportunity to assess the strengths and weaknesses of a division of student affairs. This is particularly the case when an outside consultant is employed to offer independent, objective, and, perhaps, innovative suggestions to the way programs, services, and initiatives are managed within the division. Program review is particularly helpful when based on the Council on the Advancement of Standards (CAS) (www.cas .edu/), the professional standards for the student affairs field.

Student Characteristics. The overall characteristics of the institution need not change in order for a shift in students served by the division to take place. Increases in students served over time, changes in the nature of how students consume services (e.g., online versus in person), the addition of new facilities, and other factors can cause minor or seismic shifts in the way students are served by the division. In addition to these, student characteristics change over time. Often discussed generationally (e.g., Generation X, Millennial Generation), the success of any student affairs division and the choice of model for practice must coincide with the nature of the student body served.

Changing from One Model to Another

Our emphasis in this book is on the importance of student engagement and success. The research and practice for the contemporary student affairs division directs us to transform models to ones that maximize student learning. It should come as no surprise that we believe that a model is ripe for change when it is incongruent with institutional mission. Additionally, models that are completely disconnected from the academic mission are good candidates for transformation. As described in the chapters delineating the models, even the most mundane services can be fashioned in such a way to achieve learning goals. Models that compete with academic mission have, in our minds, no place in colleges and universities. Finally, models that fail to encourage student growth and development at higher levels of cognitive, moral, social, and other development should also be refashioned.

Philosophical Shifts. Any change in the model used for your student affairs division requires an accompanying change in the philosophical and theoretical approaches used by the division's professionals. Table 9.1 provides examples of shifts that may be necessary as you consider the adoption of a new model for practice. The shift from the left to the right column entails a change to a learning and engagement-focused approach to student affairs practice. We believe that student affairs cannot change to the innovative models without these or similar shifts in approach.

Tools to Bring About Change

A change from one model to another cannot be a unilateral decision made by the SSAO. For change to take effect, consensus must be built among the division's professionals. As you consider ways to change your student affairs division from one model to another, we suggest two tools that may be of assistance to this task: SWOT Analysis and Lewin's Force Field Analysis.

SWOT Analysis. "SWOT" stands for strengths, weaknesses, opportunities, and threats (Andrews, 1980). This tool can be used in the renewal or transformation of a student affairs division through the assessment of internal divisional strengths, internal divisional weaknesses, external opportunities, and external threats. A simple 2 × 2

Table 9.1 Shifts in Philosophy Necessary for a Change in Models

FROM THIS VIEW	TO THIS VIEW
Administrators	Educators
Bureaucrats	Teachers
Task	Learning
Control	Openness
Efficiency	Effectiveness
Telling	Asking
Involvement	Engagement
Separate	Together
Independence	Collaboration

design can help student affairs leaders assess these elements of their divisions (see Table 9.2 for an example).

Lewin's Force Field Analysis. A classic in the field of organizational development, Kurt Lewin (1946) developed the Force Field Analysis as a way to assess the organizational forces that drive and inhibit change. Lewin suggested the following steps as a way to understand how change might be achieved. His approach will be described in the context of a change in the model of student affairs practice.

> *Step 1:* Begin the force field analysis by describing your current model of student affairs practice with as much detail as possible. As suggested in Chapter 10, the primary and secondary models used in the division can be assessed using the Models of Student Affairs Practice Inventory (see Appendix B).

Table 9.2 SWOT Analysis Example

INTERNAL DIVISIONAL STRENGTHS	INTERNAL DIVISIONAL WEAKNESSES
• Presence of an experienced professional staff.	• Underfunded in most departments.
• Excellent facilities including a new student center and renovated residence halls.	• Lack of academic emphasis (e.g., residential learning communities) in the residence life program.
• Institutional commitment to professional development.	• The presence of two 30 plus year professional staff members who are highly resistant to change.
	• Lack of administrative support (e.g., associate vice presidents) in the SSAO office.

EXTERNAL OPPORTUNITIES	EXTERNAL THREATS
• Recent commitment of $200,000 by an outside donor to enhance the student affairs program.	• Continued pressure by the parents' association regarding the lack of congruence between the academic and student affairs missions.
• Presence of a well regarded masters program in student affairs that acts as a feeder for professional staff, particularly diverse staff by race, sex, and sexual orientation.	• Increased pressure to use student affairs-based facilities for revenue generating activities (e.g., conferences, meetings).
• Upcoming arrival of a new president with experience in student affairs.	• A long-standing and influential Board of Trustees member who is antagonistic to student affairs.

Table 9.3 Force Field Analysis to Assess Driving and Resisting Forces

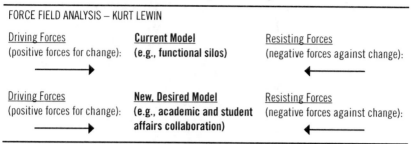

FORCE FIELD ANALYSIS – KURT LEWIN		
Driving Forces (positive forces for change):	**Current Model** (e.g., functional silos)	Resisting Forces (negative forces against change):
Driving Forces (positive forces for change):	**New, Desired Model** (e.g., academic and student affairs collaboration)	Resisting Forces (negative forces against change):

Step 2: The second step is to describe the desired model for student affairs practice. Steps 1 and 2 can be facilitated by using the template in Table 9.3.

Step 3: After determining the existing and desired models, list all the forces *driving* the decision to keep the existing model. In similar fashion, list all the forces driving the decision to change to the desired model.

Step 4: List all forces *resisting* change toward keeping the existing model. Then, list all the forces resisting change to the desired model.

Step 5: When you have finished your inventory of the driving and resisting forces for each model, discuss each force. Which forces are critical? Which can be changed? Evaluate the strength (1 = weak 10 = strong) of each force and rank the forces by strength. This visual representation will give you a better idea of the opportunities and challenges that will prevail as the division changes its model.

Step 6: Following the assessment and ranking, discuss ways to strengthen or add *driving* forces toward the desired model and ways to weaken or remove *resisting* forces.

Identifying the Steps to Change Your Model

Now that you have examined the driving and resisting forces regarding change, you want to identify the steps necessary to change your model of student affairs practice. Table 9.4 presents a graphic that you can use to generate a list of steps or activities needed to make the change from one model to another. These steps should be determined in the context of the supporting and resisting changes identified through the Force Field Analysis. Examples of steps toward the desired change are illustrated in Table 9.4.

Through the Force Field Analysis, you may find that the negative forces are too strong and necessitate temporarily abandoning or changing your approach. You may also find that the steps identified to move you from one model to another might take excessive time and resources, neither of which is available to the division. We do not recommend, however, that you completely abandon the effort to change your model from one that no longer serves the learning and engagement goals for your division and institution to one that is a better fit for your long-term goals. The examination that occurs through the Force Field Analysis can help you identify opportunities that may present themselves at later dates. You may be able to undertake activities including changing policy, engaging in staff development, managing the campus environment, conducting retreats, undertaking strategic planning, changing hiring expectations, writing grants,

Table 9.4 Where You Want to Be . . . and How You Get There . . . .

WHERE YOU ARE NOW . . . (TRADITIONAL MODEL)	STEPS NEEDED FOR CHANGE . . .	WHERE DO YOU WANT TO GO? (INNOVATIVE MODEL)
Functional Silos (based on inventory—see Appendix B)	Privilege student learning by sponsoring a professional development session to discuss the findings of the NSSE survey.	Academic and Student Affairs Collaboration
	Provide seed money for activities that enhance faculty-student affairs collaborations.	
	Front load resources through a First-Year Experience Program to better assure student success.	
	Reposition staff to better enable academic-student affairs collaborations.	
	Assign a staff member to the charge of assessing student learning goals.	
	Steer the organization toward continuous improvement by adjusting staffing patterns.	

and hiring consultants that move the division toward the desired model.

Getting Started—Small Wins

As you undertake the process of change, it is useful to consider that issues seldom get solved because people define them in ways that overwhelm their ability to take action. The identification of intervening steps can help you discover small wins that can add up to significant change.

> A small win is a concrete, complete, implemented outcome of moderate importance. By itself a small win may seem unimportant. A series of wins at small but significant tasks, however, reveals a pattern that may attract allies, deter opponents, and lower resistance to subsequent proposals. (Weick, 1984, p. 43)

The wisdom of small wins was reiterated by Pascarella and Terenzini (1991) in a student affairs context:

> Instead of singular, large, specially designed and campuswide programs to achieve a particular institutional goal, efforts might more profitably focus on ways to embed the pursuit of that goal in *all* appropriate institutional activities . . . rather than seeking large levers to pull in order to promote change on a large scale, it may well be more effective to pull more levers more often. (p. 655, emphasis in original)

Pulling more levers and seeking small wins may involve enlisting campus leaders invested in improvement. Student affairs leaders can use data as indisputable evidence for the need to change and to demonstrate the success of their programs and initiatives. Data can be used as a tool to win others over to the cause of changing models from outmoded traditional approaches to engagement-oriented innovative ones. Faculty allies can be recruited and critics persuaded. Opportunities may be taken advantage of to motivate others toward a common vision of student success. Students can be involved in the process of articulating the success of student engagement initiatives. These small wins may release student affairs staff, faculty, and institutional leaders from traditional structures, roles, and territoriality and encourage collaboration.

Conclusion

There are many ways to effect change in organizations. Student affairs divisions have long histories of changing, often quite quickly, when the need arises. The student affairs field is one that has been marked by innovation and creativity from its earliest founding. The transformation from traditional models based on administrative need, teaching students, and providing programs to innovative models based on student-centeredness, learning approaches, and collaborating on programs follows that same tradition.

Questions for Discussion

- What professional and personal reflection is necessary among staff members before change can be effected within a division of student affairs?
- What are your motivations for change?
- Are the changes proposed substantial or inconsequential?
- What resources can you take advantage of to inform yourself of the ways that change is effected in organizations?

10

REDESIGNING YOUR STUDENT AFFAIRS DIVISION

In the previous chapters we introduced traditional and innovative models of student affairs practice based on Project DEEP, the literature of the field, experiences and observations from over 40 years of involvement in student affairs, and work as consultants and speakers at colleges and universities in the United States and countries around the world. Whether you have been a student affairs educator for many years or are new to the profession, we think familiarity with the models likely will lead to a better understanding of the division of student affairs within which you work as well as provide you with ways of thinking about student affairs practice. It is highly likely that none of the models we have identified represents a perfect depiction of the division of student affairs with which you are most familiar, and in many cases large divisions may incorporate elements from several models included in this book.

In this final chapter we introduce ideas for redesigning and sustaining a division of student affairs. We think a good place to start with divisional redesign is to identify with as much specificity as possible the predominant student affairs organizational model currently in place. This process can be accomplished by using the Models of Student Affairs Practice Inventory located in Appendix B of this volume. As many staff as possible should complete the form to obtain a composite view of the division's model. Realistically, staff with various responsibilities may view the organizational model differently but assuming that consensus can be reached, a point of departure can be established.

Let's use as an example Mid Central University (MCU), a hypothetical regional university with roots in baccalaureate teacher education but now has expanded programs to include some master's programs and a few doctoral-level programs. MCU just completed its decennial regional accreditation process and the accreditation team's report indicated that student affairs has drifted from the institution's primary mission, that being to support and enhance undergraduate learning for traditional college students. An example of the drift was a significant investment in the construction and staffing of a new childcare facility even though there was a very limited need for this service. To make ends meet the childcare program opened its doors to the children of community members who had no association with the university. Even so, the childcare program had difficulty meeting its budgetary obligations from year to year and, in some years, funds had to be reallocated from other programs to bring the budget into balance. What has evolved at MCU and been uncovered during the accreditation visit is a misalignment between the enacted mission and vision of the division of student affairs and the mission that the larger institution expects. Accordingly, the accreditation team recommended that student affairs staff members revisit the division's mission and vision with an eye toward aligning it with the University's mission and vision. Completing the Models of Student Affairs Practice Inventory (see Appendix B) will provide assistance in getting a picture of how staff members perceive the organization and purposes of the division. If the consensus of this process indicates that the "real" model of student affairs practice, meaning how staff members go about their work rather than how they would like to go about their work, is inconsistent with what is needed at MCU, then it is time to rework the conceptual approach taken to frame student affairs practice at MCU. This process could involve several steps.

Aligning Mission and Vision

What we learned from our analysis of student affairs models included in the previous chapters is that the mission and vision of student affairs must be aligned very closely with the mission and vision of the institution. The programs, services, and experiences provided should complement what is needed at the institution. For example, at an institution that primarily serves commuter students, who live at home, and work significant hours to pay for their education, a student services approach can make very good sense. Students do not spend much of their free time on campus and they need quick answers to their questions. They need services that they avail themselves of on a periodic rather than continuous basis. Commuter students at this institution might find that they need tutoring help in a particular course and as a consequence they drop in for help at the campus learning support center. Once they get back on track with the course's requirements, they may not go back because, in their mind, they do not need additional assistance and do not have the time.

In contrast, the student services approach might not work as well at a residential institution where virtually all students live on campus and seek to be engaged deeply in the life of the college outside the classroom. A student services approach would not provide the depth of involvement that the college seeks to provide for students and, equally importantly, that students seek. In the case of a tutoring program, students might seek assistance before they experience difficulties in their courses and may continue to be tutored throughout an entire semester or academic year with an eye toward becoming a tutor at the institution in subsequent academic years.

In the example of MCU previously outlined, how can the misalignment of divisional and institutional missions occur? Drift can occur as a consequence of new staff members being hired who do not have experiences at similar institutions and/or who have not had a thorough acculturation to the nature of their new institution. Drift also might occur when new senior leaders are appointed who do not study the history of their new institution, and/or do not understand the powerful influence that the institutional culture can have on how student affairs programs and services are offered (Kuh, Schuh, Whitt, & Associates, 1991).

Conducting a thorough examination of the division's mission and vision is not a matter of a meeting or two. It can take significant time because the division's mission and vision reflect not only what the staff say the division ought to do, but what they actually do. As a consequence, the alignment process of the division's mission and vision with that of the institution may require recalibrating the mission and vision of the various units that comprise the division. It may mean extending beyond student affairs and engaging in discussions with staff from units with which student affairs staff interact on a regular basis. An example of this extended conversation might be discussions with the coordinator of the first year writing program or the administrator who is responsible for undergraduate education. Simply aligning missions and vision statements will not necessarily result in adequate redesign of the division but it is an important start. Other steps are necessary and are introduced in the next section of this chapter.

Practical Steps

In no particular order, the division needs to examine three important elements: human resources, financial resources, and physical facilities. Each of these elements needs to be positioned in such a way as to support the newly designed mission and vision.

Human Resources. Staff, quite obviously, are needed to organize, design, deliver, and assess programs and services from the division. But not all staff have the appropriate background, training, and perspective that fit all institutions of higher education. A staff member, for example, from a metropolitan, commuter institution, may experience a difficult adjustment, absent of an extended orientation to the new institution, in moving to a residential, baccalaureate institution. This assertion does not suggest that such adjustments are impossible, because many examples of successful transitions exist, but it does claim, justifiably so in our opinion, that moving from one institution or type of institution to another can require significant adjustments in perspectives.

New staff are not the only ones who need to make sure that their approaches are consistent with that of their institution. Staff who have served for a significant length of time need to make sure that, as the institution and the division change their mission and vision, they, too, realign their thinking and approaches to their professional practice. An example might be the housing director who was hired to correct a budgetary mess but, upon accomplishing that challenging task, is now criticized for not devoting enough time on developing residentially based learning communities. The director, in this example, did a wonderful job of cleaning up a fiscal mess, but the focus has shifted and so, too, must the perspective.

In the case of MCU, staff may need to engage in a series of meetings or retreats designed to "unpack" the accreditation team's report. They will need to develop strategies to stay focused on delivering the kinds of programs, services, and experiences that are consistent with what the larger institution needs. This assessment must include a reexamination of the institution's mission and vision. If student affairs has been engaged in drift as critiqued by the accreditation team and that drift has resulted in experiences for undergraduates that are less than robust, then refocusing the work of the various units would be in order. In addition to retreats and meetings, this work might involve external consultants, visits to institutions that have missions and visions similar to MCU, and/or participation in workshops offered by professional organizations designed to help the staff refocus their work. These strategies, and perhaps others, can be employed so that student affairs staff align their work with what MCU needs.

Financial Resources. While we argue that staff are the central building block of a student affairs division, the financial resources available to them are essential in their ability to deliver what MCU needs from student affairs. We start our commentary on financial resources by recommending that a long view of the history of financial resources for student affairs be taken. Over the past decade, for example, has the mix of financial resources changed, or has it stayed relatively the same for student affairs? For example, has division funding involved a shift in funding from the institution's general fund to student fees or fees for service? More on this topic follows in this section.

Measures of change also could be examined from the amount of resources on a per student basis devoted to student affairs. Setting auxiliary services such as housing and food service aside, what percentage of the institution's budget has been devoted to student affairs over the past decade? Has the amount increased, declined, or stayed about the same? The answer to this question will serve as a proxy for how successful the division of student affairs has been in securing campus resources for its programs and services. If the amount has declined, perhaps student affairs has been diminished in terms of its importance on campus but if the amount has increased, then what has resulted from the increased funding?

Not only is the percentage of budget an important measure, so, too, is a comparison of how MCU's student affairs budget compares with similar institutions. Most institutions have a set of self-identified peer institutions with which it compares itself. How does the student affairs budget at MCU, as a percentage of institutional expenditures, compare with its peer institutions? How much money is spent on a per student basis for student affairs at MCU when compared with peer institutions? If MCU spends less using either measure, then additional questions need to be explored, such as why is student affairs at MCU faring less well than at its peer institutions? On the other hand, if MCU is spending more, what added value has resulted from these expenditures?

Finally, as previously suggested, a study of how the mix of financial resources has changed over time is worth conducting. Student affairs typically receives its funding through a mix of funding made of the institution's general fund (state appropriation and tuition for public institutions; tuition at private, not-for-profit or for profit institutions), student fees, and fees for services. If the mix has changed, does that suggest that students are being assessed more directly for the services and programs in which they participate? Is the amount of student fee money increasing in an effort to keep tuition increases low? Who controls student fee revenues? And, if more fees for services are being levied, such as fees for registering with career services, fees for parking, fees for visits to the student health services and so on, what does this trend represent in terms of institutional philosophy about the cost of attendance?

Facility Resources. As important as human and fiscal resources are, the physical resources of a division of student affairs are central to the delivery of programs, services, and learning experiences. If, for example, the amount of outdoor space devoted to recreation is very limited, it might be impossible to have a robust intramural touch football, rugby, or soccer league. Without swimming pools, recreational or intramural swimming may be severely limited, and having an inadequate number of meeting rooms or available office space may curtail the development of student organizations, academic clubs, service organizations, and the like.

Clearly, some aspects of student affairs will be more facility intensive than others. Residence halls and student unions require a great deal of space and commonly are financed through long-term revenue bonds. Making sure that the facilities are kept up to date and in good repair are essential to generating sufficient revenue to keep the facilities attractive and fiscally sound. Long-term repair and renovation plans ought to be in place along with sinking funds developed to provide the fiscal resources necessary to take care of necessary renovations such as replacement of roofs, windows, heating and air conditioning units, and so on.

Other aspects of student affairs are less facility intensive and have resources provided by the institution. Examples of these are judicial affairs, international programs, academic advising, and multicultural affairs. These units require office and meeting space but do not require specialized facilities, as would be the case for a health service or childcare center. That does not mean that routine audits of space are unnecessary or that facilities can be allowed to fall into disrepair for units that are not facility-intensive. But units such as judicial affairs or tutoring services are not nearly as facility dependent as residence halls or health centers that simply cannot function if facilities are inadequate.

Conducting routine audits of facilities, preparing long-term repair and renovation plans, and developing funds to pay for renovation and improvement are central to keeping student affairs contemporary and aligned with what the institution needs. Tired, old fashioned facilities in disrepair will signal that student affairs is not an institutional priority and will communicate unfavorable messages to students, their parents, and others interested in the student experience.

Staying Contemporary

MCU went through an accreditation process that resulted in questions being raised about the extent to which the division of student affairs as well as non-student affairs units had drifted away from the institutional mission. The result was that many units on campus underwent an extensive review and made changes to realign their activities with MCU's mission and vision. Student affairs was no exception and by conducting a thorough study of its human, financial, and fiscal resources, it recalibrated divisional work so that it was consistent, once again, with what MCU and its students expect and need. But the question that arose in the mind of the senior leadership of the student affairs division was this: How do we stay contemporary with what MCU needs? Moreover, the leaders wondered how they could avoid repeating some of the mistakes of the past that led to a drift away from the central purpose of student affairs, that is, supporting and enhancing undergraduate student learning at MCU. That is an ongoing challenge for student affairs—how does the division stay contemporary with what the institution needs?

Keeping the Mission and Vision of Student Affairs and the Institution Aligned

Besides making sure that the mission and vision of student affairs and the institution are aligned (as previously discussed), reviewing the strategic plans of student affairs and its units is necessary to make sure that the plans are consistent with those of the institution. Annual reports, for example, ought to illustrate what has been accomplished with respect to how student affairs supports and advances the larger institution. Proposals for new programs should focus on how the new initiative will advance the institution in ways that are consistent with the vision and mission. Assessments of current programs similarly should focus on how the unit's activities contribute to the goals of the division and mission of the institution. At a minimum this activity should be conducted on an annual basis.

Providing Appropriate Infrastructure

Regardless of the model of student affairs practice employed, student affairs staff require an adequate infrastructure to conduct their work. Elements of this infrastructure include fiscal resources, a professionally trained staff, effectively used facilities, and well-planned and coordinated programs and services.

Reviewing Fiscal Resources. The review of fiscal resources previously outlined and outlined in more detail as follows is conducted with the intention of providing adequate and appropriate infrastructure for the work of the division. The division's and comprising unit budgets need to be more than simply determining if resources are adequate to deliver the portfolio of student affairs. Budgets represent much more than that. They reflect organizational priorities and aspirations. So, an annual review of the revenues (general fund, fee for service, student fees) that are designed to support student affairs in the next fiscal year should be conducted. Is the mix stable? In what direction is the mix trending? Are programs being curtailed or eliminated due to lack of funding? If so, why is there a lack of funding? What new programs are being initiated? How are they being funded? Are staff salaries keeping up with the market? These questions are examples of the kind of analysis that needs to be conducted to determine the extent to which budgetary support is adequate or trending in a direction that is likely to lead to significant challenges in the future.

Keeping Staff Up to Date. While this volume is not dedicated to staff development, a division of student affairs that is contemporary in its approaches is one where the staff, regardless of their length of time in the field, are on the cutting edge of professional practice. That suggests that the division wholly supports staff development initiatives that keep the staff fresh and contemporary. Among the strategies that will contribute to an up to date staff are the following:

(a) An in-depth orientation program for new staff,
(b) Support of staff who attend conferences, and present programs at professional conferences,
(c) Encouragement of staff to attend extended development programs such as the National Housing Training Institute,
(d) Making it possible for staff to teach courses as appropriate,
(e) An awards program that celebrates top notch performance in the division,
(f) Poster sessions and other presentations of excellent initiatives and an assessment project of programs and services, and
(g) Use of technology such as web sites and Facebook to promote public awareness of divisional programs and initiatives.

Jackson, Moneta, and Nelson (2009) and Komives and Carpenter (2009) provide other strategies and techniques related to developing and sustaining staff members. In the final analysis, providing an infrastructure to support staff is an important element in keeping the division up to date.

Conducting Facility Audits. In addition to budget allocation and staff development, the existence and effective use of facilities is an important consideration in building an infrastructure that supports the divisional and institutional mission. Previously we mentioned that some student affairs units are facility intensive, such as campus recreation, while others have more modest facility requirements, such as judicial affairs. Regardless, yearly facility audits should be conducted and long-term facility repair and renovation plans updated on an annual basis. Rather than waiting for a disaster, such as, for example, a mid-winter heating system failure in a large residence hall, facilities need to be repaired according to a plan rather than an emergency. This approach suggests careful planning as well as prudent fiscal management to make sure that adequate funds are available to insure that work can be undertaken. Moreover, institutional leaders should be reminded that facilities will have an influence on attracting students. Tired, run down high profile facilities such as residence halls, student unions, or recreation facilities may result in prospective students looking elsewhere to pursue higher education.

Assessing Programs and Services. Staying aligned with what the institution wants and needs also requires information. A story illustrates this point. The late Ed Koch, former Mayor of New York City, was attributed to walking around the city and asking residents how he was doing. New Yorkers, so the story goes, were free with their advice. This form of anecdotal assessment provided Mayor Koch and his staff with information about how citizens evaluated city programs and services.

We do not suggest that collecting anecdotal information should serve as the cornerstone of an assessment program in student affairs, but we do strongly recommend that a program of data collection and analysis be a central part of programs and services in student affairs. Assessment for accountability and improvement (see Ewell, 2009) needs to be a foundation upon which the work of student affairs educators (Schuh & Associates, 2009) is built. Staff tend to resist conducting assessments for a variety of reasons, among them are (a) lack of time and resources, (b) fear of results, (c) lack of administrative support, and (d) lack of skills (Schuh, 2012). All of these concerns or issues can be overcome with a thoughtful approach to incorporating assessment into the work of the student affairs division. One simple approach is for staff to ask the following question when proposing new student programs, services, or learning experiences: How will we determine if it works?

The fact is that assessment is very much a part of virtually all aspects of higher education and an element in the accreditation process (see, for example, Southern Association of Colleges and Schools Commission on Colleges, 2012). An ongoing program of assessment in student affairs is essential for this area to stay aligned with what the larger institution wants, needs, and aspires. As Sandeen and Barr (2006, p. 131) asserted, "this issue (assessment) is now very important to the successful practice of student affairs." Without the information generated by ongoing assessments, leaders will be unable to assert empirically that the work of student affairs is producing the kind of outcomes that the institution seeks.

Closing the Loop

It is easy for student affairs staff to get caught up in the problem of the day and lose sight of the bigger picture. This observation is not offered as criticism because in many respects student affairs staff members are the front line institutional representatives charged with resolving issues related to campus crises. Miser and Cherrey concluded, rightly so in our view, "The effective management of crisis is an essential skill for student affairs administrators" (2009, p. 602). In addition to campus crises, student affairs staff also manage conflict on campus as Roper and Matheis pointed out: "When conflict arises, student affairs leaders must have the ability to view conflict as a potentially positive dynamic, convene key individuals, assess the dynamics of the situation, identify the appropriate process, and facilitate towards a successful outcome" (2011, p. 454). Crises and conflicts are nearly impossible to predict, and often require staff to defer what they are doing until the situation is resolved. That means that staff often are behind in their routine work and may not feel like they have the time to look at the larger picture.

While we concede that student affairs staff are challenged and at times consumed by their often unpredictable work, we also assert that staff must be able to step back from the crisis of the day and take a longer view of their work and that of the unit for which they are responsible. This assertion is especially true for unit heads and senior leaders in student affairs. We believe that divisional staff, at least on an annual basis, must review the mission and goals of their areas of responsibility and pay careful attention to the assessment data collected during the previous 12 months. This review will help determine the extent to which the division of student affairs and its units are on track or in need of realigning with what is desired of student affairs. If this work is undertaken on an annual basis, the changes necessary may not be much more than fine tuning the operation including devoting a two percent increase in funding from the operating budget to the repair and rehabilitation fund or offering a specialized retreat for staff before the next academic year begins. If this work is not done on an annual basis our view is that the division and its units have the potential to find themselves in a situation similar to the example of MCU—the focus of an accreditation report where the external reviewers found that significant drift had student affairs no longer contributing to the university as it should have.

Conclusion

In this final chapter we have presented ideas related to organizational renewal for the division of student affairs. Much more could be provided, quite obviously, but we think we have identified, at a minimum, some salient ideas that will be of value to student affairs educators. Our approach is both simple and complex, in that the elements that we present in many ways are obvious—staying aligned with the larger institution in terms of mission and vision, providing appropriate infrastructure to support the work of the division, and assessing the extent to which goals have been achieved. These steps are neither novel nor conceptually difficult. While the design is simple, the implementation is complex, given all of the demands of the time and expertise of student affairs educators. Our view is that to stay contemporary, the division cannot afford to ignore these steps related to renewal.

Our approach is thorough and systematic and one that we believe is well illustrated by the institutions we studied. We think this approach has a great deal of promise and will lead to advancing student affairs and the student experience at virtually any institution that adopts this approach.

Questions for Consideration

- What does student affairs look like at colleges and universities with high levels of student engagement?
- What role does student affairs play in promoting student success—graduation rates?
- What similarities in student affairs practice exist across institutions that perform well in terms of promoting student success?
- Is it possible that widely divergent approaches to student affairs can work equally well to foster student success?
- How do these approaches differ from established student affairs models?
- What is your institution doing on an annual basis to make sure that the mission of the division of student affairs and its units are consistent with the institution's mission?
- How is a solid infrastructure (facilities, staffing, budget) sustained for student affairs at your institution? What can you point to that illustrates renewal for student affairs at your institution?
- How is assessment for improvement and accountability sustained at your institution?

Appendix A
DEEP Research Method

This appendix briefly summarizes the research methods used in the Documenting Effective Educational Practices (DEEP) project, a two-year study carried out under the auspices of the National Survey of Student Engagement (NSSE) Institute for Effective Educational Practice at the Indiana University Center for Postsecondary Research. A more complete explanation of the research methodology is in Kuh, Kinzie, Schuh, Whitt, & Associates' *Student Success in College* (2005/2010) that includes a freshening of DEEP findings from the original publication of the book. Details about the approach to conducting the update are summarized at the end of this appendix

Introduction

The purpose of the DEEP project was to develop a comprehensive understanding of what 20 high-performing institutions do to promote student engagement and success. A research team was assembled and used a qualitative case study design (Merriam, 2002) to discover and document the policies, programs, practices, and conditions associated with higher than predicted student engagement and success.

Research Team

The DEEP research team consisted of 24 people intentionally chosen for their different areas of expertise and background. Some were primarily scholars; others were current or former academic and student affairs practitioners. The team was large enough to allow two multiple day site visits to each school (for a total of 40 visits) between fall 2002 and winter 2004.

DEEP team members met for three days in August 2002 to review the research process, discuss site visit procedures and logistics, and develop data collection protocols. The team met four times during the data collection phase by conference call or face-to-face meetings. Site visit teams communicated regularly via e-mail and telephone before, during, and following site visits to discuss data analysis procedures and interpretations, make decisions about various aspects of the work, and conduct data analysis.

Sample

An ideal-typical case selection process was used, whereby the researchers identified institutions representing "models" or desirable examples of colleges and universities with demonstrable track records for promoting student success (LeCompte & Preissle, 1993). Sample institutions were drawn from a potential pool of 700 four-year colleges and universities that participated in the NSSE between 2000 and 2002. The initial pool of 700 was narrowed down to institutions that had higher-than-predicted student engagement results and higher-than-predicted six-year graduation rates. Regression models calculated the predicted student engagement scores and graduation rates. The number of institutions that met these two criteria exceeded the target of 20 schools, which was the maximum number the project resources (e.g., financial, personnel, time) could accommodate. At this point additional criteria were considered: institutional size, type (e.g., 4-year institution), control (e.g., public or private), and geographic locale (region, rural/urban).

Data Collection

Teams of three to five researchers visited each of the 20 DEEP schools for the first site visit. Prior to the site visit, an on-campus DEEP site visit coordinator was identified to facilitate the research, gather documents for team review, and schedule interviews and focus groups. In advance, the site visit team reviewed written or web-based documents, such as institutional histories, catalogs, admissions materials, policy statements, student handbooks, organizational charts, student newspapers and other campus publications or videos, accreditation reports, and institutional self-studies. Reviewing campus websites alerted the visiting team to current issues and events. NSSE survey data for the visiting institution were also reviewed for possible lines of inquiry and exploration.

On site, the research team obtained data through interviews, focus groups, observation, and document analysis about the programs, policies, and practices that contributed to student success. The five NSSE clusters of effective educational practice (i.e., level of academic challenge, active and collaborative learning, student-faculty interactions, enriching educational experiences, and supportive campus environment) were a conceptual map to guide data collection and analysis. The teams also sought to discover programs, policies, and practices that were not encompassed by the NSSE framework but that respondents identified as related to student engagement and success. Peer debriefing among site visit team members occurred on site to test assumptions and determine themes and interpretations. A final meeting was held with key informants (e.g., provost, site coordinator) for feedback and verification purposes.

Following the initial site visit, site team members drafted an "interim report," which described the college or university context; featured relevant policies, programs, and practices; and identified factors and conditions that respondents and other data sources suggested were related to student engagement and success. The interim report summarized tentative themes warranting additional consideration and identified unanswered questions and topics for exploration during the second visit. The interim report was sent to the campus site visit coordinator with the request that it be distributed widely on campus for member checking.

Second site visit teams were usually composed of two or three people, at least one of whom was a member of the first site visit group and one of whom was new to the campus. This approach ensured both continuity and "fresh eyes." During the second visit, debriefing meetings were held with groups of faculty, students, staff, and others. The interim report was discussed in an effort to correct errors and identify practices needing further attention. Snowball sampling was used to identify additional respondents from whom site team members could learn different or potentially instructive views. Following the second visit, a final report was produced and sent to the institution with a request for additional member checking, feedback, and commentary. This document became the primary data source for analysis. Both the interim and final site visit reports included descriptive and interpretative material so that readers could make explicit connections between the goals of the study, the findings, and emerging themes (Merriam, 2002).

In all, team members interacted individually or in groups with more than 2,500 people (1,233 students, 750 faculty members, and 526 others, including student affairs professionals, librarians, and instructional technology staff). Some people were interviewed more than once. Team members sat in on approximately 60 classes, attended more than 30 campus events, dined in about 20 campus locations, rode buses, participated in campus tours, walked on campus, and visited student centers.

Data Analysis

Analyzing qualitative data from multiple sites is an iterative process (Coffey & Atkinson, 1996). In this study, data collection and analysis became more systematic with each site visit. This iterative, emergent design allowed team members to continually improve the amount and quality of the information gathered. Through a hermeneutic and dialectic process (Guba & Lincoln, 1989), different interpretations, claims, concerns, and issues were shared, understood, considered, critiqued, and acted upon. The objective was to elicit ongoing interpretive impressions from research team members and institutional stakeholders—honoring and simultaneously testing their constructions and interpretations of tentative claims against the collected data. Intra- and inter-site data analysis was conducted. To analyze the data in the richest way possible, different combinations of research team members met during data collection and analysis when circumstances allowed (e.g., professional meetings, conference calls).

During the data analysis phase, voluntary team members identified key data elements from the reports. These elements were the smallest units (e.g., phrases, sentences, paragraphs) that stood alone and revealed meaningful information (Lincoln & Guba, 1985). To manage the process, NUD*IST/NVivo software (Richards, 2002) was employed. NUD*IST required the NSSE staff and select research teams members to read data line by line, considering the meaning of each word, sentence, and idea (Creswell, 1998).

Trustworthiness

Triangulation, peer debriefing, member checking, and searching for disconfirming evidence to establish credibility were employed to establish trustworthiness (Creswell & Miller, 2000; Lincoln & Guba, 1985). Preliminary hypotheses, assumptions, and interpretations were challenged through peer debriefings during site visits and afterward via e-mail and conference calls. Interim and final reports were distributed to the entire research team to inform their data gathering at subsequent site visits. Interim and final reports were shared with respondents to confirm or challenge their accuracy and credibility. NSSE Institute staff reviewed every interim report to scrutinize data and preliminary interpretations.

To provide evidence that the inquiry decisions were logical and defensible, an audit trail was established (Lincoln & Guba, 1985; Whitt & Kuh, 1991). This trail included raw data (e.g., tapes, interview notes, and documents), field notes, and interview and document summary forms. Case analysis forms (e.g., multiple drafts of site visit reports), evidence of member checking, and materials relating to research team intentions, including notes of debriefings and staff meeting minutes and correspondence, also became part of this trail.

Update to Student Success in College

We conducted a follow-up study in 2009 to determine to what extent the conditions for student success were still in place six years following our initial case studies. To conduct this update, we examined empirical measures, namely NSSE results and graduation rates, to examine how current performance compared to when we identified the DEEP schools. All 20 DEEP institutions had administered NSSE at least once since our visit, and 16 institutions had results from more than three administrations, allowing for an even more robust examination over time. On balance, every institution looked much the same, and some improved their student engagement scores slightly. Graduation rates were mostly comparable to 2002, but interestingly, seven schools increased their graduation rates by at least six percent, and three increased by 10%. We also asked our primary contacts at the institutions to respond to key questions about the status of programs, practices and policies identified with student success, new initiatives and evidence of effectiveness, and their efforts to sustain education-ally effective practice. We also followed up with contacts via tele-phone, email, and face-to-face meetings to learn more about what had transpired. Results of this update were reported in a new Preface and Epilogue to *Student Success in College* (Kuh, Kinzie, Schuh, Whitt, & Associates, 2005/2010).

Appendix B

Models of Student Affairs Practice Inventory
Manning, Kinzie, & Schuh

Please check off the characteristics that apply to the student affairs division or department on your campus.

_____ 1. Students are viewed as equals in the running of the institution.

_____ 2. Academic affairs administrators "sound like" student affairs administrators and student affairs administrators "sound like" academic affairs administrators.

_____ 3. Student development theory is the main theoretical underpinning for the division/department.

_____ 4. Academic and student affairs cede responsibility for each other's experiences to the other and tend to stay out of the way.

_____ 5. Student affairs staff provide structural support for the intense academic environment.

_____ 6. Academic and student affairs leaders are aware of developments in each other's areas.

_____ 7. Student leadership is a major objective of the division/department.

_____ 8. Activities, decisions, and programs are the responsibility of the students.

_____ 9. Student affairs assumes that some students come to college inadequately prepared for academic work and the institution is committed to providing that support.

_____ 10. The complementary nature of academic and student affairs experiences is not recognized or acted upon.

_____ 11. Student and academic affairs missions are both designed to contribute to the total student learning experience: from admission through graduation.

_____ 12. Administrative and organizational clarity exist within the division of student affairs.

_____ 13. Significant interactions occur between student and academic affairs around the common purpose of enhanced student learning.

_____ 14. Administrative silos are torn down in order to provide students with the best possible experience.

_____ 15. Assumption that students require different programs, services, and environments that are best offered by distinct and separate offices.

_____ 16. Services, programs, and policies are well and/or adequately delivered without or with minimal division-level coordination.

_____ 17. Atmosphere of care and support is created.

_____ 18. Attention of student affairs units is focused on areas where students are most in need of support.

_____ 19. Student affairs possesses a high level of trust in students and they are intimately involved in running the majority of campus programs and services.

_____ 20. Business and consumer orientations are prevalent.

_____ 21. Student affairs and academic affairs programs, services, and activities compete for resources, student time, and mission priority.

_____ 22. Competition exists among departments for resources and student attention.

_____ 23. Student and academic affairs maintain their distinct functions but capitalize on the strengths of student learning from their unique perspective.

_____ 24. Due to joint student-academic affairs efforts, students have increased opportunities for learning in in- and out-of-classroom settings.

_____ 25. Duplication of effort due to lack of coordination is the norm between academic and student affairs.

_____ 26. Efficiency and effectiveness are the main concerns in delivery of student affairs functions.

_____ 27. Student affairs is organized on the belief that students may need extra support to succeed in college.

_____ 28. Faculty and student affairs staff are divided into in- and out-of-classroom activities respectively.

_____ 29. Faculty are free to concentrate their efforts on teaching, research, and service.

_____ 30. Functions and services are clustered together.

_____ 31. Growth and development come from out-of-class experiences that are independent from the formal academic curriculum.

_____ 32. Students drive campus activities, programs, and services.

_____ 33. High level of professionalism and expertise occur within the individual departments/offices of the student affairs division.

_____ 34. Student affairs staff work with faculty to develop a rich intellectual community.

_____ 35. Academic and student affairs are unaware of the contributions that each can make to the other.

_____ 36. Highest priority is creating an intellectual environment.

_____ 37. Student and academic affairs respect each other's professionalism and try not to interfere.

_____ 38. Independent, stand-alone budgets are the norm within each department.

_____ 39. _The Student Learning Imperative_ and/or _Learning Reconsidered_ form the philosophy of your on campus model.

_____ 40. Individual relationships between students and student affairs educators are not as crucial as the overall reputation of the office.

_____ 41. Inefficient delivery of programs and services occurs because academic units are unaware of the activities of student affairs.

_____ 42. Decentralization of supervision, professional development, and, oftentimes, goals are commonplace.

_____ 43. Student and academic affairs are independent though they do communicate with each other on important issues.

_____ 44. Learning occurs everywhere in a seamless manner.

_____ 45. Level of service available in the name of student support is very high.

_____ 46. Student learning experiences offered by academic and student affairs are uncoordinated with one another's efforts.

_____ 47. Student organizations are living laboratories to teach programming, budgeting, decision making, and conflict resolution.

_____ 48. The main purpose of student affairs is to deliver services, not provide a developmentally oriented education to students.

_____ 49. Departments within the division of student affairs operate independently of one another.

_____ 50. Student affairs operationalizes the assumption that students are more satisfied when services are conveniently organized and provided.

_____ 51. Only faculty teach courses, including First Year Experience, Leadership, or other student affairs-oriented subject matter.

_____ 52. Out-of-classroom learning is important but secondary to inside the classroom learning.

_____ 53. Out-of-classroom learning is the main goal of the student affairs division/department.

_____ 54. Planning between academic and student affairs is undertaken in an effort to avoid conflicts, not to collaborate about student learning and engagement.

_____ 55. Powerful partnerships are forged from the strengths of academic and student affairs.

_____ 56. Student affairs staff strategically and purposefully build student involvement into campus activities and programs.

_____ 57. Programs and services may lack the "polish" of professionally managed experiences.

_____ 58. Separate orientation and support services are tailored to the unique needs of particular students or student populations.

_____ 59. Students run the institution.

_____ 60. Services are accessed on a periodic rather than daily basis.

_____ 61. Specialization and narrowness of focus in academic and student affairs are valued over coordination and cooperation.

_____ 62. Student affairs activities are crafted to support, not compete with the academic mission.

_____ 63. Student affairs functions are to support the goals of education, not provide an education in and of themselves.

_____ 64. Student affairs is clear about their role as supporting the academic mission.

_____ 65. Student affairs is often responsible for initiating the collaborative efforts with academic affairs.

_____ 66. Student affairs staff are responsible for the choices made about the services, programs, and environment molded to advance student engagement.

_____ 67. Student affairs staff encourage and have high levels of expectation about the involvement of students in decision making and governance.

_____ 68. Student affairs staff often face ethical dilemmas over the extensive use of student employees.

_____ 69. Student affairs staff spend little energy on co-curricular programs that are not related to the academic mission.

_____ 70. Student and academic affairs missions are distinct but each respects and acknowledges the contributions of the other to student learning.

_____ 71. Student employees fill positions normally reserved for full time staff.

_____ 72. Student empowerment and leadership are at the center of the student affairs philosophy on campus.

_____ 73. Student involvement and leadership are at the core of the student affairs philosophy.

_____ 74. Student learning transcends administrative hierarchies and functional area boundaries.

_____ 75. Student success and academic rigor are of primary importance.

_____ 76. Students are highly invested in co-curricular life.

_____ 77. Students are highly invested in the running of the institution because of their deep involvement.

_____ 78. The academic mission is the highest priority at the institution.

_____ 79. The emphasis is on student learning, regardless of where it is occurring.

_____ 80. Student energies, time, and talents are channeled into activities shown to maximize student learning and development.

_____ 81. The high level of service to students is labor intensive and expensive.

_____ 82. The lines between in- and out-of-classroom are blurred.

_____ 83. Through campus employment, students can gain skills that prepare them for post-graduation employment.

_____ 84. Student learning has the potential to be a result of any student experience—in- and outside the classroom.

_____ 85. Unwillingness of academic and student affairs to work together is commonplace.

_____ 86. Well-developed programs, services, and policies are established for in- and out-of-classroom contexts.

_____ 87. Student affairs may sometimes overprotect, coddle, or fail to adequately challenge students.

_____ 88. Whole student development is maximized through well-integrated and coordinated student and academic affairs.

Scoring

EXTRA-CURRICULAR

3. _____
7. _____
28. _____
29. _____
47. _____
53. _____
66. _____
86. _____
_____ Total

FUNCTIONAL SILOS

12. _____
15. _____
16. _____
22. _____
33. _____
38. _____

42. _____
49. _____
_____Total

STUDENT SERVICES
20. _____
26. _____
30. _____
40. _____
48. _____
50. _____
60. _____
63. _____
_____Total

COMPETITIVE AND ADVERSARIAL
21. _____
25. _____
35. _____
41. _____
46. _____
51. _____
61. _____
85. _____
_____Total

CO-CURRICULAR
 4. _____
10. _____
31. _____
37. _____
43. _____
52. _____
54. _____
70. _____
_____Total

SEAMLESS LEARNING

6. _____
11. _____
14. _____
39. _____
44. _____
79. _____
82. _____
84. _____
_____ Total

ETHIC OF CARE

9. _____
17. _____
18. _____
27. _____
45. _____
58. _____
81. _____
87. _____
_____ Total

STUDENT DRIVEN

32. _____
56. _____
68. _____
71. _____
73. _____
76. _____
80. _____
83. _____
_____ Total

STUDENT AGENCY

1. _____
8. _____
19. _____

57. _____
59. _____
67. _____
72. _____
77. _____
_____ Total

ACADEMIC-STUDENT AFFAIRS COLLABORATION

2. _____
13. _____
23. _____
24. _____
55. _____
65. _____
74. _____
88. _____
_____ Total

ACADEMIC CENTERED

5. _____
34. _____
36. _____
62. _____
64. _____
69. _____
75. _____
78. _____
_____ Total

PRIMARY MODEL (highest number of points): _____
SECONDARY MODEL (second highest points): _____

References

Allen, K., & Cherrey, C. (2000). *Systemic leadership: Enriching the meaning of our work.* Lanham, MD: University Press of America.

Alpert, D. (1985). Performance and paralysis: The organizational context of the American research university. *Journal of Higher Education, 56*(3), 1–19.

Ambler, D. (2000). Organizational and administrative models. In M.J. Barr, M.K. Desler, & Associates, *The handbook of student affairs administration* (pp. 121–133). San Francisco, CA: Jossey-Bass.

American Association for Higher Education (AAHE), American College Personnel Association (ACPA), & National Association of Student Personnel Administrators (NASPA). (1998). *Powerful partnerships: A shared responsibility for learning.* Washington, DC: American College Personnel Association.

American College Personnel Association (ACPA) (1996). *The student learning imperative.* Washington, DC: Author.

American College Personnel Association (ACPA) & National Association of Student Personnel Administrators (NASPA). (1997/1999). *Principles of good practice for student affairs.* Washington, DC: Author.

American College Personnel Association (ACPA) & National Association of Student Personnel Administrators (NASPA). (2004). *Learning reconsidered: A campus-wide focus on the student experience.* Washington, DC: Author.

American Council on Education (ACE). (1937). The student personnel point of view. Washington, DC: Author. Retrieved from http://www.bgsu.edu/colleges/library/cac/sahp/word/THE%20STUDENT%20PERSONNEL.pdf

American Council on Education (ACE). (1949). The student personnel point of view. Washington, DC: Author. Retrieved from www.bgsu.edu/colleges/library/cac/sahp/pages/1949SPPVrev.pdf-2010-12-02

Andrews, K.R. (1980). *The concept of corporate strategy* (2nd ed.). Homewood, IL: Irwin.

Appleton, J.R., Briggs, C.M., & Rhatigan, J.J. (1978). *Pieces of eight: The rites, roles, and styles of the dean by eight who have been there.* Portland, OR: National Association of Student Personnel Administrators.

Arum, R., & Roksa, J. (2011). *Academically adrift: Limited learning on college campuses.* Chicago, IL: University of Chicago Press.

Association of American Colleges and Universities (AAC&U). (2007). College learning for the new global century: A report from the National Leadership Council for liberal education and America's promise. Washington, DC: Author. Retrieved from www.aacu.org/leap/documents/GlobalCentury_final.pdf

Association of American Colleges and Universities (AAC&U). (2012). A crucible moment: College learning and democracy's future. Washington, DC: Author. Retrieved from www.aacu.org/civic_learning/crucible/documents/crucible_508f.pdf

Association of College and University Housing Officers International Residential College Task Force (ACUHO-I). (1996, April). The residential nexus: A focus on student learning. *Talking Stick: Bringing Academics to the Residence Halls, 13*(7), 6–10.

Astin, A.W. (1977). *Four critical years.* San Francisco, CA: Jossey-Bass.

Astin, A.W. (1984). Student involvement: A developmental theory for higher education. *Journal of College Student Personnel, 25*(4), 297–308.

Astin, A.W. (1985). *Achieving educational excellence.* San Francisco, CA: Jossey-Bass.

Astin, A.W. (1990). Student involvement: A developmental theory for higher education. *Journal of College Student Personnel, 40,* 518–529.

Astin, A.W. (1991). *Assessment for excellence: The philosophy and practice of assessment and evaluation in higher education.* American Council on Education Series on Higher Education. Washington/New York, NY: American Council on Education and Macmillan.

Astin, A.W. (1993). *What matters in college? Four critical years revisited.* San Francisco, CA: Jossey-Bass.

Astin, A.W. (1999). *Involvement in Learning* revisited: Lessons we have learned. *Journal of College Student Personnel, 40,* 587–598.

Baldridge, J.V., Curtis, D.V., Ecker, G., & Riley, G.L. (1980). *Policy making and effective leadership.* San Francisco, CA: Jossey-Bass.

Ballard, S., & Long, P.N. (2004, November/December). Profiles in partnership: Finding strength in collaborative leadership. *About Campus, 9*(5), 16–22.

Bandura, A. (2001). Social cognitive theory: An agentic perspective. *Annual Review of Psychology, 52,* 1–26.

Banning, J. (1978). *Campus ecology: A perspective for student affairs.* Cincinnati, OH: NASPA Monograph.

Barr, M.J. (2000). The importance of institutional mission. In M.J. Barr, M.K. Desler, & Associates, *The handbook of student affairs administration* (2nd ed., pp. 25–36). San Francisco, CA: Jossey-Bass.

Barr, R., & Tagg, J.T. (1995, November/December). From teaching to learning: A new paradigm for undergraduate education. *Change, 27,* 12–25.

Baum, S, & Ma, J. (2012). *Trends in college pricing.* New York, NY: The College Board.

Benedict, A., Casper, B., Larson, L., Littlepage, G., & Panke, J. (2000). Utilizing paraprofessionals to expand student outreach. Paper presented at the National Career Development Association Annual Conference, Pittsburgh, PA.

Birnbaum, R. (1991). *How colleges work.* San Francisco, CA: Jossey-Bass.

Blau, P.M. (1970). A formal theory of differentiation in organizations. *American Sociological Review, 35,* 201–218.

Blau, P.M. (1970/1973). *The organization of academic work.* New York, NY: John Wiley & Sons.

Blau, P.M. (1972). Interdependence and hierarchy in organizations. *Social Science Research, 1*(1), 1–24.

Blimling, G.S. (2009). A legacy of scholarship in which every student affairs professional can be proud. *Journal of College Student Development, 50*(6), 712–714.

Blimling, G.S., Whitt, E.J., & Associates. (1999). *Good practice in student affairs: Principles to foster student learning.* San Francisco, CA: Jossey-Bass.

Bloland, P.A., Stamatakos, L.C., & Rogers, R.R. (1994). *Reform in student affairs: A critique of student development.* Greensboro, NC: ERIC Counseling and Student Services Clearinghouse.

Bourassa, D.M., & Kruger, K. (2001). *The national dialogue on academic and student affairs collaboration,* (pp. 9–38). New Directions for Higher Education, 116. San Francisco, CA: Jossey-Bass.

Bowen, H.R. (1977). *Investment in learning: The individual and social value of American higher education.* San Francisco, CA: Jossey-Bass.

Boyer, E.L. (1987). *College: The undergraduate experience in America.* New York, NY: Harper & Row.

Boyer, E.L. (1990). *Scholarship reconsidered: Priorities of the professoriate.* San Francisco, CA: Jossey-Bass.

Breen, D.G. (1970). Survey of selected programs for student leadership training at colleges and universities. Eric Document 044073. DeKalb, IL: Northern Illinois University.

Brown, R.D. (1972). *Student development in tomorrow's higher education: A return to the academy* (Student Personnel Series No. 16).Washington, DC: American College Personnel Association.

Bruffee, K.A. (1993). *Collaborative learning: Higher education, interdependence, and the authority of knowledge.* London: Johns Hopkins University Press.

Burke, J.C. (2004). The many faces of accountability. In J.C. Burke & Associates, *Achieving accountability in higher education* (pp. 1–24). San Francisco, CA: Jossey-Bass.

Caple, R.B. (1996). The learning debate: A historical perspective. *Journal of College Student Development, 37*(2), 193–202.

Caple, R.B. (1998). *To mark the beginning: A social history of college student affairs.* Lanham, MD: University Press of America.

Chandler, E.M. (1973/1986). Student affairs administration in transition. In G.L. Saddlemire & A.L. Rentz (Eds.), *Student affairs: A profession's heritage* (pp. 334–345). Alexandria, VA: ACPA.

Chickering, A.W. (1969). *Education and identity.* San Francisco, CA: Jossey-Bass.

Chickering, A.W. (1977). *Experience and learning: An introduction to experiential learning.* New Rochelle, NY: Change Magazine Press.

Chickering, A.W., & Gamson, Z.F. (1987). Seven principles for good practice in undergraduate education. *AAHE Bulletin, 39*(7), 3–7.

Chickering, A.W., & Reisser, L. (1993). *Education and identity* (2nd ed.). San Francisco, CA: Jossey-Bass.

The *Chronicle* 1999–2000 Almanac. *The Chronicle of Higher Education*. Retrieved from http://chronicle.com/prm/weekly/1999/facts/14stu.htm

Clothier, R.C. (1931/1986). College personnel principles and functions. In G. Saddlemire & A. Rentz (Eds.), *Student affairs: A profession's heritage* (pp. 9–20). Alexandria, VA: American College Personnel Association.

Coffey, A., & Atkinson, P. (1996). *Making sense of qualitative data: Complementary research strategies*. Thousand Oaks, CA: Sage.

Cohen, M.D., & March, J.G. (1986). *Leadership and ambiguity: The American college presidency* (2nd ed.). Boston, MA: Harvard Business School Press.

Collins, P.H. (1986). Learning from the outsider within: The sociological significance of Black feminist thought. *Social Problems, 33*(6), S14–S32.

Cook, B., & Pullaro, N. (2010). *College graduation rates: Behind the numbers*. Washington, DC: American Council on Education.

Cook, J.H., & Lewis, C.A. (2007). *Student and academic affairs collaboration: The divine comity*. Washington, DC: NASPA.

Council for the Advancement of Standards in Higher Education (CAS). (2013). *Standards*. Retrieved from http://www.cas.edu/index.php/standards/

Crane, W.J. (1963/1983). Curb service administration. In B.A. Belson & L.E. Fitzgerald (Eds.), *Thus, we spoke. ACPA—NAWDAC 1958–1975* (pp. 107–118). Carbondale, IL: ACPA.

Crawley, A. (2012). *Supporting online students: A guide to planning, implementing and evaluating services*. San Francisco, CA: Jossey-Bass.

Creswell, J.W. (1998). *Qualitative inquiry and research design: Choosing among five traditions*. Thousand Oaks, CA: Sage.

Creswell, J.W., & Miller, D.L. (2000). Determining validity in qualitative inquiry. *Theory Into Practice, 39*(3), 124–130.

Delworth, U., & Hanson, G. (1980). *Student services: A handbook for the profession*. San Francisco, CA: Jossey-Bass.

Delworth, U., & Hanson, G. (1989). *Student services: A handbook for the profession* (2nd ed.). San Francisco, CA: Jossey-Bass.

Dewey, J. (1904). *The relation of theory to practice in education*. Chicago, IL: University of Chicago Press

Dewey, J. (1916). *Democracy and education*. New York, NY: Macmillan.

Dewey, J. (1940). *Education today*. New York, NY: G.P. Putnam's Sons.

Doyle, J. (2004). Student affairs division's integration of student learning principles. *NASPA Journal, 41*, 375–394.

Dungy, G.J. (2003). Organization and functions of student affairs. In S.R. Komives, D.B. Woodard Jr., & Associates, *Student services: A handbook for the profession* (4th ed.) (pp. 339–357). San Francisco, CA: Jossey-Bass.

Dungy, G.J., & Gordon, S.A. (2011). The development of student affairs. In J.H. Schuh, S.R. Jones, S.R. Harper, & Associates, *Student services: A handbook for the profession* (5th ed.) (pp. 61–79). San Francisco, CA: Jossey-Bass.

Ellis, S.E. (2010). Introduction to strategic planning in student affairs. In S.E. Ellis (Ed.), *Strategic planning in student affairs,* (pp. 5–16). New Directions for Student Services, 132. San Francisco, CA: Jossey-Bass.

Engstrom, C.M., & Tinto, V. (2000). Developing partnerships with academic affairs to enhance student learning. In M.J. Barr, M.K. Desler, & Associates, *The handbook of student affairs administration* (2nd ed., pp. 425–452). San Francisco, CA: Jossey-Bass.

Erikson, E. (1968). *Identity: Youth and crisis.* New York, NY: Norton.

Evans, N.J., & Reason, R.D. (2001). Guiding principles: A review and analysis of student affairs philosophical statements. *Journal of College Student Development, 42,* 359–377.

Ewell, P.T. (2009, November). *Assessment, accountability and improvement: Revisiting the tension.* (NILOA Occasional Paper No. 1). Urbana, IL: University of Illinois and Indiana University, National Institute for Learning Outcomes Assessment. Retrieved from learningoutcomes assessment.org

Fenske, R. (1989). Evolution of the student services profession. In U. Delworth, G.R. Hanson, & Associates, *Student services: A handbook for the profession* (2nd ed., pp. 25–56). San Francisco, CA: Jossey-Bass.

Flowers, L. (2004). Examining the effects of student involvement on African American college student development. *Journal of College Student Development 45*(6), 633–654.

Foubert, J.D., & Grainger, L.U. (2006). Effects of involvement in clubs and organizations on the psychosocial development of first-year and senior college students. *NASPA Journal, 43*(1), 166–182.

Franklin, D.S. (2009). A study on the organizational location of the division of campus recreation. Unpublished paper, Ohio University, Athens, OH.

Freire, P. (1985). *The politics of education: Culture, power and liberation.* Hadley, MA: Bergin & Garvey.

Freire, P. (1990). *Pedagogy of the oppressed.* New York, NY: Continuum Publishing.

Frigault, R., Maloney, G., & Trevino, C. (1986). Training paraprofessionals to facilitate leadership development. *Journal of College Student Personnel, 27*(3), 281–282.

Garland, P.H., & Grace, T.W. (1993). *New perspectives for student affairs professionals: Evolving realities, responsibilities, and roles.* ASHE-ERIC Higher Education Report, No. 7. Washington, DC: The George Washington University School of Education and Human Development.

Giddens, A. (1979). *Central problems in social theory: Action, structure and contradiction in social analysis.* Berkeley, CA: University of California Press.

Gilligan, C. (1982). *In a different voice: Psychological theory and women's development.* Cambridge, MA: Harvard University Press.

Goodsell, A.M., Maher, M., & Tinto, V. (Eds.) (1992). *Collaborative learning: A sourcebook for higher education.* University Park, PA: National Center on Postsecondary Teaching, Learning, and Assessment, The Pennsylvania State University.

Griffin, K.A., & Hurtado, S. (2011). Institutional variety in American higher education. In J.H. Schuh, S.R. Jones, S.R. Harper, & Associates, *Student services: A handbook for the professional* (5th ed.) (pp. 24–42). San Francisco, CA: Jossey-Bass.

Guarasci, R. (2001). Recentering learning: An interdisciplinary approach to academic and student affairs. In A.J. Kezar, D.J. Hirsch, & C. Burack (Eds.), *Understanding the role of academic and student affairs collaboration in creating a successful learning environment,* (pp. 101–109). New Directions for Student Services, 116, San Francisco, CA: Jossey-Bass.

Guba, E.G., & Lincoln, Y.S. (1989). *Fourth generation evaluation.* Thousand Oaks, CA: Sage.

Guthrie, K.L., & Osteen, L. (Eds.). (2013). *Developing students' leadership capacity.* New Directions for Student Services, 140. San Francisco, CA: Jossey-Bass.

Hamrick, F.A., Evans, N.J., & Schuh, J.H. (2002). *Foundations of student affairs practice: How philosophy, theory, and research strengthen educational outcomes.* San Francisco, CA: Jossey-Bass.

Hamrick, F.A., & Rumann, C.B. (2012). *Called to serve: A handbook on student veterans and higher education.* San Francisco, CA: Jossey-Bass.

Harding, S. (Ed.). (1987). *Feminism and methodology: Social sciences issues.* Bloomington, IN: Indiana University Press.

Harding, S. (1991). *Whose science? Whose knowledge? Thinking from women's lives.* Ithaca, NY: Cornell University Press.

Harper, S.R., & Quaye, S.J. (Eds.). (2009). Student engagement in higher education: Theoretical perspectives and practical approaches for diverse populations. New York, NY: Routledge.

Hecht, I.D., Higgerson, M.L., Gmelch, W.H., & Tucker, A. (1999). *The department chair as academic leader.* Phoenix, AZ: The American Council on Education and Oryx Press.

Hersh, R.H. (1999). Generating ideals and transforming lives: A contemporary case for the residential liberal arts college. *Daedalus, 128*(1), 173–194.

Hirt, J.B. (2009). The importance of institutional mission. In G.S. McClellan & J. Stringer (Eds.), *The Handbook of Student Affairs Administration* (3rd ed., pp. 19–38). Washington, DC: NASPA, Student Affairs Administrators in Higher Education.

Hirt, J.B., Amelink, C.T., & Schneiter, S. (2004). The nature of student affairs work in the liberal arts college. *NASPA Journal, 42*, 94–110.

Horowitz, H.L. (1987). *Campus life: Undergraduate cultures form the end of the eighteenth century to the present.* Chicago, IL: University of Chicago Press.

Hu, S., & Kuh, G.D. (2002). Being (dis)engaged in educationally purposeful activities: The influence of student and institutional characteristics. *Research in Higher Education, 43*, 555–576.

Hussar, W.J., & Bailey, T.M. (2013). Projections of Education Statistics to 2021 (NCES 2013-008). U.S. Department of Education, National Center for Education Statistics, Washington, DC: U.S. Government Printing Office.

Jackson, M.L., Moneta, L., & Nelson, K.A. (2009). Effective management of human capital in student affairs. In G.S. McClellan, J. Stringer, & Associates, *The handbook of student affairs administration* (3rd ed., pp. 333–354). San Francisco, CA: Jossey-Bass.

Javinar, J.M. (2000). Student life and development. In L.K. Johnsrud & V.J. Rosser (Eds.), *The work and career paths of midlevel administrators*, (pp. 85–93). New Directions for Higher Education, 111. San Francisco, CA: Jossey-Bass.

Jessup-Anger, J., Wawrzynski, M.R., & Yao, C.W. (2011). Enhancing undergraduate education: Examining faculty experiences during their first year in a residential college and exploring the implications for student affairs professionals. *Journal of College and University Student Housing, 38*(1), 56–69.

Johnson, D.W., Johnson, R., & Smith, K.A. (1991). *Cooperative learning: Increasing college faculty instructional productivity.* ASHE-ERIC Higher Education Report No. 4. Washington, DC: The George Washington University, School of Education and Human Development.

Josselson, R. (1987). *Finding herself: Pathways to identity development in women.* San Francisco, CA: Jossey-Bass.

Keeling, R.P., Wall, A.F., Underhile, R., & Dungy, G.J. (2008). *Assessment reconsidered.* Washington, DC: National Association of Student Personnel Administrators.

Kezar, A. (2003a). Achieving student success: Strategies for creating partnerships between academic and student affairs. *NASPA Journal, 41*, 1–22.

Kezar, A. (2003b). Enhancing innovative partnerships: Creating a change model for academic and student affairs collaboration. *Innovative Higher Education, 28,* 137–156.

Kezar, A., Hirsch, D.J., & Burack, C. (2002). *Understanding the role of academic and student affairs collaboration in creating successful learning enrivonments.* San Francisco, CA: Jossey-Bass.

Kezar, A., & Lester, J. (2009). *Organizing higher education for collaboration: A guide for campus leaders.* San Francisco, CA: John Wiley & Sons.

Kinzie, J., & Kuh, G.D. (2004). Going DEEP: Learning from campuses that share responsibility for student success. *About Campus, 9*(5), 2–8.

Knock, G. (1988). The philosophical heritage of student affairs. In A.L. Rentz & G.L. Saddlemire (Eds.), *Student affairs functions in higher education.* Springfield, IL: Charles C. Thomas.

Kohlberg, L. (1969). Stage and sequence: The cognitive-developmental approach to socialization. In D. Goslin, *Handbook of socialization theory and research* (pp. 347–480). New York, NY: Rand McNally.

Komives, S.R., & Carpenter, S. (2009). Professional development as lifelong learning. In G.S. McClellan, J. Stringer, & Associates, *The handbook of student affairs administration* (3rd ed., pp. 371–387). San Francisco, CA: Jossey-Bass.

Komives, S., Lucas, N., & McMahon, T. (2013). *Exploring leadership: For college students who want to make a difference* (3rd ed.). San Francisco, CA: Jossey-Bass.

Kouzes, J. M, & Posner, B.Z. (2002). *The leadership challenge* (3rd ed.). San Francisco, CA: Jossey-Bass.

Kuh, G.D. (1996). Guiding principles for creating seamless learning environments for undergraduates. *Journal of College Student Development, 37,* 135–148.

Kuh, G.D. (1999). Setting the bar high to promote student learning. In G.S. Blimling, E.J. Whitt, & Associates, *Good practice in student affairs: Principles to foster student learning* (pp. 67–81). San Francisco, CA: Jossey-Bass.

Kuh, G.D. (2001a). Assessing what really matters to student learning: Inside the National Survey of Student Engagement. *Change, 33*(3), 10–17, 66.

Kuh, G.D. (2001b). The National Survey of Student Engagement: Conceptual framework and overview of psychometric properties. Bloomington, IN: Indiana University Center for Postsecondary Research.

Kuh, G.D. (2003, March/April). What we're learning about student engagement from NSSE. *Change, 35*(2), 24–32.

Kuh, G.D. (2008). *High-impact educational practices: What they are, who has access to them, and why they matter.* Washington, DC: Association of American Colleges and Universities.

Kuh, G.D. (2009). What student affairs professionals need to know about student engagement. *Journal of College Student Development, 50*(6), 683–706.

Kuh, G.D., & Ikenberry, S. (2009). More than you think, less than we need: Learning outcomes assessment in American higher education. Urbana, IL: University of Illinois and Indiana University, National Institute for Learning Outcomes Assessment.

Kuh, G.D., Kinzie, J., Buckley, J., Bridges, B.K., & Hayek, J.C. (2007). *Piecing together the student success puzzle: Research, propositions, and recommendations.* ASHE Higher Education Report, 32(5). San Francisco, CA: Jossey-Bass.

Kuh, G.D., Kinzie, J., Schuh, J.H., & Whitt, E.J. (2005). Never let it rest: Lessons about student success from high-performing colleges and universities. *Change, 37*(4), 44–51.

Kuh, G. D., Kinzie, J., Schuh, J., Whitt, E., & Associates. (2005/2010). *Student success in college: Creating conditions that matter.* San Francisco, CA: Jossey-Bass.

Kuh, G. D., Kinzie, J., Schuh, J. H., & Whitt, E. J. (2011). Fostering student success in hard times. *Change: The Magazine of Higher Learning, 43*(4), 13–19.

Kuh, G. D., Schuh, J., Whitt, E., & Associates. (1991). *Involving colleges.* San Francisco, CA: Jossey-Bass.

Kuk, L. (2009). The dynamics of organizational models within student affairs. In G. McClellan & J. Stringer (Eds.), *The handbook of student affairs administration* (pp. 313–332). Washington, DC: NASPA, Student Affairs Administrators in Higher Education.

Kuk, L., & Banning, J.H. (2009). Designing student affairs organizational structures: Perceptions of senior student affairs officers. *NASPA Journal, 46*(1), 94–117.

Kuk, L., Banning, J.H., & Amey, M.J. (2010). *Positioning student affairs for sustainable change: Achieving organizational effectiveness through multiple perspectives.* Sterling, VA: Stylus Publishing.

LeCompte, M.D., & Preissle, J. (1993). *Ethnography and qualitative design in educational research.* San Diego, CA: Academic Press.

Levine, A., & Cureton, J.S. (1998). *When hope and fear collide.* San Francisco, CA: Jossey-Bass.

Lewin, K. (1946). Force field analysis. *The 1973 Annual Handbook for Group Facilitators,* 111–13.

Lightfoot, S.L. (1986). On goodness in schools: Themes of empowerment. *Peabody Journal of Education, 63*(3), 9–28.

Lincoln, Y.S., & Guba, E. (1985). *Naturalistic inquiry.* Thousand Oaks, CA: Sage.

Lyons, J.W. (1993). The importance of institutional mission. In M.J. Barr & Associates, *The handbook of student affairs* (pp. 3–15). San Francisco, CA: Jossey-Bass.

Magolda, M.B.B. (1999). Engaging students in active learning. In G.S. Blimling, E.J. Whitt, & Associates, *Good practice in student affairs: Principles to foster student learning* (pp. 21–43). San Francisco, CA: Jossey-Bass.

Magolda, P.M. (2005). Proceed with caution: Uncommon wisdom about academic and student affairs partnerships. *About Campus, 9*(6), 16–21.

Manning, K. (2013). *Organizational theory in higher education.* New York, NY: Routledge.

Marine, S.B. (2011). "Our college is changing": Women's college student affairs administrators and transgender students. *Journal of Homosexuality, 58*(9), 1165–1186.

Martin, J., & Murphy, S. (2000). *Building a better bridge: Creating effective partnerships between academic affairs and student affairs.* Washington, DC: National Association of Student Personnel Administrators.

McCormick, A.C., Kinzie, J., & Gonyea, R.M. (2013). Student engagement: Bridging research and practice to improve the quality of undergraduate education. In M.B. Paulsen (Ed.), *Higher education: Handbook of theory and research, 28* (pp. 47–92). Dordrecht, The Netherlands: Springer.

McCoy, D.L. (2011). Multicultural student services at public institutions. In D. Stewart (Ed.), *Multicultural student services on campus: Building bridges, re-visioning community* (pp. 140–153). Sterling, VA: Stylus.

McKeachie, W.J., Pintrich, P.R., Lin, Y., & Smith, D. (1986). *Teaching and learning in the college classroom: A review of the research.* Ann Arbor, MI:

National Center for Research to Improve Postsecondary Teaching and Learning, University of Michigan.

Merriam, S. (2002). *Qualitative research and case study applications in education.* San Francisco, CA: Jossey-Bass.

Michalak, S.J., & Robert, J.F. (1981). Research productivity and teaching effectiveness at a small liberal arts college. *Journal of Higher Education, 52*(6), 578–597.

Miller, M.A. (2012, January). *From denial to acceptance: The stages of assessment* (NILOA Occasional Paper No. 13). Urbana, IL: University of Illinois and Indiana University, National Institute for Learning Outcomes Assessment.

Miller, M.A., & Ewell, P. (2005). *Measuring up on college-level learning.* San Jose, CA: National Center for Public Policy and Higher Education.

Miser, K.M., & Cherrey, C. (2009). Responding to campus crisis. In G.S. McClellan, J. Stringer, & Associates, *The handbook of student affairs administration* (3rd ed., pp. 602–622). San Francisco, CA: Jossey-Bass.

Morgan, G. (1997). *Images of organization.* Thousand Oaks, CA: Sage.

Mueller, K.H. (1961). *Student personnel work in higher education.* Boston, MA: Houghton Mifflin.

National Association of Student Personnel Administrators (NASPA). (1989). *Points of view.* Washington, D.C.: Author.

National Commission on Excellence in Education. (1983). *A nation at risk.* Washington, DC: Author.

National Survey of Student Engagement (NSSE). (2002). *From promise to progress: How colleges and universities are using student engagement results to improve collegiate quality.* Bloomington, IN: Indiana University Center for Postsecondary Research.

National Survey of Student Engagement (NSSE). (2003a). *Converting data into action: Expanding the boundaries of institutional improvement.* Bloomington, IN: Indiana University Center for Postsecondary Research.

National Survey of Student Engagement (NSSE). (2003b). Final report, Alverno College. Bloomington, IN: Unpublished paper.

National Survey of Student Engagement (NSSE). (2003c). Final report, George Mason University. Bloomington, IN: Unpublished paper.

National Survey of Student Engagement (NSSE). (2003d). Final report, Gonzaga University. Bloomington, IN: Unpublished paper.

National Survey of Student Engagement (NSSE). (2003e). Final report, Longwood University. Bloomington, IN: Unpublished paper.

National Survey of Student Engagement (NSSE). (2003f). Final report, Macalester College. Bloomington, IN: Unpublished paper.

National Survey of Student Engagement (NSSE). (2003g). Final report, University of Maine–Farmington. Bloomington, IN: Unpublished paper.

National Survey of Student Engagement (NSSE). (2004a). *Converting data into action: Expanding the boundaries of institutional improvement.* Bloomington, IN: Indiana University Center for Postsecondary Research.

National Survey of Student Engagement (NSSE). (2004b). Final report, The Evergreen State University. Bloomington, IN: Unpublished paper.

National Survey of Student Engagement (NSSE). (2004c). Final report, University of Kansas. Bloomington, IN: Unpublished paper.

National Survey of Student Engagement (NSSE). (2012). *Promoting student learning and institutional improvement: Lessons from NSSE at 13.* Bloomington, IN: Indiana University Center for Postsecondary Research.

Nesheim, B.E., Guentzel, M.J., Kellogg, A.H., McDonald, W.M., Wells, C.A., & Whitt, E.J. (2007). Outcomes for students of student affairs-academic affairs partnership programs. *Journal of College Student Development, 48*(4), 435–454.

Newton, F.B., Ender, S.C., & Gardner, J.N. (2010). *Students helping students: A guide for peer educators on college campuses.* San Francisco, CA: Jossey-Bass.

Noddings, N. (1984). *Caring: A feminine approach to ethics and moral education.* Berkeley, CA: University of California Press.

Nuss, E.M. (2003). The development of student affairs. In S. Komives & D. Woodard (Eds.), *Student services: A handbook for the profession* (pp. 65–88). San Francisco, CA: Jossey-Bass.

Osteen, L., & Coburn, M.B. (2012). Considering context: Developing students' leadership capacity. In K. L. Guthrie & L. Osteen (Eds.), *Developing students' leadership capacity* (pp. 5–15), New Directions for Student Services, 140. San Francisco, CA: Jossey-Bass.

Pace, C.R. (1980). Measuring the quality of student effort. *Current Issues in Higher Education, 2,* 10–16.

Pace, C.R. (1982). *Achievement and the quality of student effort.* Washington, DC: National Commission on Excellence in Education.

Pascarella, E.T. (2001). Identifying excellence in undergraduate education: Are we even close? *Change, 33*(3), 19–23.

Pascarella, P.T., & Terenzini, E.T. (1991). *How college affects students.* San Francisco, CA: Jossey-Bass.

Pascarella, P.T., & Terenzini, E.T. (2005). *How college affects students: A third decade of research.* San Francisco, CA: Jossey-Bass.

Perozzi, B. (Ed.). (2009). *Enhancing student learning through college employment.* Indianapolis, IN: Dog Ear Publishing.

Pike, G.R. (1993). The relationship between perceived learning and satisfaction with college: An alternative view. *Research in Higher Education, 34*(1), 23–40.

Price, J. (1999). Merging with academic affairs: A promotion or demotion for student affairs? In J. Schuh & E. Whitt (Eds.), *Partnerships between academic and student affairs,* (pp. 75–83). New Directions for Student Services, 87. San Francisco, CA: Jossey-Bass.

Radford, A.W. (2011). *Learning at a distance. Undergraduate enrollment in distance education courses and degree programs.* (NCES 2012–154). Washington, DC: U.S. Department of Education, National Center for Education Statistics.

Reason, R.D., & Kimball, E.W. (2012). A new theory-to-practice model for student affairs: Integrating scholarship, context, and reflection. *Journal of Student Affairs Research and Practice, 49*(4), 359–376.

Reisser, L., & Roper, L. (1999). Using resources to achieve institutional missions and goals. In G.S. Blimling, E.J. Whitt, & Associates, *Good practice in student affairs* (pp. 113–131). San Francisco, CA: Jossey-Bass.

Rendón, L.I. (1994). Validating culturally diverse students: Toward a new model of learning and student development. *Innovative Higher Education, 19*(1), 33–51.

Renn, K.A., & Reason, R.D. (2013). *College students in the United States: Characteristics, experiences, and outcomes.* San Francisco: Jossey-Bass.

Rentz, A.L., & Saddlemire, G.L. (1988). *Student affairs functions in higher education.* Springfield, IL: Charles C. Thomas.

Rhatigan, J.J. (2000). The history and philosophy of student affairs. In M.J. Barr, M.J. Desler, & Associates, *The handbook of student affairs administration* (pp. 3–24). San Francisco, CA: Jossey-Bass.

Rhatigan, J.J. (2003). The history and philosophy of student affairs. In S. Komives & D. Woodard (Eds.), *Student services: A handbook for the profession* (pp. 3–24). San Francisco, CA: Jossey-Bass.

Rhatigan, J.J. (2009). From the people up: A brief history of student affairs administration. In G.S. McClellan, J. Stringer, & Associates, *The handbook of student affairs administration* (3rd ed., pp. 3–18). San Francisco, CA: Jossey-Bass.

Rhatigan, J.J., & Schuh, J.H. (1993). The dean over 75 years: Some key themes. *NASPA Journal, 30*, 83–92.

Richards, L. (2002). *Using N6 in qualitative research.* Melbourne, Australia: QSR International.

Roberts, D.C. (1981). *Student leadership programs in higher education.* ACPA Media Monograph Series, 30. Cardondale, IL: Southern Illinois University Press.

Roberts, D.C. (1998). Student learning was always supposed to be the core of our work: What happened? *About Campus, 3*(3), 18–22.

Roberts, D.C. (2012). The student personnel point of view as a catalyst for dialogue: 75 years and beyond. *Journal of College Student Development, 53*(1), 2–18.

Romer, R. (1995). Making quality count in undergraduate education. Denver, CO: Denver Education Commission of the States.

Roper, L., & Matheis, C. (2011). Conflict resolution. In J.H. Schuh, S.R. Jones, S.R. Harper, & Associates, *Student services: A handbook for the profession* (5th ed., pp. 433–447). San Francisco: Jossey-Bass.

Rudolph, F. (1990). *The American college and university: A history.* Athens, GA: University of Georgia Press.

Saddlemire, G.L. (1988). Student activities. In A.L. Rentz & G.L. Saddlemire (Eds.), *Student affairs functions in higher education.* Springfield, IL: Charles C. Thomas.

Sanchez, F. (2013). *Negotiating with hurricanes: A system response to student crisis.* Featured speech at the annual conference of the National Association of Student Personnel Administrators, Orlando, FL.

Sandeen, A. (1991). *The chief student affairs officer: Leader, manager, mediator, educator.* San Francisco, CA: Jossey-Bass.

Sandeen, A. (2001). Organizing student affairs divisions. In R.B. Winston, Jr., D.G. Creamer, T.K. Miller, & Associates, *The professional student affairs administrator* (pp. 181–209). New York, NY: Routledge.

Sandeen, A. (2004). Educating the whole student: The growing academic importance of student affairs. *Change, 36*(3), 28–33.

Sandeen, A., & Barr, M.J. (2006). *Critical issues for student affairs.* San Francisco, CA: Jossey-Bass.

Sanford, N. (1962). *The American college.* New York, NY: Wiley.

Sax, L.J., & Harper, C.E. (2011). Using research to inform practice. In J. Schuh, S.R. Jones, S.R. Harper, & Associates, *Student Services: A handbook for the profession* (5th ed., pp. 499–514). San Francisco, CA: Jossey-Bass.

Schlossberg, N.K. (1989). Marginality and mattering: Key issues in building community. In D.C. Roberts (Ed.), *Designing campus activities to foster a sense of community,* (pp. 5–15). New Directions for Student Services, 48. San Francisco, CA: Jossey-Bass.

Schroeder, C.C. (1999a). Forging educational partnerships that advance student learning. In G.S. Blimling, E.J. Whitt, & Associates, *Good practice in student affairs: Principles to foster student learning* (pp. 133–156). San Francisco, CA: Jossey-Bass.

Schroeder, C.C. (1999b). Partnerships: An imperative for enhancing learning and institutional effectiveness. In J.H. Schuh & E.J. Whitt (Eds.), *Creating successful partnerships between academic and student affairs,* (pp. 5–18). New Directions for Student Services, 87. San Francisco, CA: Jossey-Bass.

Schroeder, C.C. (2003). How are we doing at engaging students? Charles Schroeder talks to George Kuh. *About Campus,* 8(1), 9–16.

Schroeder, C.C., & Hurst, J.C. (1996). Designing learning environments that integrate curricular and cocurricular experiences. *Journal of College Student Development, 37,* 174–181.

Schuh, J.H. (1983). When the measles come to college: Implications for student affairs administrators. *The College Student Affairs Journal, 5*(2), 32–36.

Schuh, J. (1999). Guiding principles for evaluating student and academic affairs partnerships. In J.H. Schuh & E.J. Whitt (Eds.), *Creating successful partnerships between academic and student affairs* (pp. 85–92). New Directions for Student Services, 87. San Francisco, CA: Jossey-Bass.

Schuh, J.H. (2007). Changing student services through assessment. In G.L. Kramer (Ed.), *Fostering student success in the campus community* (p. 61–80). San Francisco, CA: Jossey-Bass.

Schuh, J.H. (2012). *Assessment in student affairs: One more thing to do or central to student affairs practice?* Keynote speech delivered at University of Tennessee Assessment Conference, Knoxville, TN.

Schuh, J.H., & Associates. (2009). *Assessment methods for student affairs*. San Francisco, CA: Jossey-Bass.

Schuh, J.H., & Gansemer-Topf, A.M. (2010). The role of student affairs in student learning assessment. National Institute for Learning Outcomes Assessment Occasional Paper. Retrieved from http://www.learningout comeassessment.org/occasionalpapers.htm

Schuh, J.H., & Whitt, E.J. (Eds.). (1999). *Creating successful partnerships between academic and student affairs*. New Directions for Student Services, 87. San Francisco, CA: Jossey-Bass.

Schwartz, R.A. (1997). How deans of women became men. *The Review of Higher Education, 20*, 419–436.

Schwartz, R.A. (2002). The rise and demise of deans of men. *The Review of Higher Education, 26*, 217–236.

Seifert, T.A., Arnold, C., Burrow, J., & Brown, A. (2011). *Supporting student success: The role of student services within Ontario's postsecondary institutions*. Toronto: The Higher Education Quality Council of Ontario.

Shaffer, R.H. (1961/1986). Student personnel problems requiring a campus-wide approach. In G.L. Saddlemire & A.L. Rentz (Eds.), *Student affairs: A profession's heritage* (pp. 183–191). Alexandria, VA: ACPA.

Shutt, M.D., Garrett, J.M., Lynch, J.W., & Dean, L.A. (2012). An assessment model as best practice in student affairs. *Journal of Student Affairs Research and Practice, 49*(1), 65–82.

Simon, H.A. (1957). *Administrative behavior*. New York, NY: Free Press.

Smith, R.L., Jr., & Director, E.O. (2006). Task force report on the organizational structure of the division of Educational and Student Services (ESS). Iowa City, IA: University of Northern Iowa.

Snyder, T.D., & Dillow, S.A. (2012). *Digest of education statistics 2011* (NCES 2012–001). National Center for Education Statistics, Institute of Education Sciences, U.S. Department of Education, Washington, DC.

Sorcinelli, M.D. (1991). Research findings on the seven principles. In A.W. Chickering & Z.F. Gamson (Eds.), *Applying the seven principles for good practice in undergraduate education,* (pp. 13–25). New Directions for Teaching and Learning, 47. San Francisco, CA: Jossey-Bass.

Southern Association of Colleges and Schools Commission on Colleges. (2012). *The principles of accreditation: Foundations for quality enhancement*. Decatur, GA: Author.

Strange, C.C., & Banning, J.H. (2001). *Educating by design: Creating campus learning environments that work*. San Francisco, CA: Jossey-Bass.

Study Group on the Conditions of Excellence in American Higher Education. (1984). *Involvement in learning: Realizing the potential of American higher education*. Washington, DC: National Institute of Education.

Sullivan, B. (2010). Organizing, leading, and managing student services. In D. Hardy Cox & C.C. Strange (Eds.), *Achieving student success: Effective student services in Canadian higher education* (pp. 165–191). Montreal & Kingston: McGill-Queens University Press.

Tagg, J. (2003). *The learning paradigm college.* Boston, MA: Anker Publishing

Thelin, J.R. (2003). Historical overview of American higher education. In S.R. Komives, D.B. Woodard, Jr., & Associates, *Student services: A handbook for the profession* (4th ed., pp. 3–22). San Francisco, CA: Jossey-Bass.

Thelin, J.R. (2004). *A history of American higher education.* Baltimore, MD: The Johns Hopkins University Press.

Thelin, J.R., & Gasman, M. (2011). Historical overview of American higher education. In J.H. Schuh, S.R. Jones, S.R. Harper, & Associates, *Student services: A handbook for the profession* (5th ed., pp. 3–23). San Francisco, CA: Jossey-Bass.

Tinto, V. (1993). *Leaving college: Rethinking the causes and cures of student attrition* (2nd ed.). Chicago, IL: University of Chicago Press.

Tinto, V. (1996). Reconstructing the first year of college. *Planning for Higher Education, 25*(1), 1–6.

Tinto, V. (2012). *Completing college: Rethinking institutional action.* Chicago, IL: University of Chicago Press.

Torres, V. (2007). *One size does not fit all: Traditional and innovative models of student affairs practice* (review). *The Journal of Higher Education, 78*(6), 718–720.

Tull, A., & Freeman, J. (2008). Chief student affairs officer titles: Standardization of titles and broadening of labels. *NASPA Journal, 45*(2), 265–281.

U.S. Department of Education. (2006). *A test of leadership: Charting the future of U.S. higher education.* Washington, DC: Author.

U.S. Department of Education. (2011). *Digest of Education Statistics.* Washington, DC: U.S. Department of Education, National Center for Education Statistics, Integrated Postsecondary Education Data System (IPEDS).

U.S. Department of Education. (2012). *Digest of Education Statistics 2011.* Washington, DC: National Center for Education Statistics, U.S. Department of Education. Retrieved from http://nces.ed.gov/programs/digest/d11/

U.S. Department of Education. (2013). Advance release of selected 2012 tables. Washington, DC: National Center for Education Statistics, U.S. Department of Education. Retrieved from http://nces.ed.gov/programs/digest/2012menu_tables.asp

Wawrzynski, M.R., Heck, A.M., & Remley, C.T. (2012). Student engagement in South African higher education. *Journal of College Student Development, 53*(1), 106–123.

Weber, M. (1947). *The theory of social and economic organization.* London: Oxford University Press.

Weick, K. (1976). Educational organizations as loosely-coupled systems. *Administrative Science Quarterly, 21*, 1–21.

Weick, K.E. (1984). Small wins: Redefining the scale of social problems. *American Psychologist, 39*(1), 40–49.

Wheatley, M. (2010). *Leadership and the new science: Learning about organization from an orderly universe.* San Francisco, CA: Berrett-Koehler.

Whitt, E.J. (2011). Academic and student affairs partnerships. In J.H. Schuh, S.R. Jones, S.R. Harper, & Associates, *Student services: A handbook for the profession* (5th ed., pp. 482–496). San Francisco, CA: Jossey-Bass.

Whitt, E.J., & Kuh, G.D. (1991). Qualitative research in higher education: A team approach to multiple site investigation. *Review of Higher Education, 14,* 317–337.

Whitt, E.J., Nesheim, B.E., Guentzel, M.J., Kellogg, A.H., McDonald, W.M., & Wells, C.A. (2008). "Principles of good practice" for academic and student affairs partnership programs. *Journal of College Student Development, 49*(3), 235–249.

Winston, R.B., & Ender, S.C. (1988). Use of student paraprofessionals in divisions of college student affairs. *Journal of Counseling & Development, 66*(10), 466–473.

Wolf-Wendel, L., Ward, K., & Kinzie, J. (2009). A tangled web of terms: The overlap and unique contribution of involvement, engagement, and integration to understanding college student success. *Journal of College Student Development, 50,* 407–428.

Yeater, E.A., Miltenberger, P.A., Laden, M.R., Ellis, S., & O'Donohue, W. (2001). Collaborating with academic affairs: The development of a sexual assault prevention and counseling program within an academic department. *NASPA Journal, 38,* 438–450.

Young, R.B. (1996). Guiding values and philosophy. In S.R. Komives, D.B. Woodard, Jr., & Associates, *Student services: A handbook for the profession* (3rd ed., pp. 83–105). San Francisco, CA: Jossey-Bass.

Zohar, D. (1997). *Rewiring the corporate brain: Using the new science to rethink how we structure and lead organizations.* San Francisco, CA: Berrett-Koehler.

Index

Page numbers in italic indicate figures and tables.